CARRAIG THURA HOTEL
(OVF ~~~ ~~ KILCHURN CASTLE)

GW00690040

Superb
place to
Bedroo
Bathroo
Prices:
Evenin
service ....
Open March to November

Break your journey north in style, without breaking the bank.

Just off the main A74 route to Scotland, in the heart of the Borders, lies a hotel fit for a king. The Auchen Castle Hotel is set in its own magnificent fifty acre grounds.

It has its own loch, brimming with fat trout. It has twenty five comfortable bedrooms, all with colour television, and all with private bathrooms or showers. It has an excellent restaurant. And it has a warm, friendly, country house atmosphere.

In short it's the sort of hotel you'd think you couldn't afford to stay in. But at around £27 for dinner, bed and breakfast, you might even feel tempted to stay a day or two longer than you planned.

Auchen Castle Hotel and Restaurant, Moffat, Dumfriesshire. Egon Ronay, **Tourist Board 4 Crowns Commended.** A.A., recommended. For further details and reservations, telephone Beattock (06833) 407.

CULLIGRAN COTTAGES
Glen Strathfarrar
Struy, Nr. Beauly IV4 7JX

Salmon & Trout fishing on the River Farrar. Guided tours of the deer farm, bicycles for hire, all within a national nature reserve.

For Brochure/Prices
Tel: (046376) 285
Frank & Juliet Spencer Nairn

GLEN MHOR HOTEL

Ness Bank, Inverness
Tel: 0463 234308

Beautiful riverside location near Town centre. Ample car park. All modern facilities and services. Superb cuisine, shellfish and local specialities in Riverview Restaurant, chargrills and carvery in Nico's. Under personal supervision of owners who can arrange your fishing for you, if required.

MONSTER HOLIDAY OFFERS!
5% discount off normal 7-day Dinner, Bed & Breakfast rate, plus a free Jacobite Cruise (excluding 12th July - 13th Sept.). Cheap weekends January to May and September to December.

Write to **MONSTER HOLIDAY OFFER, GLEN MHOR HOTEL, INVERNESS** for details

---

BANCHORY LODGE HOTEL
TEL: (033 02) 2625
Banchory AB3 3HS

*Hosts:*Mr & Mrs D.B. Jaffray

25 bedrooms. Closed January.
Picturesque and tranquil setting overlooking River Dee.
Country house with private fishing and luxurious accommodation.

Grantown-on-Spey Caravan and Camping Park

Pleasant partly wooded site of 23 acres with hard standings for caravans and accommodation for 170 touring caravans and 180 tents. No advance booking. Laundry, sanitary facilities, showers; shop, children's play area; games room & television room. Dogs allowed on leads. ¼-mile from town centre with shops, restaurants, fishing, golfing, tennis and riding nearby. Ski slopes within easy reach. Closed between October and March.

SEAFIELD AVENUE, GRANTOWN-ON-SPEY
(Badenoch & Strathspey District Council)
Tel: (0479) 2474

Strathspey Lodges

Centrally situated in the delightful town of Grantown-on-Spey, Strathspey Lodges offer high class comfort with quality furnishings and fittings throughout. Ideal location for exploring the whole of the Highlands with a wide variety of sports and leisure facilities all year round. Each lodge has 3 bedrooms, 2 double, 1 bunk, large lounge/dining room, modern kitchen and bathroom. Colour TV and linen included. Complimentary bottle of wine on arrival.

Package includes: 7 nights self-catering accommodation. First £5 worth of electricity free.

Price per unit: From £90 to £245 based on 6 persons sharing. Package starts Saturday.

Enquiries and Reservations: Mrs. C. Lawson, Strathspey Lodges, Arnish, Market Road, Grantown-on-Spey. Tel: 0479 2339. Or at any ABTA travel agent.

Allt-Chaorain House Hotel

CRIANLARICH
PERTHSHIRE FK20 8RU
Telephone (08383) 283

Scottish Tourist Board
COMMENDED

GOOD ROOM AWARD

"Welcome to my home". Allt-Chaorain House is a small family hotel situated in an elevated position, 500m from the roadside and 1 mile west of Crianlarich on the A82. This peaceful and secluded position gives us commanding views of Ben More and Strathfillan from the south-facing sun lounge.

With 9 comfortable bedrooms, most with private facilities and "Taste of Scotland" home cooking. The friendly and relaxing atmosphere will unwind you as you sit by the log fire exchanging your day's experiences with other guests who have been walking, fishing or touring the Central Highlands.

Come by road/rail and share the beauty and history of Scotland, which lies at our doorstep.

A PASTIME PUBLICATION
will help you
to find a Happy Holiday for all

SCOTLAND HOME OF GOLF

SCOTLAND FOR FISHING

SCOTLAND FOR THE MOTORIST

See our Guides on Sale
at Your Local Newsagent
and Book Shop.

PASTIME PUBLICATIONS
LIMITED

NEW FOR 1987

THESE TWO NEW GUIDES are full of indispensable information for anyone wishing to play golf or go fishing whilst away from home. They contain details of golf clubs and fishing grounds which welcome visitors and nearby hotels which can cater for them and provide all the facilities they need. With other interesting information and features and tips from such celebrities as Tony Jacklin, Jack Charlton and Trevor Housby, these guides will make it easy to plan your golf or fishing trip and be assured of a welcome at a convenient hotel.

England for Golf and England for Fishing are published by Pastime Publications in association with the English Tourist Board and will be on sale from January 1987. They cost £1.10 each and are available from all good bookshops or by post, price £1.50 each (inc p&p), from:

Pastime Publications Ltd, 15 Dublin Street Lane South, Edinburgh EH1 3PX.

(Please make cheques payable to Pastime Publications Ltd.)

AVAILABLE January 1987

THIS ARTICLE IS BY THE SCOTTISH TOURIST BOARD AND EXPLAINS THEIR CLASSIFICATION AND GRADING OF ACCOMMODATION IN SCOTLAND

STAY WHERE YOU SEE THE SIGN OF A REAL SCOTTISH WELCOME

We've made sure there's a comfortable welcome waiting at hundreds of places to stay in Scotland.

Now there's no need to puzzle over which hotel, guest house, B & B or self-catering accommodation best suits you.

We've introduced a new easy to understand classification and grading scheme so you can find at a glance *exactly* what you're looking for.

WHAT DOES CLASSIFICATION MEAN?

The *classifications,* from 'Listed' to five crowns, are awarded according to the *range* of facilities available. In hotels, guest houses and B & Bs, a 'Listed' classification guarantees, for example, that your bed conforms to a minimum size, that hot and cold water is available at all reasonable times, that breakfast is provided and that there is adequate heating according to the season.

In self-catering accommodation, one crown means that you have a minimum size of unit, at least one twin or double bedroom, dining and cooking facilities suitable for the number of occupants, and a refridgerator.

Naturally, more crowns mean more facilities. A five crown establishment will provide many extras for your holiday comfort. To name just two, in five crown hotels *all* rooms have 'en suite' bathrooms, and five crown self-catering units provide the labour-saving fittings of home, including a dishwasher.

All classifications have been checked by our fully-trained team of independent officers.

CLASSIFICATION AND GRADING OF ACCOMMODATION IN SCOTLAND

Scottish Tourist Board

HIGHLY COMMENDED

Facilities

WHAT ABOUT GRADING?

While classification is all about facilities, *grading* is solely concerned with their *quality*. The grades awarded — 'Approved', 'Commended' or 'Highly Commended' — are based upon an independent assessment of a wide variety of items, ranging from the appearance of the buildings and tidiness of the gardens, to the quality of the furnishings, fittings and floor coverings. Cleanliness is an absolute requirement — and, of course, our officers know the value of a warm and welcoming smile.

Like classification, grading is carried out by the Scottish Tourist Board's expert team.

You can find excellent quality in all kinds of places to stay in Scotland, irrespective of the range of facilities offered: for example, a 'Listed' B & B, with the minimum of facilities, but offering excellent quality, would be awarded a 'Highly Commended' grade while a five crown self-catering property would be graded as 'Approved' if the quality of its extensive facilities was assessed as average.

SO HOW DOES THE NEW SCHEME HELP YOU PLAN YOUR HOLIDAY?

Quite simply, it offers a guarantee of both the range of facilities and their quality. Many of the establishments listed in this brochure have been inspected and this is highlighted in their entries. When you choose accommodation that has been classified, or classified and graded, you have the reassurance that what is being offered has been independently checked.

Equally, if you're on a touring holiday, and booking accommodation as you go, the new scheme can help you. All places to stay which have been inspected bear a distinctive blue oval sign by their entrance showing the classification and grade awarded. And if you call in at a Tourist Information Centre you can ask for a list of local establishments that have joined the scheme, which will include those which are shown in this brochure as *awaiting inspection* at time of going to press.

Whatever kind of accommodation you're looking for, you can be sure the new classification and grading scheme will help you find it.

Please note that where self-catering establishments offer a number of units of differing classifications and grades, their entry in this brochure is shown as 'Up to' the highest award held. You should ascertain the specific classification and grade of an individual unit at time of booking.

Please also note that establishments are visited annually and therefore classifications and grades may therefore change from year to year.

YOUR HOLIDAY IN SCOTLAND
USEFUL INFORMATION ABOUT SCOTLAND

TRAVEL

Bookings for rail, sea and air travel to Scotland and within Scotland should be made through your travel agent, or directly to British Rail, airlines and ferry companies. The Scottish Tourist Board will be glad to give you information but cannot make your bookings for you.

Seats may be booked in advance on the main long-distance coaches, aircraft and for berths and cabins in the steamers to the islands. Sleeping berths on trains should always be booked well in advance. It is necessary to book seats for 'extended' coach tours and also for day coach outings operated from most holiday and touring centres.

Car hire bookings should also be made in advance wherever possible, especially for July and August. Taxis are readily available in Edinburgh, Glasgow, and other major centres at controlled charges. Taxis are generally available in most communities, but in smaller, less populous areas charges may vary considerably.

DRIVING

The 'Rules of the Road' are the same in Scotland as in the rest of the U.K. While there is limited motorway mileage in Scotland, the roads are uniformly good. In the remoter areas there is a considerable mileage of one-way roads, with frequent passing-places. Please, never use these passing-places as lay-bys — or for overnight parking of caravans. Slow-moving traffic (and motorists towing caravans), are asked to pull in to let faster traffic through.

When touring in the far north and west particularly, remember that petrol stations are comparatively few, and distances between them may be considerable. Some petrol stations close on Sundays. Fill your tank in good time, and keep it as full as possible.

Remember, it is now law that the driver and front passenger must wear seat belts.

SCOTLAND'S WEATHER

Did you know that in June, places in the north of Scotland have an average of 18-20 hours of daylight each day, and that resorts on the east coast are particularly noted for their hours of sunshine?

June has those marvellous long evenings when it's light till very late, and the palm trees which grow on the west coast must say something about how warm it is.

Yes, we do have to admit, it does sometimes rain in Scotland; but rainfall is surprisingly low despite the age-old myths. The rainfall in the Edinburgh area, for example, is almost exactly the same as that around London — and Rome for that matter. And don't forget, even if you do get caught in a shower, that Scotland is well-endowed with a whole host of indoor attractions to keep you entertained till long after the sun has come out again.

PUBLIC HOLIDAYS

The Bank Holidays which are also general holidays in England do not apply in Scotland. Most Bank Holidays apply to banks and to some professional and commercial offices only, although Christmas Day and New Year's Day are usually taken as holidays by everyone. Scottish banks are closed in 1987 on 1 and 2 January, 17 April, 4 and 25 May, 3 August, 25 and 28 December. In place of the general holidays, Scottish cities and towns normally have a Spring Holiday and an Autumn Holiday. The dates of these holidays vary from place to place, but they are almost invariably on a Monday.

MONEY

Currency, coinage and postal rates in Scotland are the same as in the rest of the U.K. Scotland differs from England in that Scottish banks issue their own notes. These are acceptable in England, at face value, as are Bank of England notes in Scotland. Main banks are open during the following hours:

Monday, Tuesday, Wednesday: 0930-1230; 1330-1530

Thursday: 0930-1230; 1330-1530; 1630-1800

Friday: 0930-1530

Some city centre banks are open daily 0930-1530 and on Saturdays.

In rural areas, banks post their hours clearly outside and travelling banks call regularly.

SHOPPING

The normal shopping hours in Scotland are 0900-1730, although bakeries, dairies and newsagents open earlier. Many shops have an early closing day (1300) each week, but the actual day varies from place to place and in cities from district to district.

Many city centre shops also stay open late on one evening each week.

EATING

Lunch in restaurants and hotels outside the main centres is usually served between 1230 and 1400. Dinner usually starts at 1900 or 1930 and may not be served much after 2100. Where you know you may arrive late it is advisable to make arrangements for a meal in advance. An alternative to dinner is High Tea, usually served between 1630 and 1830.

A TASTE OF SCOTLAND

When eating out, don't forget to sample a 'Taste of Scotland'. Look out for the 'Stockpot' sign at hotels and restaurants. This indicates that the establishment offers traditional Scottish recipes using the best of Scottish produce: Scottish soups with intriguing names like Powsowdie or Cullen Skink; Aberdeen Angus steaks or venison or game in season; salmon or trout from Scottish rivers, or herring or haddock cured in a variety of ways; and a choice of some 30 varieties of Scottish cheese — these are some of the 'Tastes

of Scotland' which add to the enjoyment of a holiday. For your free copy of the 1987 booklet, write to: Taste of Scotland Ltd, 23 Ravelston Terrace, Edinburgh EH4 3EU.

LICENSING LAWS

Currently in Scotland, the hours that public houses and hotel bars are open to serve drinks are the same all over the country. 'Pubs' are open from 1100 to 1430 and from 1700 to about 2300 hours, Monday to Saturday inclusive and most are now licensed to open on Sundays. In addition, some establishments may have obtained extended licences for afternoon or late night opening.

Hotel bars have the same hours as 'pubs', and are open on Sundays from 1230 to 1430 and 1830 to 2300. Residents in licensed hotels may have drinks served at any time. Some restaurants and hotels have extended licences allowing them to serve drinks with meals until 0100 in the morning. Persons under the age of 18 are not allowed to drink in licensed premises.

COMING FROM OVERSEAS?

Visitors to Scotland from overseas require to observe the same regulations as for other parts of the U.K. As a general rule they must have a valid passport and, in certain cases, visas issued by British Consular authorities overseas: check with a local Travel Agent, or where appropriate, the overseas offices of the British Tourist Authority.

Currency: Overseas visitors who require information about the import and export of currency, cars, or other goods, on personal purchases and belongings, shopping concessions, etc., should consult a Travel Agent or Bank or the overseas offices of the B.T.A.

Driving: Motorists coming from overseas who are members of a motoring organisation in their own country may obtain from them full details of the regulations for importing cars, motor cycles, etc., for holiday and touring purposes into the U.K. They can drive in Britain on a current Driving Licence from their own country, or with an international Driving Permit, for a maximum period of 12 months. Otherwise, a British Driving Licence must be obtained: until the Driving Test is passed it is essential to be accompanied by a driver with a British licence.

CONTENTS

Pastime Publications Ltd gratefully acknowledge the assistance of The Scottish Tourist Board, Area Tourist Boards, Drew Jamieson and others in compiling this guide.

No part of 'Scotland for Fishing' may be published or reproduced in any form without prior consent of the Publisher.

Published by Pastime Publications Limited, 15 Dublin Street Lane South, Edinburgh EH1 3PX. Tel: 031-556 1105/0057.

While every care has been taken to ensure accuracy, Pastime Publications cannot accept any responsibility for errors or omissions in the information provided. Readers are also advised to check holiday dates and prices before booking.

© **COPYRIGHT PASTIME PUBLICATIONS LTD. 1987**
15 Dublin Street Lane South, Edinburgh EH1 3PX

First published by The Scottish Tourist Board 1970

Typesetting by Newtext Composition Ltd.
Printed & Bound by G.A. Pindar & Son Ltd.
U.K. Distribution by W.H.S. Distributors

Worldwide distribution by
The British Tourist Authority
BTA

INDEX

A PASTIME PUBLICATION
will help you
to find a Happy Holiday for all

SCOTLAND HOME OF GOLF

SCOTLAND FOR FISHING

SCOTLAND FOR THE MOTORIST

See our Guides on Sale at Your Local Newsagent and Book Shop.

PASTIME PUBLICATIONS
LIMITED

Welcome to Scotland . . . .

Welcome to Scotland, to another season of spectacular angling sport — we hope!

Last season had its ups and downs. A cold, wet spring slowed up the start of the brown trout fishing, but some rivers had their best runs of salmon for many years. The Spey had a particularly good summer. The Border Esk had good runs of salmon and sea trout. The Tweed had a tremendous run of salmon in late October after being held up at Norham Bridge with the low water, and the Annan had a good run in early November when the rains came at last.

Highlight of the year was a new contender for the record rainbow trout — a 21 pound 4 ounce specimen from Loch Awe. Although this was initially an escapee from the fish cages it had put on a lot of weight in the wild.

1987 will see some changes. A new Protection Order came into force on 7th October 1986 for the River Tay catchment area from the top of the Dochart down to Perth. It is now a criminal offence to fish for trout, grayling and other freshwater fish, without a written permit.

Also, on the legislative front, the 1986 Salmon Act is now in force. The full implications of this Act are still to be appreciated and it may be a season or two before much effect is noticed at the riverside. The test will be whether it ultimately puts more salmon in the rivers for anglers to pursue.

This year should be the year to "Take a Friend Fishing". Angling is no longer the country's fastest growing sport and has not always had a good Press recently. Now is the time to do something about it. Declare our faith in our sport, support the Angling Foundation and "Take a Friend Fishing" in 1987.

TAKE A FRIEND FISHING

Big Fish and Blue Waters JIM McLANAGHAN

Big fish and blue waters, these are the boasts of the world-famous big-game angling centres such as Cairns in Australia. Whangaroa in New Zealand and the Bahamas. A new venue has evolved over the past two decades however which, although not offering tailwalking marlin or high-flying makos, can provide world-class sport in beautifully rugged surroundings. This Valhalla is Scotland.

Giant porbeagles only a few pounds below the world record, five-hour battles with huge skate, tackle-shattering world-record halibut are only a few of the piscatorial pleasures awaiting the angler who ventures north into Europe's greatest untapped potential angling grounds.

Big-game angling has come late to Scotland and only since the late-sixties has some of its true potential begun to emerge. The well-known skate grounds of Ullapool, Orkney, Shetland and Caithness gave us our first taste of the ton-up fish, resulting in the British and European record of 226½ lbs. from Shetland — on a beachcasting reel! New grounds are being constantly discovered such as Portpatrick, just north of the Border and, more prolifically, the Isle of Mull where Brian Swinbank has carved a notch for himself in the legend of Scottish big fish. The shore angler too has a part to play, or if he's lucky even the fish of a lifetime. One such fellow hooked, played and successfully beached a common skate from the shoreline at Achiltibuie just north of Ullapool. The weight? — an impressive 154 lbs. Beats flatty-bashing, doesn't it? Eddy Wason of Ayr had a similar experience from the pier at Loch Aline, opposite Mull, when he hooked and beat a skate of 98 lbs. on a beachcaster. Two very separate incidents but potentially repeatable at any stance which gives access to deep water and there are countless thousands all along our rugged West coast.

Sharks have shared our seas for centuries with our angling ancestors. It was not until one day in 1971 that one was officially recorded on rod and line. That fish, taken by Dietrich Burkel at East Tarbet on the Mull of Galloway weighed 176 lbs. and added another important species to our big fish lists. John O'Kelly from Manchester took another small 90 pounder a year later from the other side of Luce Bay and English businessman Jim Wood had a huge fish of 275 lbs. on *22 lb.* line which took him *12 hours!* to land. He told very few people and never claimed a record. Several fish per year now began to fall to rod and line as more and more anglers tackled these superb scrappers. One place above all others began to produce fish regularly and of well-above-average size. This was Sumburgh Head, the most southerly tip of Shetland. Peter White, Erik Manson and Ray Phillips took four fish in one day several years ago. The weights were mind-boggling at 195 lbs., 372 lbs., 404 lbs. and 450 lbs. Erik Manson had the two smaller (?) fish, Peter White 404 lbs. and Ray Phillips the 450 lbs. The three largest fish all obliterated the Scottish record but Ray declined to claim his fish as a record, leaving Peter to do so — that record still stands. A footnote is that Ray's fish was only 15 lbs. below the all-tackle world record!!!

The waters which scour our most northerly headlands are so rich in fishlife that to describe it would appear pure fiction in a sport which has become synonomous with tall tales. The record lists tell the facts and it is evident that this abundant fishlife attracts our most desirable and yet most elusive big fish — the halibut. The Pentland Firth is subjected to huge tide races, more than 10 knots in places, and any fish which can live in this environment must be immensely strong and this the halibut is — and more. Reels destroyed, rods broken, fish jumping back *out* of boats — all well-documented events which add to the legend and mystic of the 'Butt'. These fish can regularly be brought to the surface without any fight at all and as the bemused angler wonders what all the stories are about, it flips, gets its nose down and goes, with or without the angler's consent. It is this immensely fast and strong dive which can wreck gear so easily if the angler has not backed off his clutch in advance. Halibut of over 600 lbs. have been recorded but it says much for this fish that the current record stands at 234 lbs.

Whereas most potentially big fish tend to be elusive and require highly specialised gear, our most popular and arguably most game fish requires little more than most anglers would use for salmon. This is the tope. Reasonably abundant all up the west coast, there are places which have become known — indeed famous — as hotspots for this medium-sized shark. Luce Bay and the Mull of Galloway — names to conjure with for most species of big fish — have grown to prominence as one of Britain's premier tope areas. The eastern side of Luce Bay provides some tremendous sport with smaller tope, 15-30 lbs. and some huge catches have been recorded. One boat-load of anglers from Irvine boasted 77 tope in one day. The Mull of Galloway on the western side of the bay does not normally produce such huge numbers but it does produce some huge fish. Skipper Steven Woods of Drummore had reported an eighty-pound plus fish but declined claiming it as a record. Two brothers fishing at the Kailieness buoy had a catch of eight tope in one day — all over 50 lbs. Such catches occur but once in a lifetime but sometime somewhere in Scotland it will be somebody's turn and, as the record lists show, the visiting angler has a better-than-average chance. I had one such day off Portpatrick, fishing for tope. I had a dozen thornbacks over the Scottish specimen weight (15 lbs.). I threw a Scottish record back twice (same fish), an undulate ray! I caught no tope though but I ended the day with a 76 lbs. common skate. See what I mean about potential!

With the hunt for big fish, came the slow realization that angling pressure alone could seriously threaten any local population to the extent of the fishery being no longer viable. Fortunately for Scotland, the acceptance of this fact was nurtured into a determination to not only protect but to conserve our valuable sporting fish. One club which helped show the way was the Mull of Galloway Big Game Club, whose founding members incorporated into their club constitution a rule that 'no tope shall be killed'. The governing body for sea angling in Scotland, the Scottish Federation of Sea Anglers, has also included conservation in its rules and this covers not only tope but also skate. It is my opinion that ANY fish which is not wanted for eating should be returned, unharmed, to the water. Surprisingly, help is coming from the most unexpected quarters — Japan, Germany, Russia . . . As technology advances, cameras are nowadays as cheap and convenient as at any time previously and instead of hauling a large dead dish ashore most people are taking photographs and returning the fish alive. Long may it continue! It is also the nicest form of one-up-manship as you draw your wallet out saying 'You should see the one that I threw back'.

The 'Old and the New' — a contrast for coarse angling

DAVE CARNELL

As Scottish coarse fishing has increased in popularity and the National teams have increased in competitiveness, two particular venues have come to the forefront in the provision of quality sport in Scotland. These two waters, Kilbirnie Loch in Ayrshire and Strathclyde Park Loch at Motherwell provide a marked contrast between an old-established 'traditional' loch and a modern, artificially-created water purpose-built for a variety of water-based recreational activities.

Kilbirnie Loch

Kilbirnie Loch was the venue for the 1983 Four Nations Home International and has been nominated again for the return of this match to Scotland in 1987. Tucked away in the rolling hills of Ayrshire this prolific loch consistently yields both quality and quantity and remains a jewel amongst Britain's renowned roach waters.

All the banks fish equally well, although fishing into the wind usually produces the best results. With an average depth of only four or five feet, the approach should be kept simple. A waggler float, often up to 12 inches in length to help the drift, should be set so that the bait falls slowly through the entire depth. No finesse is needed here. Lines can be stepped up to three or four pounds breaking strain, fished straight through to a 14 or 16 forged hook. Particle baits such as sweetcorn, wheat or tares will help to single out the larger fish, while bunches of maggots, delivered among lashings of loose feed, with or without soft ground bait, will guarantee a succession of fish of all sizes.

Kilbirnie Loch can only be described as Scottish coarse fishing at its very best.

Strathclyde Park Loch

By diverting a 1½ mile loop of the River Clyde and excavating over 100 acres of wasteland between Hamilton and Motherwell, the local authorities of Strathclyde set out to create a water sports complex worthy of hosting 1986 Commonwealth Games events. By subsequently adopting a positive fish-stocking policy, the water is now also well on its way to becoming a national fishery and a possible World Championship venue by the early 1990's. In 1977 some 4,000 fingerling tench were introduced from a nearby pond. In 1980 a programme of 4 batches, each consisting of 6,000 mixed coarse species was agreed and the most recent stocking of another 6,000 fish took place on 17th November 1986.

The depth of water varies, up to 25 feet in the old channel of the River Clyde. The method of fishing can be equally varied, with the resident species responding well to float, leger or pole. Most swims have six to eight feet of water under the rod tip so there is no need to fish at a great distance. However, the 'secret' of the Park is to locate the depth where the bankside pebbles and stones merge into the mud of the bottom of the loch. For some reason the fish elect to patrol up and down this crease and these anglers who locate this will return the best weights.

While roach, up to 2 pounds, remain the dominant species, large bream, as heavy as 8 pounds — a species hitherto unknown north of the Borders — help make Strathclyde Park a very exciting prospect for the future. Other species present include common carp to 15 pounds, perch to 3 pounds, pike to 10 pounds, tench to 3 pounds and eels to 3 pounds. Also included in the permit is a two mile stretch of the River Clyde and one mile of the Avon, waters which contain dace to 1 pound and chub to 3 pounds, as well as trout, grayling and even salmon, which are not for catching at present. The head of fish in the loch has not yet reached the desired level but in a good year catches of over 150 fish have been recorded by anglers and weights of 50 to 60 pounds have been taken on occasions. Given reasonable spawning conditions over the next few years, this venue will certainly be well worth a visit.

Loch Tummel

Catch Your First Trout

DREW JAMIESON

No matter how many mighty salmon you may go on to catch in shining rivers — or how huge a marlin, shark or swordfish you may haul from the blue ocean — that first exciting tug from your first trout is the moment forever ingrained upon your memory. If that first trout should be a lively, spotted beauty coaxed from clear waters amid the wild scenery of Scotland, so much richer will be that memory.

To most beginners the perception of the 'typical' Scottish angler is an awesome figure in chest-waders, wielding a double-handed rod, up to his armpits in a rushing salmon river, or a deerstalkered enthusiast in plus-fours, drifting a tiny boat down a gale-swept loch in pursuit of monster sea trout.

There is no need to be overawed by the "professional" fisherman as there are ample opportunities for novices of all ages to be introduced gently to the ranks of trout fishing and to catch their first trout — and their lifelong addiction — in the rivers and lochs of Scotland.

The simplest, and arguably most civilized, way to do this, is to join a custom-built trout-fishing holiday package. There are several fishing schools and many hotels in this guide which organise holidays specifically to put the visitor in touch with good quality trout as quickly and as often as possible. Instructors are on hand who are not just competent at passing on their knowledge and skills, but are "characters" from whom one will absorb the atmosphere, ethics, ambience and the spirit of what trout fishing is all about.

Instruction can vary from formal lessons to benign supervision and is usually tailored to the individual's needs and desires.

Transport, permits, boats, tackle, food and accommodation may all be provided in some packages — each hotel or school can advise upon enquiry. In addition to instruction on the mechanics of casting a fly, you will probably get a brief introduction to the habits of the trout, the types of fly and tackle to use and when to use them, the safety aspects of the sport plus all the peripheral nature-lore, which makes trout angling so much more a way of life, rather than just a pastime.

Those visitors who wish to take the challenge a bit less seriously and be more independent, have other opportunities. Many of the new generation of smaller 'put and take' fisheries specifically encourage the beginner. Special "Beginners' Ponds" may be set aside appropriately stocked with obliging trout. Tackle may be hired and friendly advice is on hand to help with the casting and the landing of that first trout, and the second, and the third . . . These are usually bank-fishing venues which is a comfortable way to start if you are not too happy about boats. For those anglers with aspiring youngsters eager to come to grips with boat fishing, some fisheries offer "Father and Son" (or "Father and Daughter") boats at discount rates where Dad can do his own instruction and get another member of the family "hooked" on his passion, thus ensuring future Scottish trouting holidays for the family.

For the beginner, the requirements to start trout fishing are minimal. If you wish to buy your tackle, rather than hire it, any reputable tackle-dealer will kit you out with a suitable fly rod, around the 9 to 9½ foot mark, a balanced line and reel and an assortment of local fly patterns guaranteed to slay the local trout. Warm and waterproof clothing and footwear are essential, whilst a hat and polaroid sun glasses are important safety measures to keep any badly cast flies and hooks from doing damage. Midge repellent and sunburn cream can make life comfortable. For those determined to teach themselves to cast a fly, I would recommend flattening the barb on the hook for the first few hours, just in case it lodges in your ear or finger. It will come out easier and less painfully and will still catch any trout which takes it. Once you can guarantee the safety of yourself and your neighbouring anglers, then the barb can be retained.

At the end of the day; if fly fishing is

too difficult, or instructional courses are not your scene, you can always tip-toe away on your own up some hill burn. Lost among the moors and surrounded by curlews you can flick a small red worm on the end of your fly rod and pick the small dark burn trout out from peat-stained pools. They may not be the biggest trout you'll ever catch, but they taste the sweetest and look the prettiest. If its your first trout, it is the trout you will remember for the rest of your life.

SCOTTISH FEDERATION OF SEA ANGLERS
OFFICIALS

President

Mr. M. L. Rowlands, 45 Lochbank, Ladywell, Livingston, West Lothian EH54 6EH. Telephone: (0506) 30149

Vice Presidents:

Mr. D. M. Mackay (1985), 56 Drumfork Road, Helensburgh G84 7TY Telephone: (0436) 6980.
Mr. S. Thompson (1986), 19 Craigpark Avenue, Prestwick Telephone (02092) 70200.
Mr. R. B. Walker (1987), Springvale Cottage, Halket By Lugon, Ayrshire. Telephone: (050585) 593.

Hon Treasurer:

Mr. J.K. Crawford (1986), 6 Duchray Drive, Ralston, Paisley, Renfrewshire Telephone 041 882 2851.

Secretary Adminstrator:

Mrs. Cath Watson (1985), 25 Wardie Road, Edinburgh EH5 3LH. Telephone: 031 225 7611 (Office).

Hon Fish Recorder

Mr. R. B. Burn (1986), 7 Oswald Road, Ayr. Telephone: Ayr (0292 28) 648.

REGIONAL SECRETARIES

Clyde

Mrs. E.A.H. Walker, Springvale Cottage, Halket by Lugton, Ayrshire KA3 4EE.
Tel: Uplawmoor (0505 85) 593.

Central

Mr. J. Haggarty, 18 Boswell Drive, Kinghorn, Fife. Tel: Kinghorn (0592) 890405.

West

Mr. G. Long, 119 High Road, Saltcoats, Ayrshire.

North East

Mr. P.P. King, 25 Thornhill Place, Forres, Morayshire. Tel: (0309) 74472.

Eastern

Mr. G.A. Walker, 12/4 Murrayburn Place, Edinburgh. Tel: 031-442 3750.

Highlands & Islands

Mrs W.A. Dowie, 43, Mackenzie Place, Maryburgh, Ross-shire. Tel: Dingwall (0349) 61850.

Why Not Join A Club?

THE FOLLOWING CLUBS AND ASSOCIATIONS ARE IN MEMBERSHIP OF THE FEDERATION:

Aberdeen Airport Angling Club
Hon. Sec. I.G. Duncan Esq., 13 Parkhill Circle, Dyce, Aberdeen AB2 0FN.
Aberdeen Thistle Sea Angling Club
Hon. Sec. D. Kinnaird Esq., Newpark, Newmachar, Aberdeenshire AB5 0PB. (Tel: 0224 722142).
Albion Sea Angling Club
Hon. Sec. A. Semple Esq., 13 Ashgill Road, Lambhill, Glasgow G22 6QJ.
Anderson Mavor, Angling Section
Hon. Sec. J. Robertson Esq., 2 Ochiltree Court, Rimbleton, Glenrothes, Fife.
Ardrossan & District Sea Angling Club
Hon. Sec. I.B. McClymont Esq., 41 Corrie Crescent, Saltcoats, Ayrshire KA21 6JL.
Arran Sea Angling Association
Hon. Sec. Mrs. S. Alison, 7 Brathwic Terrace, Brodick, Isle of Arran KA27 8BW.
Auchtermuchty Angling Club
Hon. Sec. S. Szylack Esq., 24 Low Road, Auchtermuchty, Fife. (Tel: 735).
Ayr Sea Angling Club
Hon. Sec. D. Neil Esq., 30 Woodfield Road, Ayr, Ayrshire.
"856" Sea Angling Club
Hon. Sec. R.R. Welsh Esq., 6 Hall Street, Innerleithen, Peebleshire. (Tel: 830412).
Balgownie Angling Club
Hon. Sec. T. Ross Esq., c/o 26 Cardens Knowe, Bridge of Don, Aberdeen.
B.B.C. Club, Sea Angling Section
Hon. Sec. Miss E. Forsyth, 62 Thornwood Avenue, Glasgow G11 7PF.
Beaverbank Angling Club
Hon. Sec. D. Cridge Esq., 63 Sommerville Gardens, South Queensferry, West Lothian.
Beechams Sea Angling Club
Hon. Sec. A. Frew Esq., 4 Merrick Place, Bourtreehill, Irvine, Ayrshire.
Bell Rock Sea Angling Club
Hon. Sec. A. Burnett Esq., 6 Gardner Lane, Arbroath, Angus DD11 4HQ. (Tel: Arbroath 79911).
Bellshill Sea Angling Club
Hon. Sec. R. Price Esq., 44 Harvey Way, Bellshill ML4 1TF.
Breakaway Sea Angling Club
Hon. Sec. J. Kinniburgh Esq., 107 Batson Street, Glasgow.
Britoil (Glasgow) Sea Angling Club
Hon. Sec. S.J. Forrest Esq., 31 Loudoun Crescent, Kilwinning, Ayrshire KA13 6TS. (Tel: 0294 58639).
Buckhaven & District Sea Angling Club
Hon. Sec. D. Williams Esq., 50 Lomond Gardens, Methil, Fife KY8 3JL.
Callander Sea Angling Club
Hon. Sec. R. Pywell Esq., 42 Stirling Road, Callander, Perthshire. (Tel: 30933).
Civil Service Sports Association
Hon. Treasurer A. Ferguson Esq., Civil Service Sports Centre (Angling), Castle Road, Rosyth, Fife.
Clyde Specimen Hunters Sea Angling Club
Hon. Sec. G. Kinnear Esq., 9 Kiloch Drive, Barrhead, Renfrewshire. (Tel: 041-881 4925).
Cockenzie & Port Seton Royal British Legion Sea Angling Club
Hon. Sec. J. Whyte Esq., 99 North Seton Park, Port Seton, East Lothian.
Cupar, St. Andrews & District Sea Angling Club
Hon. Sec. J. O'Brien Esq., 40 King Street, Kirkcaldy, Fife. (Tel: Kirkcaldy 263065).
Daily Record & Sunday Mail Angling Club
Hon. Sec. J. McKie Esq., Buying Dept., Scottish Daily Record & Sunday Mail Ltd., Anderston Quay, Glasgow G3 8DA. (Tel: 041-242 3380).
Dalbeattie & District Sea Angling Club
Hon. Sec. J. Moran Esq., 12 Church Crescent, Dalbeattie, Kirkcudbrightshire.
D.K.L. No. 18 Fishing Section
Hon. Sec. E.J. Watson Esq., 74 Cumbrae Crescent South, Castlehill, Dumbarton.
Drumfork Sea Angling Club
Hon. Sec. W. Buchan Esq, 11 Fisher Place, Helensburgh, Dunbartonshire. (Tel: Helensburgh 71507).
Dunoon Sea Angling Club
Hon. Sec. W.C. Wilson Esq., 35 Spence Court, Queen Street, Dunoon, Argyllshire.
Dysart Sailing Club (Sea Angling Section)
Hon. Sec./Fishing Convener, H.F. Greig Esq., c/o Dysart Sailing Club, The Harbour, Dysart, Fife.
Eastern Sea Angling Club
Hon. Sec. J. Gordon Esq., 42 Pennelton Place, Bo'mains, Bo'ness, West Lothian.
East Kilbride Inland Revenue Angling Club
Hon. Sec. G. Berry Esq., 1 Mossingal, Whitehills 3, East Kilbride.

16

East Sutherland Sea Angling Club
Hon. Sec. W. Yates Esq., 21 Johnstone Place, Brora, Sutherland KW9 6PF.
Edina Sea Angling Club
Hon. Sec. R. Combe Esq., 38 Craiglockhart Terrace, Edinburgh EH14 1AJ. (Tel: 031-443 7209).
Edinburgh Golden Hook Sea Angling Club
Hon. Sec. D.T. Roberts Esq., 21 Perth Street, Edinburgh EH3 5DW.
Edinburgh Meadowbank Sea Angling Club
Hon. Sec. A. McCreadie Esq., 2 Hawkins Terrace, Penicuik, Midlothians.
Elgin Sea Angling Club
Hon. Sec. D. Clarke Esq., 24 Bezack Street, New Elgin, Morayshire. (Tel: 46889).
Fereneze Sea Angling Club
Hon. Sec. A. Henderson Esq., 20F Divernia Way, Auchenback, Barrhead G78 2JN. (Tel: 041-880 6465).
Ferranti Sea Angling Club
Hon. Sec. S. Watson Esq., 14 Clerwood Loan, Edinburgh. (Tel: 031-334 6016).
Firth of Clyde Sea Angling Association
Hon. Sec. J. Galt Esq., 22 Helmsdale Avenue, Blantyre G72 9NY.
Flounders Match & Specimen Group
Hon. Sec. I. King Esq., 60 Dundee Road, Broughty Ferry, Dundee, Angus.
Forfar Seahawks Angling Club
Hon. Sec. I.C. Hardie Esq., Quikoe Cottage By Forfar, Angus.
Gala Sea Angling Club
Hon. Sec. L. Thin Esq., 10 Aster Court, Galashiels, Selkirkshire TD1 2LN. (Tel: 55088).
Gareloch & Loch Long Civil Service Angling Club
Hon. Sec. W. Greaves Esq., 24 Camsaill Road, Rosneath, Dumbartonshire. (Tel: Clynder 600).
Giffnock North Amateur Athletic Club - Angling Section
Hon. Sec. J. Sherman Esq., 12 Kilmartin Place, Arden G46 8DS.
Glaxo Sports & Social Club, Angling Section
Hon. Sec. W. MOseley Esq., 19 Beacon Terrace, Ferryden, Montrose, Angus DD10 0RN.
Glenrothes Royal British Legion Sea Angling Club
Hon. Sec. J. McGuinness Esq., 163 Inverary Avenue, Glenrothes, Fife KY7 4QS.
Glen Urquhart Sea Angling Club
Hon. Sec. A. Whyte Esq., Kinnarid, Drumnadrochit By Inverness IV3 6XD.

Hamilton & District Sea Angling Club
Hon. Sec., A.P. Brown Esq., 32 Swisscot Walk, Fairhill, Hamilton ML3 8DX. (Tel: 427085).
Harris Sea Angling Club
Hon. Sec. A.B. Deas Esq, Invercarse, Kendebig, Isle of Harris PA85 3HQ.
Harrow Hotel Sea Angling Club
Hon. Sec. D.M. Johnson Esq., 2 Westhouses Avenue, Mayfield, Dalkeith, Midlothian. (Tel: 031-660 1197).
Highland Omnibuses Employees Sea Angling Club
Hon. Sec. D.J. Mackay Esq., 35 Dell Road, Inverness. (Tel: Inverness 230136).
Innes Angling Club
Hon. Sec. J. McInnes Esq., 16 Nelson Street, Inverness.
Inverness Royal British Legion Angling Club
Hon. Sec. A.J. Ralph Esq., 81 McIntosh Road, Inverness.
Irvine Sea Angling Club
Hon. Sec. A. Pauley Esq., 122 Braehead, Girdle Toll, Irvine, Ayrshire KA11 1BG. (Tel: Irvine 212872).
Johnstone Castle Sea Angling Club
Hon. Sec. F. Brown Esq., 107 Elm Drive, Johnstone, Renfrewshire.
Keppoch Inn Angling Club
Hon. Sec. A. Forsyth Esq., 26 Trentham Court, Westhill, Inverness IV1 2DF. (Tel: 0463 792412).
Kilsyth Broch Sea Angling Club
Hon. Sec. G. Derrick Esq., 35 Gateside Avenue, Kilsyth, Glasgow G65 9BW.
Kinghorn Sea Angling Club
Hon. Sec. G.T. Morris Esq., 8 Burt Avenue, Kinghorn, Fife. (Tel: Kinghorn 890055).
Kingsmills Sea Angling & Sporting Club
Fishing Convener: I.M. Wilson Esq., 119 Culduthel Road, Inverness.
Kirkton Sea Angling Club
Hon. Sec. S. Hoskins Esq., 50 Craigmount Road, Dundee DD2 4QF.
Leachly Angling Club
Hon. Sec. A. MacMillan Esq., 43 Bruce Gardens, Inverness IV3 5EW. (Tel: 221840).
Lennox Sea Angling Club
Hon. Sec. R.N. Elder Esq., 191 Crosslet Road, Dumbarton G82 2LQ. (Tel: 63845).
Leukaemia Research Fund Sea Angling Club
Hon. Sec. G.A. Walker Esq., 12/4 Murrayburn Place, Edinburgh. (Tel: 031-442 3750).
Lochaber Sea Angling Club
Hon. Sec. G. Band Esq., 24 Abrach Road, Inverlochy, Fort William, Inverness-shire.
Locharbriggs & District Social Club Ltd.
Hon. Sec. J. Kerr Esq., 70 Gledhill Crescent, Locharbriggs, Dumfries DG1 1XD.
Lothian & Borders Police, Sea Angling Section
Hon. Sec. Sgt. A. Thomas, Court & Records Dept., Police Headquarters, Fettes Avenue, Edinburgh. (Tel: 031-226 7181 Extn. 296).
Luggy's Sea Strikers Sea Angling Club
Hon. SEc. P. Iannatta Esq., 20 Bank Avenue, Downfield, Dundee, Angus DD 38NY. (Tel: 825706).
McDermott Fishing & Sea Angling Club
Hon. Sec. C. Logie Esq., Tarras Cottage, Forres, Morayshire.
Moorpark Sea Angling Club
Hon. Sec. T. Murty Esq., 18 Moorpark Square, Renfrew, Renfrewshire.
Mull of Galloway Big Game Club
Hon. Sec. R.B. Burns Esq., 7 Oswald Road, Ayr, Ayshire. (Tel: 0292 281648).
Nairn Thistle Angling Club, Kirkcaldy
Hon. Sec. H.F. Grieg Esq., 24 James Grove, Kirkcaldy, Fife. (Tel: 0592 62584).
Newburgh Sea Angling Club
Hon. Sec. A. Shand Esq., 12 Wheatland, Pitmedden, Ellon, Aberdeenshire AB4 0GF.
Nitshill Sea Angling Club
Hon. Sec. H. Gilliland Esq., 128 Pinmore Street, Nitshill, Glasgow G53. (Tel: 041-881 6267).
Norscot Angling Association
Hon. Sec. V. Goudie Esq., c/o Norscot Base, Greenhead, Lerwick, Shetland. (Tel: 2983).

Please mention this Pastime Publications guide.

North Berwick Sea Angling Club
Hon. Sec. L. Thomson Esq., 19 Gilbert Avenue, North Berwick, East Lothian. (Tel: 0620 2243).
Northfield Sea Angling Club
Hon. Sec. R. Reid Esq., 5 Burdiehouse Drive, Edinburgh. (Tel: 031-664 8942).
North West Skye Sea Angling Club
Hon. Sec. L. Shurmer Esq., 13 Skindin By Dunvegan, Isle of Skye.
Orkney Islands Sea Angling Association
Hon. Sec. J. Geddes Esq., Quarryfield, Orphir. (Tel: Orphir 311).
Ormille Lodge Angling Club
Hon. Sec. I. Myles Esq., 32 Sweyn Road, Thurso, Caithness KW14 7NW. (Tel: Thurso 2000).
Park Stores Angling Club
Hon. Sec. W. Gordon Esq., 14 Trafalgar Street, Edinburgh EH6 4DG. (Tel: 031-554 6659).
Port of Leith Sea Angling Club
Hon. Sec. J. Ramsay Esq., 18 Pilton Crescent, Edinburgh EH5 2HX.
Possilpark Garage Angling Club
Treasurer: F. O'Brien, Flat 15D, 109 Wester Common Road, Glasgow G22 5NJ. (Tel: 041-336 6714).
Prestwick Sea Angling Club
Hon. Sec. Mrs. M. Templeton, 'Trebor', 15 Teviot Street, Ayr. (Tel: 0292 268072).
R.A.F. Kinloss Sea Angling Club
Hon. Sec. Sgt. S. Tomlinson, 61 Highfield, Forbeshill, Forres, Morayshire. (Tel: Forbes 75259).
R.A.F. Lossiemouth Sea Angling Club
Hon. Sec. C/T Bean Esq., E.E.S., R.A.F. Lossiemouth, Morayshire IV30 6SD.
Ranza Angling & Social Club
Hon. Sec. R. Brockett Esq., c/o Ranza Angling & Social Club, 1159 Royston Road, Glasgow.
R.A. Range Hebrides Sea Angling Club
Hon. Sec. Mrs. Macleod, R.A. Range Balivanich, Isle of Benbecula, Outer Hebrides PA88 5LF.
Reform Club, Angling Section
Hon. Sec. W. Blacker Esq., 6 Linthouse Buildings, Linthouse, Glasgow G51 4RG. (Tel: 041-440 1641).
Ross's Sea Angling Club
Hon. Sec. H. Bowden Esq., 7L Bucklemaker Court, Dundee DD3 6TQ.
Ross-shire Sea Angling Club
Hon. Sec. Mrs. W. Downie, 43 McKenzie Place, Maryburgh, Conon Bridge, Ross-shire. (Tel: 0349 61850).
Royal Air Force Leuchars Angling Club
Hon. Sec. W.O., K. Farrell, c/o G.R.F., R.A.F. Leuchars, St. Andrews, Fife.
Royal British Legion Sea Angling Club
Hon. Sec. P. Lamont Esq., c/o Royal British Legion Club, High Street, Invergordon, Ross-shire.
Royal Infirmary of Edinburgh Sea Angling Club
Hon. Sec. W. Wilson Esq., 9 Gordon Avenue, Poltonhall, Bonnyrigg. (Tel: 031-663 0091).
Saltcoats Argyle Seahawks Sea Angling Club
Hon. Sec. M. Nelson Esq., 19 Braeside, Girdle Toll, Irvine. (Tel: 0294 216628).
Saltcoats Sea Angling Association
Hon. Sec. R. beames Esq., 2 Coranbae Place, Burton, Alloway, Ayr, Ayrshire.

"71" Sea Angling Club
Hon. Sec. R.S.M. Smith Esq., Army Careers Information Office, Charlotte House, 78 Queen Street, Glasgow G1.
Shetland Association of Sea Anglers
Hon. Sec. Miss C. Scott, 18 Cheyne Crescent, Lerwick, Shetland. (Tel: Lerwick 3792).
Shotts Bon-Accord Angling Club
Hon. Sec. I. Keiley Esq., 12 Hunter Street, Shotts, Lanarkshire.
Silver Lure Sea Angling Club
Hon. Sec. G.V.R. Griffiths Esq., 43 Ingleby Drive, Dennistoun, Glasgow G31. (Tel: 041-554 1423).
South Queensferry Angling Club
Hon. Sec. B.D. Plasting Esq., 53 Sommerville Gardens, South Queensferry, West Lothian EH30 9PN. (Tel: 031-331 1605).
State Hospital Angling Group
Hon. Sec. J. Cooper Esq., 8 Lampits Road, Westend, Carstairs Junction, Lanark ML11 8RR.
Stevenson Sea Angling Association
Hon. Sec. G. Long Esq., 119 High Road, Saltcoats, Ayrshire.
Stornoway Sea Angling Club
Hon. Sec. F.G. Jefferson Esq., No.1 Sheshader Point, Isle of Lewis. (Tel: 0851 870214).
Strathclyde Police Recreation Association, Sea Angling Section
Hon. Sec. F. Kirkham Esq., Greenock Police Office, Rue End Street, Greenock, Renfrewshire.
Strathclyde Secondary Schools Angling Association
Hon. Sec. H. Hamilton-Willows Esq., 142 Barrachnie Road, Garrowhill, Baillieston, Glasgow G69 6PJ.
Tartan Sea Eagles Sea Angling Club
Hon. Sec. R. McIntyre Esq., 28 St. Margarets Avenue, Dalry, Ayrshire.
Towerlands Sea Angling Club
Hon. Sec. J.G. Macnab Esq., 27 Wilson Avenue, irvine, Ayrshire KA12 0TW. (Tel: 76886).
Walker & Albert Sea Angling Club
Hon. Sec. J. Bishop Esq., 22 Maitland Drive, Cupar, Fife KY15 5EU. (Tel: 0334 53476).
Westfield Angling Club
Hon. Sec. R.P. Elliot Esq., 9 Lomond Place, Kinross KY13 7BH.
Whitfield Labour Club, Angling Section
Hon. Sec. A. Perrie Esq., 13 Doon Terrace, Dundee DD4 8EW. (Tel: 452589).

JUNIOR CLUB MEMBERSHIP (HONORARY)
Crookston Castle Secondary School Sea Angling Club
Hon. Sec. T. Craig Esq., Science Department, 126 Brockburn Road, Glasgow G53 5RX.
Cumbernauld Sea Angling Club
Hon. Sec. Martin Smith Esq., 28 Rowan Road, Cumbernauld.
Kilmarnock Academy Sea Angling Club
Hon. Sec. Philip Kerr Esq., c/o Kilmarnock Academy, Kilmarnock, Ayrshire.
Rosehall High School Angling Club
Hon. Sec. R. Macdonald Esq., Rosehall High School, Woodhall Avenue, Coatbridge. (Tel: 31166).
St. Ambrose High School Sea Angling Club
Hon. Sec. T. Lennon Esq., St. Ambrose High School, Blair Road, Coatbridge ML5 2EW.
St. Gerard's Secondary School Sea Angling Club
Hon. Sec. E. A. Hara Esq., 6 Aberdour Street, Glasgow G31 3NH. (Tel: 041-554 8703).

SCOTTISH FEDERATION FOR COARSE ANGLING

The Federation was formed in 1975 to promote and encourage the sport of Coarse Angling in Scotland. It is recognised by the Scottish Sports Council as being the governing body for Coarse Angling throughout Scotland.

Objects and Functions

To obtain waters for coarse angling.
To assist with fisheries management.
To assist with stocking of waters.
To promote and develop coarse angling in Scotland.
To promote and organise competitions and league matches.
To provide team representation at the World Championships (CIPS-FIPS-ED).
To organise international events for Scottish anglers.

Members

At present, seven clubs are affiliated to the Federation. Individual membership of the Federation is available although it is preferred that individuals join clubs affiliated to the Federation. The annual subscription for Club Membership of the SFCA is £10 with a joining fee of £5.00.
Individual membership is offered at £2.00.

Coaching and Courses

Some SFCA member clubs hold 'in class' coaching sessions for novice anglers, while others operate 'on the bank' instruction thus providing knowledge under varying conditions.

Committee Structure

The affairs of the Federation are at present conducted by a Management Committee comprising the Chairman, Hon. Secretary, Hon. Treasurer and Club Representatives.
A Development and a Match Angling Committee also exist to deal with specific projects.

Office Bearers

Chairman and Hon. Treasurer
Mr. A.H. Keir, 'Tigh-na-Fleurs', Mill O'Gryfe Road, Bridge of Weir, Renfrewshire. Tel: Bridge of Weir 612580.

Hon. Secretary
Mr. J. McMenemy, 53 Rossland Crescent, Bishopton, Renfrewshire. Tel: Bishopton 862460

Team Manager
Mr. C. Palmer, 64 Dawson Place, Bo'ness. Tel: Bo'ness 823953

Press Officer
Mr. D. Carnell, 6 Kathleen Park, Helensburgh. Tel: 0436 78725.

Competition

Summer and Winter Club Leagues are held each year. Overall results provide the Scottish Team and Individual champions.
Scottish National Junior Open Championship.

All Scotland championship — Scottish residents only.

Scottish Federation Open.

Scottish Federation Cup —Federation members only.

Home International Series.

International friendlies against other countries.

Participation in the World Championships.

Scottish Pole Angling Championship.
Member clubs also arrange club match programmes throughout spring, summer and autumn.

Specimen Group

A newly formed and active element of the Federation. Objectives include:
Providing an efficiently managed fishery befitting the Federation membership.
Continually updating the 'Available Waters Register' for the benefit of all Scottish coarse anglers and visitors.

Clubs

Barochan Freshwater Angling Club:
Mr. A. Keir, 'Tigh-na-Fleurs', Mill O'Gryfe Road, Bridge of Weir, Renfrewshire. Tel: Bridge of Weir 612580.

Border Coarse Angling Club:
Mr. J. Wilson, 36 Portland Place, Carlisle.

Central Match Angling Club:
Mr. C. Palmer, 64 Dawson Place, Bo'ness. Tel: Bo'ness 823953.

Linlithgow C.A.C.:
Mr. E. Gilbert, 12 Clarendon Road, Linlithgow.

Edinburgh Coarse Anglers:
Mr. R. Stephens, 68 Meadowhouse Road, Edinburgh. Tel: 031-334 7787.

Milton C.A.C.:
Mr. B. Gough, 66/2 Fountainwell Terrace, Sighthill, Glasgow. Tel: 041-557 1311

Forth and Clyde C.A.C.
Mr. P. Morrisey, 18 Daiglen, Tillicoultry, Clacks. Tel: 0259 50757

GAME ANGLING CLUBS

CLUB	SECRETARY	CLUB	SECRETARY
Aberfeldy Angling Club	R.M. Stewart, Police House No.1 Kenmore Street, Aberfeldy, Perthshire.	Dunkeld & Birnam Angling Association	D.F. Scott, 3 County Place, Bankfoot, Tayside.
Airdrie Angling Club	Roy Burgess, 21 Elswick Drive, Caldercruix.	Earlston Angling Association	Mr. Lothian, 10 Westfield Street, Earlston. Tel: 559.
Annan & District Angling Club	J. Glen, 110 High Street, Annan.	Eckford Angling Association	R.B. Anderson, W.S., Royal Bank Buildings, Jedburgh. Tel: 3202.
Atholl Angling Club	W. McEwan, The Corner House, Blair, Atholl. Tel: Blair Atholl 246.	Elgin & District Angling Association	I. Mackay, Rowan Bank, 28 Rose Avenue, Elgin, Moray.
Badenoch Angling Association	Mrs. J. Waller, 39 Burnside Avenue, Aviemore.	Esk & Liddle Fisheries Association	R.J.B. Hill, Solicitor, Bank of Scotland Buildings, Langholm.
Berwick & District Angling Association	J. Moody, 12 Hillcrest, East Ord, Berwick-upon-Tweed. Tel: 305692.	Esk Valley Angling Improvement Association	Kevin Burns, 53 Fernieside Crescent, Edinburgh.
Blairgowrie, Rattray & District Angling Association	W. Matthew, 4 Mitchell Square, Blairgowrie. Tel: (0250) 3679.	Eye Water Angling Club	W.S. Gillie, 2 Tod's Court, Eyemouth.
Brechin Angling Club	D.E. Smith, 3 Friendly Park, Brechin.	Ford & Etal Estates Fishing Club	Mr. W.M. Bell, Heatherslaw, Cornhill on Tweed. Tel: Crookham 221.
Castle Douglas & District Angling Association	Ian Bendall, Tommy's Sports Shop, Castle Douglas, Tel: 0556 2851.	Fyvie Angling Association	G.A. Joss, Clydesdale Bank PLC, Fyvie, Turriff.
Chatton Angling Association	A. Jarvis, 7 New Road, Alnwick.	Gordon Fishing Club	W.A. Virtue, Kirkaig, Manse Street, Galashiels.
Coldstream & District Angling Association	Mr. E.M. Patterson, 27 Leet Street, Coldstream. Tel: 2719.	Greenlaw Angling Association	A. Lamb, Waterford, Wester Row, Greenlaw. Tel: 246.
Cramond Angling Club	R. Whyte, 23 Brunswick Street, Edinburgh.	Hawick Angling Club	R. Sutherland, 2 Twirlees Terrace, Hawick. Tel: 75150.
Dalbeattie Angling Association	N. Parker, 30 High Street, Dalbeattie. Tel: 0556 610448.	Inverness Angling Club	J. Fraser, 33 Hawthorn Drive, Inverness.
Devon Angling Association	R. Breingan, 33 Redwell Place, Alloa.	Irvine & District Angling Club	A. Sim, 51 Rubie Crescent, Irvine.
Dreghorn Angling Club	Dr. D.D. Muir, 6 Pladda Avenue, Broomlands, Irvine.	Jedforest Angling Club	Mr. A. Whitecross, 42 Howden Road, Jedburgh. Tel: 63615.
Dumfries & Galloway Angling Association	D.G. Conchie, Curriestanes Lane, Dalbeattie Road, Dumfries.	Kelso Angling Association	Mr. Hutchison, 53 Abbotseat, Kelso. Tel: 23440.

CLUB	SECRETARY	CLUB	SECRETARY
Kemnay Angling Club	A. Calder, 22 Kendal Road, Kemnay.	New Galloway Angling Association	N. Birch, Galloway View, Balmaclellan, Castle Douglas. Tel: New Galloway 404.
Killin, Breadalbane Angling Club	Douglas Allan, 12 Ballechroisk, Killin. Tel: (05672) 362.	North Uist Angling Club	Secretary, 19 Dunossil Place, Lochmaddy, North Uist.
Kilmaurs Angling Club	J. Watson, 7 Four Acres Drive, Kilmaurs.	Peeblesshire Trout Fishing Association	D.G. Fyfe, 39 High Street, Peebles. Tel: 20131.
Kintyre Fish Protection & Angling Club	S.R. Martin, Dunallister Kilkerran Road, Cambeltown.	Peeblesshire Salmon Fishing Association	Blackwood & Smith W.S., 39 High Street, Peebles.
Kyles of Bute Angling Club	R. Newton, Viewfield Cottage, Tighnabruaich, Argyll.	Perth & District Anglers Association	J.A. Lipski, 'Sunnybrae', 211 Glasgow Road, Perth PH2 0NB.
Ladykirk & Norham Angling Association	Mr. R.G. Wharton, 8 St. Cuthbert's Square, Norham. Tel: (0289) 82467.	Pitlochry Angling Club	R. Harriman, Sunnyknowe, Nursing Home Brae, Pitlochry. Tel: (0796) 2484.
Lairg Angling Club	J.M. Ross, Post Office House, Lairg, Sutherland. Tel: Lairg 2010.	Rannoch & District Angling Club	J. Brown Esq., The Square, Kinloch Rannoch. Tel: Kinloch Rannoch 331.
Larbert & Stenhousemuir Angling Club	A. Paterson, 6 Wheatlands Avenue, Bonnybridge, Stirlingshire.	River Amond Angling Association	H. Meikle, 23 Glen Terrace, Deans, Livingston.
Lauderdale Angling Association	D.M. Milligan, 41 High Street, Haddington.	St. Andrews Angling Club	Secretary, 54 Nicholas Street, St. Andrews.
Lochgilphead & District Angling Club	H. McArthur, The Tackle Shop, Lochnell Street, Lochgilphead.	St. Boswells & District Angling Association	Mr. Q. McLaren, Rowanbrae, Tweedside Road, Newtown St. Boswells. Tel: 22568.
Loch Keose Angling Association	c/o Tourist Information Centre, Stornoway, Lewis.	St. Marys Loch Angling Club	Mr. J. Miller, 8/5 Criaghouse Gardens, Edinburgh. Tel: 031-447 0024
Loch Lomond Angling Improvement Association	R.A. Clements, C.A., 224 Ingram Street, Glasgow.	Stanley & District Angling Club	D.J. Jeffrey, Airntully, Stanley. Tel: Stanley 463.
Loch Rannoch Conservation Association	Mrs. Steffen, Coilmore Cottage, Kinloch Rannoch.	Selkirk & District Angling Association	Mr. A. Murray, 40 Raeburn Meadows, Selkirk. Tel: 21534.
Melrose & District Angling Association	I.P. Graham, Dunfermline House, Buccleuch Street, Melrose. Tel: 2148.	Stormont Angling Club	The Factor, Scone Estates Office, Scone Palace, Perth.
Morebattle Angling Club	Mr. H. Fox, Orchard Cottage, Morebattle.	Stranraer & District Angling Association	Ted Ainsworth, c/o Creach More Golf Club, Stranraer.
Murthly & Glendelvine Trout Angling Club	Chairman, P.M. Castle-Smith, The Boat of Murthly, By Dunkeld, Perthshire.		

CLUB	SECRETARY	CLUB	SECRETARY
Strathmore Angling Improvement Association	Mrs. A. Henderson, 364 Blackness Road, Dundee. Tel: Dundee 68062.	Upper Nithsdale Angling Association	W. Forsyth, Solicitor, 100 High Street, Sanquhar, Dumfriesshire. Tel: Sanquhar 241.
Turriff Angling Association	I. Masson, 14 Mains Street, Turriff.	Whiteadder Angling Association	Mr. J. Boyd, St. Leonard's, Polwarth, Greenlaw. Tel: Duns 82377.
Upper Annandale Angling Association	J. Black, 1 Rosehill, Grange Road, Moffat. Tel: Moffat 20104.		

SCOTTISH FRESHWATER FISH RECORDS

Bream	5lb 15oz 12dm. = 2.71kg. Castle Loch, Dumfriesshire. H. Wood, 1973.
Carp	15lb 8oz, = 7.004kg, Lanark Loch, J. Neilson, 1983.
Char *(Salvelinus Alpinus)*	2lb 5oz = 1.408kg, Loch Dubhalochain, Knoydart Estate, S. Rex. 1982.
Dace	1lb 3oz 8dm. = 0.553kg. River Tweed, Coldstream, G. Keech, 1979.
Eel *(Anguilla Anguilla)*	4lb 6oz, = 1.908kg, Loch nr Blairgowrie. S. Richmond. 1979.
Grayling	2lb 9oz, 4dm.
Perch	4lb $1/4$oz = 1.82kg Loch Lubnaig. J. Stevenson, 1984.
Powan	1lb 7oz, 0.625kg, Loch Lomond, J. M. Ryder, 1972
Roach	2lb 1oz, 8dm, 0.948kg, River Tay, Perth. G. Shuttelworth, 1972.
*Salmon	64lb, 29.02kg, River Tay, Caputh, Miss G. W. Ballantyne, 1922.
Tench	4lb 14$^7/_8$oz = 2.24kg, Spectacle Loch, Penninchance Estate, Mrs. B. Gilber, 1982.
*Trout brown	19lb 9oz 4dm 8.800kg, Loch Quoich, Inverness-shire, J.A.F. Jackson, 1978.
*Trout, sea	20lb, = 9.071kg, River Tweed, Peebles, G. Leavy, 1983.

*Denotes British Record.

No records exist for the following species but qualifying weights listed: **Crucian Carp** 2lb; **Chub** 4lb; **Gudgeon** 4oz; **Rudd;** 2lb.

In the case of fish over the British Record Weight, please telephone either Peterborough (0733) 54084 (day) or 25248 (night) for advice. For enquiries and claims for Scotland, please contact the chairman of the Scottish Federation for 'Coarse Angling, Mr. Alisdair Keir, 'Tigh-na-Fleurs', Mill O'Gryfe Road, Bridge of Weir, Renfrewshire. Tel: Bridge of Weir 612580. Any fish not required by its captor may be retained by Glasgow Museums to build up their collection of native Scottish freshwater fish.

SCOTTISH MARINE FISH RECORDS
BOAT AND SHORE (rod and line caught)

B - Boat Records   S - Shore Records   Spec - Specimen Quanifying Weight

Species		lb	oz	dm	kg	Place of Capture	Angler	Year	Spec lb
ANGLERFISH	B	45	0	0	20.412	Sound of Mull	D. Hopper	1978	20
Lophius piscatorius	S	38	0	0	17.237	Blairmore Pier Loch Long	L.C. Hanley	1970	15
ARGENTINE	B		5	3	0.147	Arrochar	I.I. Millar	1978	4oz
Argentina sphyraena	S	OPEN AT ANY WEIGHT							
BASS	B	8	14	3	4.025	Balcary Bay	D. Shaw	1975	6
Dicentrarchus labrax	S	13	4	0	6.010	Almorness Point	G. Stewart	1975	6
BLACKFISH	B	3	10	8	1.658	Heads of Ayr	J. Semple	1972	2½
Centrolophus niger	S	OPEN AT ANY WEIGHT							Any
BLENNY, SHANNY	B	OPEN AT ANY WEIGHT							1oz
Blennius pholis	S	0	1	10	0.046	Carolina Port Dundee Docks	M.S. Ettle	1983	1oz
BLENNY, TOMPOT	B	OPEN AT ANY WEIGHT							Any
Blennius gattorugine	S		2	12	0.078	Portpatrick	G. Dods	1988	2oz
BLENNY VIVIPAROUS	B		10	0	0.283	Craigendoran	T. Lambert	1977	7oz
Zoarces viviparus	S		11	3	0.317	Craigendoran	D. Ramsay	1975	7oz
BLENNY, YARRELL'S	B	OPEN AT ANY WEIGHT							Any
Chirolophis ascanii	S		2	1	0.059	Gourock	D. McEntree	1979	2½oz
BLUEMOUTH	B	3	2	8	1.431	Loch Shell	Mrs. A. Lyngholm	1976	2½
Helicolenus dactylopterus	S	OPEN AT ANY WEIGHT							Any
BREAM, BLACK	B	2	9	0	1.162	Kebock Head, Lewis	T. Lumb	1974	1
Spondyliosoma cantharus	S	1	13	8	0.836	Gareloch	A.L. Harris	1973	1
BREAM, RAY'S	B	6	3	13	2.829	West of Barra Head	J. Holland	1978	4
Brama brama	S	6	6	8	2.905	Portobello	G. Taylor	1973	4
BREAM, RED	B	4	10	0	2.097	Ardnamurchan	R. Steel	1969	1
Pagellus bogaraveo	S	OPEN AT ANY WEIGHT							Any
BRILL	B	1	4	0	0.567	Portpatrick	J. Dickson	1984	1
Scophthalmus rhombus	S	1	2	0	0.510	Killintrinnon Lighthouse	P. Baisbrown	1971	1
BULL HUSS	B	20	3	8	9.171	Mull of Galloway	J.K. Crawford	1971	15
Scyliorhinus stellaris	S	15	8	0	7.031	West Tarbet Mull of Galloway	A.K. Paterson	1976	10
BUTTERFISH	B	OPEN AT ANY WEIGHT							Any
Pholis gunnellus	S		1	2	0.032	Gourock	D. McEntree	1978	1oz
CATFISH, COMMON	B	12	4	8	5.570	Hopeman	N. Pickard	1984	7
An a Chichas lupus	S	12	12	8	5.797	Stonehaven	G.M. Taylor	1978	4
COALFISH	B	28	4	0	12.814	Eyemouth	L. Gibson	1982	12
Pollachius virens	S	11	7	8	5.202	Loch Long	S. Mather	1976	7
COD	B	46	0	8	20.879	Gantocks	R. Baird	1970	25
Gadus morhua	S	38	0	0	17.237	Balcary Point	K. Burns	1981	15
DAB	B	2	12	4	1.254	Gairloch	R. Islip	1975	1½
Limanda limanda	S	2	5	0	1.049	Cairnryan	A. Scott	1969	1½
DAB, LON ROUGH	B		5	0	0.142	Helensburgh	R. Gregg	1983	4oz
Hippoglossoides platessoides	S		5	8	0.155	Coulport	I. McGrath	1975	4oz
DOGFISH, BLACK-MOUTHED	B	2	13	8	1.288	Loch Fyne	J.H. Anderson	1977	1½
Galeus melastromus	S	OPEN AT ANY WEIGHT							Any
DOGFISH, LESSER-SPOTTED	B	3	15	8	1.800	Kebock Hotel	J. MacDonald	1977	3
Scyliorhinus caniculus	S	4	8	0	2.040	Ayr Pier	J. Beattie	1968	3
DRAGONET, COMMON	B		4	8	0.127	Largs	T. McGowan	1978	4oz
Callionymus lyra	S		4	9	0.129	Gareloch	J. Moffat	1983	4¼oz

24

Species	lb	oz	dm	kg	Place of Capture	Angler	Year	Spec lb

B - Boat Records   S - Shore Records   Spec - Specimen Qualifying Weight

Species	lb	oz	dm	kg	Place of Capture	Angler	Year	Spec lb
EEL, COMMON	B 1	13	7	0.834	Gareloch	P. Fleming	1976	1½
Anguilla anguilla	S 3	0	0	1.360	Ayr Harbour	R.W. Morrice	1972	2
EEL, CONGER	B 48	0	0	21.771	Luce Bay	E.J. Clarke	1978	30
Conger conger	S 45	0	0	20.411	Scrabster Pier	P.G. Bell	1966	25
FLOUNDER	B 2	10	0	1.190	Fairlie	J. Roberston Snr.	1976	2½
Platichthys flesus	S 4	11	8	2.140	Musselburgh	R. Armstrong	1970	2½
GARFISH	B 1	11	8	0.779	Brodick	R. Stockwin	1970	1
Belone belone	S 1	11	0	0.764	Bute	Miss McAlorum	1971	1
GOBY, BLACK	B	1	4	0.035	Cairnryan	J. Price	1976	1oz
Gobius niger	S	2	4	0.063	Inveraray	F. O'Brien	1980	1oz
GURNARD, GREY	B 2	7	0	1.105	Caliach Point	D. Swinbanks	1976	1¾
Eutrigla gurnardus	S 1	5	0	0.595	Peterhead	A. Turnbull	1973	1
	1	5	0	0.595	Port William	J.W. Martin	1977	1
GURNARD, RED	B 2	6	0	1.077	Galiach Point	Mrs. A. Yard	1975	1½
Aspitrigla cuculus	S 1	2	5	0.519	Gareloch	G. Smith	1981	12oz
GURNARD, STREAKED	B OPEN AT ANY WEIGHT							Any
Trigloporus lastoviza	S 1	6	8	0.637	Loch Goil	H.L. Smith	1971	1
GURNARD, TUB	B 5	5	0	2.409	Luce Bay	J.S. Dickinson	1975	3½
Trigla lucerna	S 1	1	0	0.481	Carrick Bay	A.E. Maxwell	1978	12oz
HADDOCK	B 9	14	12	4.501	Summer Isles	M. Lawton	1980	6
Melanogrammus aeglefinus	S 6	12	0	3.601	Loch Goil	G.B. Stevenson	1976	3
HAKE	B 18	5	8	8.321	Shetland	B. Sinclair	1971	10
Merluccius merluccius	S	11	7	0.324	Gourock	S. Moyes	1979	8oz
HALIBUT	B 234	0	0	106.136	Scrabster	C. Booth	1979	50
Hippoglossus hippoglossus	S OPEN AT ANY WEIGHT							Any
HERRING	B 1	2	0	0.510	Loch Long	R.C. Scott	1974	14oz
Clupea harengus	S	11	11	0.331	Port Logan	R. Smith	1984	10oz
LING	B 57	8	0	26.082	Stonehaven	I. Duncan	1982	20
Molva molva	S 12	4	0	5.557	Scrabster	A. Allan	1984	6
LUMPSUCKER	B 4	11	4	2.133	Innellan	G.T. Roebuck	1976	3
Cyclopterus lumpus	S 4	14	12	2.232	Craigendoran	G. Court	1981	3
MACKEREL	B 3	12	0	1.701	Ullapool	E. Scobie	1965	2
Scomber scombrus	S 2	5	8	1.063	Wick	W. Richardson	1969	2
MEGRIM	B 3	12	8	1.715	Gareloch	P. Christie	1973	2
Lepidorhumbus whiffiagonis	S OPEN AT ANY WEIGHT							Any
MULLET, GOLDEN GREY	B OPEN AT ANY WEIGHT							Any
Liza aurata	S	11	0	0.312	Fairlie	I. McFadyen	1972	8oz
MULLET, THICK LIPPED GREY	B 3	6	0	1.531	Luce Bay	R. Williamson	1976	3½
Crenimugil labrosus	S 6	7	8	2.934	Ayr Harbour	D.A. Smith	1984	4½
NORWAY HADDOCK	B 1	1	0	0.482	Shetland	Mrs. E.W.M. Watt	1984	14oz
Sebastes viviparus	S OPEN AT ANY WEIGHT							Any
PIPEFISH, GREATER	B OPEN AT ANY WEIGHT							Any
Syngnathus acus	S	0	13	0.023	Coulport	H. Holding	1975	Any
PLAICE	B 10	3	8	4.635	Longa Sound	H. Gardiner	1974	5
Pleuronectes platessa	S 5	8	0	2.494	Arrochar	A. Holt Jnr.	1971	3½
POLLACK	B 18	0	0	8.165	Scrabster	N. Carter	1971	10
Pollachius pollachius	S 13	14	0	6.293	Furnace, Loch Fyne	J. Arthur	1974	8
POOR COD	B 1	4	0	0.567	Arbroath	F. Chalmers	1969	1
Trisopterus minutus	S 1	0	0	0.453	Loch Fyne	F. Johnstone	1970	12oz
POUTING	B 3	8	0	1.587	Gourock	J. Lewis	1977	2
Trisopterus luscus	S 2	1	0	0.935	Gourock	D. Bradley	1976	1½
RAY, BLONDE	B 26	11	0	12.105	Caliach Point	B. Swinbanks	1977	15
Raja brachyura	S OPEN AT ANY WEIGHT							Any
RAY, CUCKOO	B 5	4	4	2.388	Gairloch	A. Bridges	1979	4
Raja naevus	S 4	11	0	2.126	Gourock	R.A.H. McCaw	1973	3¾
RAY, SPOTTED	B 6	3	4	2.813	Caliach Point	P.J. England	1977	4
Raja montagui	S 5	12	0	2.608	Cairnryan	G.C. Styles	1975	4

B - Boat Records   S - Shore Records   Spec - Specimen Qualifying Weight

Species	lb	oz	dm	kg	Place of Capture	Angler	Year	Spec lb
RAY, THORNBACK	B 29	8	10	13.399	Luce Bay	A. McLean	1982	15
Raja clavata	S 21	6	0	9.695	Crammag Head	P. Paterson	1984	10
ROCKLING, FIVE BEARDED	B OPEN AT ANY WEIGHT							Any
Ciliata mustela	S	6	6	0.181	Craigendoran	A. Shaw	1980	4½oz
ROCKLING, FOUR BEARDED	B	1	7	0.040	Gourock	S. Hodgson	1981	1¾oz
Rhinonemus cimbrius	S OPEN AT ANY WEIGHT							Any
ROCKLING, SHORE	B OPEN AT ANY WEIGHT							Any
Gaidrupaarus mediterraneus	S	14	8	0.411	Loch Long	A. Glen	1982	7oz
ROCKLING, THREE BEARDED	B 1	14	4	0.857	Stonehaven	W. Murphy	1972	1¼
Gaidropsarus vulgaris	S 2	11	x9	1.235	Kirkcudbright	A. Johnstone	1981	1½
SANDEEL, GREATER	B	8	0	0.227	Caliach Point	T.J. Ashwell	1984	6oz
Hyperoplus lanceolatus	S	2	15	0.083	Eggerness	J. Ryman	1979	2½
SCAD (HORSE MACKEREL)	B 1	7	0	0.652	Loch Shell	D. MacNeill	1976	1
Trachurus trachurus	S 3	0	14	1.384	Cockenzie	R. Dillon	1981	1
SEA SCORPION, LONGSPINED	B	2	20	0.074	Stornoway	P. Redshaw	1981	2½oz
Taurulus bubalis	S	5	9	0.157	Aberdeen	T.J. Ashwell	1982	2½oz
SEA SCORPION SHORTSPINED	B 2	3	0	0.992	Kepple Pier	R. Stevenson	1973	1¾
Myoxocephalus scorpius	S 2	3	0	0.992	Cloch, Gourock	W. Crawford	1979	1½
SHAD, TWAITE	B OPEN AT ANY WEIGHT							Any
Alosa fallax	S 2	12	0	1.247	Garlieston	J.W. Martin	1978	1½
SHARK, BLUE	B 85	0	0	38.781	Stornoway	J. Morrison	1972	50
Prionace glauca	S OPEN AT ANY WEIGHT							Any
SHARK, PORBEAGLE	B 404	0	0	183.244	Sumburgh Head	P. White	1976	100
Lamna nasus	B 404	0	0	183.244	Sumburgh Head	P. White	1978	100
	S OPEN AT ANY WEIGHT							Any
SKATE, COMMON	B 266	8	0	102.733	Score Point	R.S. MacPherson	1970	100
Raja	S 154	0	0	69.854	Achiltibuie	M.J. Traynor	1971	50
SMOOTHHOUND, STARRY	B OPEN AT ANY WEIGHT							Any
Mustelus asterias	S 7	8	0	3.402	Eggerness	B. Moore	1983	5
SOLE, DOVER	B 1	12	0	0.793	Killintrinnon	W. Hannah	1974	1
Solea solea	S	9	12	0.276	Portpatrick	G. Griffiths	1977	8oz
SOLE, LEMON	B 2	2	0	0.963	Lochgoilhead	J. Gordon	1976	2
Microstomus kitt	S 1	6	2	0.627	Peterhead	B.N. Davidson	1982	12oz
SPURDOG	B 17	12	0	8.051	Troon	J. Scott	1984	14
Squalus acanthias	S 12	8	12	5.691	Millport	R. Paterson	1983	8
TADPOLE FISH	B	14	14	0.421	Firth of Clyde	R. Donnelly	1981	8oz
Raniceps raninus	S 1	3	0	0.538	Dunbar	W. Dickson	1977	10oz
TOPE	B 62	0	0	28.122	Drummore	F. Bristow	1975	45
Galeorhinus galeus	S 54	4	0	24.606	Loch Ryan	D. Hastings	1975	30
TOPKNOT	B OPEN AT ANY WEIGHT							Any
Zeugopterus punctatus	S	8	8	0.241	Peterhead	G.M. Taylor	1975	6oz
TORSK	B 18	7	2	7.005	Pentland Firth	D.J. Mackay	1982	8
Brosme brosme	S OPEN AT ANY WEIGHT							Any
TURBOT	B 25	4	0	11.453	Mull	I. Jenkins	1982	15
Scophthalmus maximus	S 1	3	1	0.540	Troon	A. Crowther	1976	1
WEEVER, GREATER	B OPEN AT ANY WEIGHT							Any
Trachinus draco	S 1	1	14	0.508	Mull of Galloway	Mr. W. Allison	1984	1
WHITING	B 6	8	0	2.948	Girvan	A.M. Devay	1969	3
Merlangius merlangus	S 3	0	0	1.360	Gourock	d. McTehee	1970	2
WHITING, BLUE (POUTASSOU)	B 1	12	0	0.793	Loch Fyne	J.H. Anderson	1977	8oz

B - Boat Records   S - Shore Records   Spec - Specimen Qualifying Weight

Species	lb	oz	dm	kg	Place of Capture	Angler	Year	Spec lb
Micromesistius poutassou	S OPEN AT ANY WEIGHT							Any
WRASSE, BALLAN	B 4	12	4	2.061	Calgary Bay, Mull	K.J.F. Hall	1983	🐷
Labrus bergylta	S 5	0	0	2.268	Girvan	T. McGeehan	1971	3½
WRASS, CORKWING	B OPEN AT ANY WEIGHT							Any
Crenilabrus melops	S	5	4	0.149	Loch Long	G. Elder	1978	4oz
WRASSE, CUCKOO	B 3	0	0	1.361	Scrabster	Mrs. H. Campbell	1969	1¼
Labrus mixtus	S 1	2	0	0.510	Neist Point, Skye	Q.A. Oliver	1972	12oz
WRASSE GOLDSINNY	B 0	0	12	0.021	Lochaline	D.D. Morrison	1983	1oz
Ctenolabrus rupestris	S	1	13	0.051	Loch Goil	T. Lambert	1977	1½oz
WRASSE, SMALL MOUTHED ROCK COOK	B OPEN AT ANY WEIGHT							Any
Centrolabrus expletus	S	1	9	0.044	Finnart	A. Elder	1981	1½oz

The above records are based on information received up to 23rd December, 1984 by the S.F.S.A. Honorary Fish Recorder, Mr. R. B. Burn, 7 Oswald Road, Ayr KA8 8NY.

USEFUL ADDRESSES IN SCOTTISH SPORT FISHERIES

Scottish Tourist Board, 23 Ravelston Terrace, Edinburgh EH4 3EU.
Tel: 031-332 2433

Department of Agriculture and Fisheries for Scotland, Chesser House, Gorgie Road, Edinburgh EH11 3AW.
Tel: 031-443 4020.

Inspector of Salmon Fisheries, Chesser House, Gorgie Road, Edinburgh EH11 3AW.
Tel: 031-443 4020.

Freshwater Fisheries Laboratory, Faskally, Pitlochry, Perthshire PH16 5LB.
Tel: Pitlochry (0796) 2060.

Marine Laboratory, Victoria Road, Torry, Aberdeen.

Secretary, Scottish River Purification Boards Association, City Chambers, Glasgow G2 1DU.
Tel: 041-227 4190.

Scottish Sports Council, 1-3 St. Colme Street, Edinburgh EH3 6AA.
Tel: 031-225 8411.

Nature Conservancy Council, 12 Hope Terrace, Edinburgh.
Tel: 031-447 4784.

Forestry Commission, 231 Corstorphine Road, Edinburgh EH12.
Tel: 031-334 0303.

North of Scotland Hydro Electric Board, 16 Rothesay Terrace, Edinburgh EH3.
Tel: 031-225 1361.

Institute of Fisheries Management, Secretary (Scottish Branch), Gordon Struthers, c/o Freshwater Fisheries Laboratory, Faskally, Pitlochry, Perthshire.

Anglers Cooperative Association, Secretary, Malcolm Thomson, 21 Heriot Row, Edinburgh EH3.
Tel: 031-225 6511.

The Salmon and Trout Association, 2 Queen's Road, Aberdeen A89 8BD.
Tel: (0224) 644276.

Scottish Angler's National Association, Secretary, D.A. Biggart, 307 West George Street, Glasgow G2 4LB.
Tel: 041-221 7206

Central Scotland Anglers Association, Secretary, Kevin Burns, 53 Fernieside Crescent, Edinburgh.
Tel: 031-664 4685.

Federation of Highland Angling Clubs, Secretary, W. Brown, Coruisk, Strathpeffer, Ross-shire.
Tel: 099 72 446.

Department of Forestry and Natural Resources. University of Edinburgh, Kings Buildings, Mayfield Road, Edinburgh EH9 3JU.
Tel: 031-667 1081.

Institute of Aquaculture, University of Stirling, Stirling FK9 4LA.
Tel: Stirling (0786) 3171.

Please mention this Pastime Publications guide.

CLOSE SEASON

The following are the statutory close season dates for trout and salmon fishing in Scotland.

TROUT

The close season for trout in Scotland is from 7 October to 14 March, both days inclusive, but many clubs extend this close season still further to allow the fish to reach better condition.

Fresh trout may not be sold between the end of August and the beginning of April, and not at any time if less than eight inches long.

SALMON

Net Fishing	Rod Fishing	River District
1 Sept-15 Feb	1 Nov-15 Feb	Add
27 Aug-10 Feb	1 Nov-10 Feb	Ailort
27 Aug-10 Feb	1 Nov-10 Feb	Aline
27 Aug-10 Feb	1 Nov-10 Feb	Alness
27 Aug-10 Feb	1 Nov-10 Feb	Applecross
27 Aug-10 Feb	1 Nov-10 Feb	Arnisdale (Loch Hourn)
27 Aug-10 Feb	16 Oct-10 Feb	Awe
27 Aug-10 Feb	1 Nov-10 Feb	Ayr
27 Aug-10 Feb	1 Nov-10 Feb	Baa & Goladoir
27 Aug-10 Feb	1 Nov-10 Feb	Badachro & Kerry (Gairloch)
27 Aug-10 Feb	16 Oct-10 Feb	Balgay & Shieldaig
27 Aug-10 Feb	1 Nov-10 Feb	Beauly
27 Aug-10 Feb	1 Nov-10 Feb	Berriedale
10 Sept-24 Feb	1 Nov-24 Feb	Bervie
27 Aug-10 Feb	1 Nov-10 Feb	Bladenoch
27 Aug-10 Feb	1 Nov-10 Feb	Broom
27 Aug-10 Feb	16 Oct-31 Jan	Brora
10 Sept-24 Feb	1 Nov-24 Feb	Carradale
27 Aug-10 Feb	1 Nov-10 Feb	Carron (W. Ross)
10 Sept-24 Feb	1 Nov-24 Feb	Clayburn (Isle of Harris (East))
27 Aug-10 Feb	1 Nov-10 Feb	Clyde & Leven
27 Aug-10 Feb	1 Oct-25 Feb	Conon
14 Sept-28 Feb	15 Oct-28 Feb	Cree
27 Aug-10 Feb	17 Oct-10 Feb	Creed or Stornoway and Laxay (Isle of Lewis)
27 Aug-10 Feb	1 Nov-10 Feb	Creran (Loch Creran)
27 Aug-10 Feb	1 Nov-10 Feb	Croe & Shiel
27 Aug-10 Feb	1 Oct-31 Jan	Dee (Aberdeenshire)
27 Aug-10 Feb	1 Nov-10 Feb	Dee (Kirkcudbrightshire)
27 Aug-10 Feb	1 Nov-10 Feb	Deveron
27 Aug-10 Feb	1 Nov-10 Feb	Don
27 Aug-10 Feb	1 Nov-10 Feb	Doon
1 Sept-15 Feb	16 Oct-15 Feb	Drummachloy or Glenmore (Isle of Bute)
27 Aug-10 Feb	16 Oct-10 Feb	Dunbeath
21 Aug- 4 Feb	1 Nov-31 Jan	Earn
1 Sept-15 Feb	1 Nov-15 Feb	Echaig
1 Sept-15 Feb	1 Nov-15 Feb	Esk, North
1 Sept-15 Feb	1 Nov-15 Feb	Esk, South
27 Aug-10 Feb	1 Nov-10 Feb	Ewe (Isle of Harris (West))
27 Aug-10 Feb	6 Oct-10 Feb	Findhorn
10 Sept-24 Feb	1 Nov-24 Feb	Fleet (Kirkcudbright)
10 Sept-24 Feb	1 Nov-24 Feb	Fleet (Sutherland)
27 Aug-10 Feb	1 Nov-10 Feb	Forss
27 Aug-10 Feb	1 Nov-31 Jan	Forth
1 Sept-15 Feb	1 Nov-15 Feb	Fyne, Shira & Aray (Loch Fyne)
10 Sept-24 Feb	1 Nov-24 Feb	Girvan
27 Aug-10 Feb	1 Nov-10 Feb	Glenelg
27 Aug-10 Feb	1 Nov-10 Feb	Gour
27 Aug-10 Feb	1 Nov-10 Feb	Greiss, Laxdale or Thunga
27 Aug-10 Feb	1 Nov-10 Feb	Grudie or Dionard
27 Aug-10 Feb	1 Nov-10 Feb	Gruinard and Little Gruinard
27 Aug-10 Feb	1 Oct-11 Jan	Halladale, Strathy, Naver & Borgie
27 Aug-10 Feb	1 Oct-10 Jan	Helmsdale
27 Aug-10 Feb	1 Oct-11 Jan	Hope and Polla or Strathbeg
10 Sept-24 Feb	1 Nov-24 Feb	Howmore
27 Aug-10 Feb	1 Nov-10 Feb	Inchard
10 Sept-24 Feb	1 Nov-24 Feb	Inner (on Jura)
27 Aug-10 Feb	1 Nov-10 Feb	Inver
10 Sept-24 Feb	1 Nov-24 Feb	Iora (on Arran)
10 Sept-24 Feb	1 Nov-24 Feb	Irvine & Garnock
27 Aug-10 Feb	1 Nov-10 Feb	Kannaird
27 Aug-10 Feb	1 Nov-10 Feb	Kilchoan
27 Aug-10 Feb	1 Nov-10 Feb	Kinloch (Kyle of Tongue)
27 Aug-10 Feb	1 Nov-10 Feb	Kirkaig
27 Aug-10 Feb	1 Nov-10 Feb	Kishorn
27 Aug-10 Feb	1 Oct-10 Jan	Kyle of Sutherland
10 Sept-24 Feb	1 Nov-10 Feb	Laggan & Sorn (Isle of Islay)
27 Aug-10 Feb	1 Nov-10 Feb	Laxford

Net Fishing	Rod Fishing	River District	Net Fishing	Rod Fishing	River District
27 Aug-10 Feb	1 Nov-10 Feb	Little Loch Broom	27 Aug-10 Feb	1 Nov-10 Feb	Pennygowan or
27 Aug-10 Feb	1 Nov-10 Feb	Loch Duich			Glenforsa & Aros
27 Aug-10 Feb	1 Nov-10 Feb	Loch Luing			
27 Aug-10 Feb	17 Oct-10 Feb	Loch Roag	27 Aug-10 Feb	1 Nov-10 Feb	Resort
27 Aug-10 Feb	1 Nov-10 Feb	Lochy	1 Sept-15 Feb	1 Nov-15 Feb	Ruel
27 Aug-10 Feb	16 Oct-10 Feb	Lossie			
10 Sept-24 Feb	1 Nov-24 Feb	Luce	27 Aug-10 Feb	1 Nov-10 Feb	Sanda
27 Aug-10 Feb	1 Nov-10 Feb	Lussa	27 Aug-10 Feb	1 Nov-10 Feb	Scaddle
		(Isle of Mull)	10 Sept-24 Feb	1 Nov-24 Feb	Shetland Isles
			27 Aug-10 Feb	1 Nov-10 Feb	Shiel
			27 Aug-10 Feb	1 Nov-10 Feb	Sligachan
27 Aug-10 Feb	1 Nov-10 Feb	Moidart	27 Aug-10 Feb	1 Nov-10 Feb	Snizort
27 Aug-10 Feb	1 Nov-10 Feb	Morar	27 Aug-10 Feb	1 Oct-10 Feb	Spey
20 Sept-24 Feb	1 Nov-24 Feb	Mullangaren,	10 Sept-24 Feb	1 Nov-24 Feb	Stinchar
		Horasary and	27 Aug-10 Feb	1 Nov-10 Feb	Sunart
		Lochnaciste			(except Earn)
		(Isle of North Uist)			
			21 Aug- 4 Feb	16 Oct-14 Jan	Tay
27 Aug-10 Feb	1 Oct-10 Feb	Nairn	27 Aug-10 Feb	6 Oct-10 Jan	Thurso
27 Aug-10 Feb	1 Nov-10 Feb	Nell, Feochan	27 Aug-10 Feb	1 Nov-10 Feb	Torridon
		and Euchar	15 Sept-14 Feb	1 Dec-31 Jan	Tweed
27 Aug-10 Feb	16 Oct-14 Jan	Ness			
10 Sept-24 Feb	1 Dec-24 Feb	Nith	10 Sept-24 Feb	1 Nov- 9 Feb	Ugie
			27 Aug-10 Feb	1 Nov-10 Feb	Ullapool
			10 Sept-24 Feb	1 Dec-24 Feb	Urr
10 Sept-24 Feb	1 Nov-24 Feb	Orkney Isles			
27 Aug-10 Feb	1 Nov-10 Feb	Ormsary (Loch	27 Aug-10 Feb	1 Nov-10 Feb	Wick
		Killisport), Loch			
		Head & Stornoway	10 Sept-24 Feb	1 Nov-10 Feb	Ythan

There is no close season for coarse fishing.

A PASTIME PUBLICATION
will help you
to find a Happy Holiday for all

SCOTLAND HOME OF GOLF

SCOTLAND FOR FISHING

SCOTLAND FOR THE MOTORIST

See our Guides on Sale
at Your Local Newsagent
and Book Shop.

PASTIME PUBLICATIONS
LIMITED

SEA ANGLING – REGULATIONS

C. MINIMUM QUALIFYING SIZES OF FISH PRESENTED FOR WEIGH-IN

1.
Bass (Dicentrarchus labrax)	30 cm	(11.8 in)
Brill (Scophthalmus rhombus)	30 cm	(11.8 in)
Coalfish (Pollachius virens) (Boat Caught)	35 cm	(13.8 in)
Coalfish (Pollachius virens) (Shore Caught)	30 cm	(11.8 in)
★ Cod (Gadus morhua)	30 cm	(11.8 in)
Dab (Limanda limanda)	20 cm	(7.9 in)
Dogfish – all species (Scyliohinus, Squalius sp)	35 cm	(13.8 in)
Eels – all species (Conger, Anguilla sp)	35 cm	(13.8 in)
Haddock (Melanogrammus aeglefinus)	27 cm	(10.6 in)
Hake (Merluccius merluccius)	30 cm	(11.8 in)
Halibut (Hippoglossus hippoglossus)	35 cm	(13.8 in)
Ling (Molva molva)	30 cm	(11.8 in)
Megrim (Lepidorhombus wiffiagonis)	25 cm	(9.8 in)
Pollack (Pollachius pollachius)	35 cm	(13.8 in)
Plaice (Pleuronectes platessa)	25 cm	(9.8 in)
Rays (Raja sp)	35 cm	(13.8 in)
Skates (Raja batis, alba, oxyrinchus sp)	11.35kg	(25 lbs)
Soles (Microstomus kitt, solea sp)	24 cm	(9.4 in)
Tope (Galeorhinus galeus)	9.10 kg	(20 lbs)
Turbot (Scophthalmus maximus)	30 cm	(11.8 in)
Whiting (Merlangius merlangus)	27 cm	(10.6 in)
Witches (Glyptocephalus gynoglossus)	28 cm	(11.0 in)
All other species	20 cm	(7.9 in)

2. A maximum of three mackerel may be presented for weigh-in.

3. TOPE AND SKATE: Common (R. batis); long-nosed (R. oxyrhinchus) or white (R. alba) are not to be brought ashore during events designated as TOPE or SKATE festivals. They are to be weighed immediately after capture and returned to the sea. (This rule does not apply to potential national record fish which must be brought ashore for weighing. In designated TOPE Competitions no minimum size for weighing will be applied as long as fish are weighed on board and returned alive.

4. Any obviously undersized fish presented for the weigh-in will result in the entrant being disqualified.

★ The minimum size for Cod for the Irish Sea South 52° North 55° is 45 cm. (17.7 ins) from 1st October to 31st December. Lochryan is not included as it comes into the Clyde area.
Northern Limits of Coordinates are from approximately Corsewall Point –Scottish Coast to Carnlough – Irish Coast.

WATERS FIT FOR FISH

The maintenance of waters fit for fish to live in and fishers to fish in has not happened by chance, but requires constant vigilance and prompt action.

The Scottish River Purification Boards have made substantial improvements to the chronic pollution of many of our industrial rivers, particularly in Central Scotland. The return of the salmon to the Clyde in 1983 is perhaps the best known achievement of recent years.

However, accidents still occur far too frequently where spillages or discharges get into the watercourse. Often it is you — the angler — who is the first one on the scene and the only witness. What can you do?

The association of Scottish River Purification Boards has recommended the following procedure which can be applied throughout Scotland.

On discovering or suspecting pollution, an angler should adopt the following procedure.

(i) Telephone the appropriate Board as soon as possible. Do not wait until you have finished fishing before you make the call.

(ii) Give the following details:
(a) Your name, address and telephone number.
(b) The exact location of the place where you have seen the pollution.
(c) A description of how the river looks, colour, dead fish etc.

(iii) If there are any dead fish, take a specimen from the river so it can be collected later by an officer of the Board.

(iv) If you have a clean bottle or unused polythene bag, take a sample of the river water and retain it for the Board's officer to collect.

KEY TO MAP

CLYDE RIVER PURIFICATION BOARD
Rivers House,
Murray Road,
East Kilbride.
Tel: East Kilbride 38181

FORTH RIVER PURIFICATION BOARD
Colinton Dell House,
West Mill Road,
Colinton,
Edinburgh EH13 0PH.
Tel: 031-441 4691

HIGHLAND RIVER PURIFICATION BOARD
Strathpeffer Road,
Dingwall IV15 9QY.
Tel: Dingwall 62021

NORTH EAST RIVER PURIFICATION BOARD
Woodside House,
Persley,
Aberdeen AB2 2UQ.
Tel: Aberdeen 6966147

SOLWAY RIVER PURIFICATION BOARD
Rivers House, Irongray Road,
Dumfries DG2 0JE.
Tel: Dumfries 720502

TAY RIVER PURIFICATION BOARD
3 South Street,
Perth PH2 8NJ.
Tel: Perth 27889

TWEED RIVER PURIFICATION BOARD
Burnbrae,
Mossilee Road,
Galashiels.
Tel: Galashiels 2425

Ian G. Fraser, Secretary,
Scottish River Purification
Boards' Association,
City Chambers, Glasgow G2 1DU.

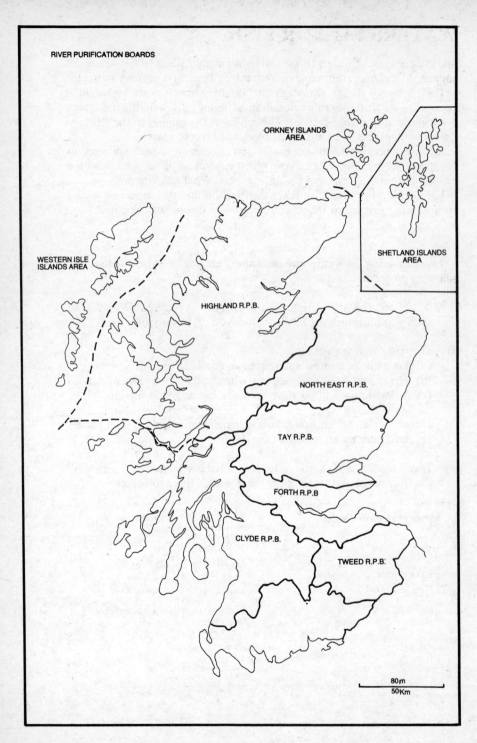

RIVER PURIFICATION BOARDS

ORKNEY ISLANDS
AREA

SHETLAND ISLANDS
AREA

WESTERN ISLE
ISLANDS AREA

HIGHLAND R.P.B.

NORTH EAST R.P.B.

TAY R.P.B.

FORTH R.P.B

CLYDE R.P.B.

TWEED R.P.B.

80 m
50 Km

KEEPING
THE WATERS CLEAN

The maintenance of waters fit for fish to live and fishers to fish in has not happened by chance, but requires constant vigilance and prompt action.

The Scottish River Purification Board have made substantial improvements to the chronic pollution of many of our industrial rivers,
particularly in Central Scotland. The return of the salmon to the Clyde in 1983 is perhaps the best known achievement of recent years.

However, accidents still occur far too frequently where spillages or discharges get into the watercourse. Often it is you — the angler — who is the first one on the scene and the only witness. What can you do?

The association of Scottish River Purification Boards has recommended the following procedure which can be applied throughout Scotland. The boundaries and addresses of the appropriate Purification Boards are shown in the Map opposite.

On discovering or suspecting pollution, an angler should adopt the following procedure:

(i) Telephone the appropriate Board as soon as possible. Do not wait until you have finished fishing before you make the call.

(ii) Give the following details:
   (a) Your name, address and telephone number.
   (b) The exact location of the place where you have seen the pollution.
   (c) A description of how the river looks, colour, dead fish etc.

(iii) If there are any dead fish, take a specimen from the river so it can be collected later by an officer of the Board.

(iv) If you have a clean bottle or unused polythene bag, take a sample of the river water and retain it for the Board's officer to collect.

COVER YOURSELF AGAINST INSECT BITES...

Don't be plagued by midges, clegs, mosquitoes and flies.

Use MIPEL™ insect repellent wipes.

A system designed for the angler by an angling entomologist, and consisting of tissues impregnated with the two most effective repellents available, neatly packaged in foil.

Non-greasy and safe to use, MIPEL™ is the only product available in Britain containing both of these chemicals from The World Health Organisation's list of effective repellents.

Slip a MIPEL™ sachet into your pocket next time you go out!

...WITH MIPEL™

ONLY £1.00 for 10, £6.50 for 100 (Including post and packing)
Please send remittance with order

AVAILABLE ONLY FROM: McCALLUMS, FREEPOST, ANNFIELD, GLENALMOND, PERTH, PH1 3BR.

be Prepared with

SHOO!

INSECT REPELLENT

NON-GREASY · ODOURLESS

FOR ANGLERS, CAMPERS, GARDENERS, AND ALL OUTDOOR PURSUITS

Shoo Insect Repellent is guaranteed effective, long lasting and economical. Handy pocket size, unbreakable bottle and now in new sachet form. It is cosmetically **SAFE** on the skin. Available at most tackle shops, chemists and general stores.

Shoo is used by Forestry Workers in the thick Highland woods where the insects are most voracious and it is found to be highly successful.

**MADE BY A. P. CUMMING, WOODSIDE LABS., BLAIRMORE, ARGYLL
TEL: (036-984) 265**

SALMON & SEA TROUT FISHING (SCOTLAND) 1987

Savills manage and let fishing on a variety of well known Scottish rivers including the Tay, Annan, Dee, Conon, South Esk and Deveron.

Fishings of various quality and price are let on a weekly basis, with and without accommodation.

If interested you should write giving us your detailed requirements.

For particulars apply:
Savills, 12 Clerk Street, Brechin, Angus DD9 6AE.

FISHING AROUND SCOTLAND

From the South to the North 7 privately-owned hotels offer fishing holidays for salmon, brown and sea-trout and sea-angling.

Send for full descriptive leaflet giving advice on best times, permits and hotel prices.

We also offer 3, 5 or 7 night centred holidays. If interested and when requesting fishing leaflet, please ask for our full colour brochure.

Inter-Hotel (Scotland)
2d Churchill Way
Bishopbriggs
GLASGOW G64 2RH
Tel: 041-762 0838

SAPLINBRAE HOUSE HOTEL

OLD DEER   Telephone: MINTLAW
MINTLAW   (0771) 23515/23643
ABERDEENSHIRE   Telex: 739032

Conference Facilities ● Sporting Activities
● Sporting Lodge ● Game Shooting ●
Fishing ● Deer Stalking ● Pony Trekking

Stag Restaurant ● Tack Room Restaurant
● Braes Snug Bar ● Ferguson Lounge

ACCOMMODATION

Single Room £27-£37 Double/Twin Room £37-£47
(All rates inclusive of VAT and full breakfast)

A B E R D E E N S H I R E

CASTLE HOTEL HUNTLY GRAMPIAN

Standing in its own grounds on the outskirts of Huntly, the Castle Hotel, hospitable as befits its heritage ... for this was formerly the ancient home of the Dukes of Gordon ... offers every comfort, spacious lounges, varied menus and well stocked cellar. Fully licensed. A.A., R.A.C., R.S.A.C., Write for illustrated brochure.

THE RIVER DEVERON PROVIDES EXCELLENT FISHING BOTH ON HOTEL WATER AND ON OTHER BEATS BY ARRANGEMENT.
TELEPHONE: HUNTLY (0466) 2696

ABERDEENSHIRE

RIVER & ESTUARY FISHING

UDNY ARMS HOTEL

What more can a fisherman ask for!

The Udny Arms Hotel
(Ideal base for a golfing holiday)
NEWBURGH, Aberdeenshire
TELEPHONE (03586) 444
TELEX 265871 (quote ABD 062)

Ask your bookshop
for
Pastime Publications
other Holiday Guides

**Scotland for the
Motorist**

**Scotland Home of
Golf**

ANGUS

SHOTCAST Ltd

SPECIALISTS IN ALL TYPES
OF FISHING TACKLE
Full Range of Accessories Available

8 Whitehall Crescent, Dundee   **Dundee 25621**

ARGYLLSHIRE

DALILEA HOUSE
AA Listed

Dalilea House, located as it is on the shores of Loch Shiel, one of the Highland's loveliest lochs, lends itself to a peaceful holiday with traditional farmhouse cooking: salmon and sea trout fishing in the loch, boating, hillwalking, or just soaking in the beauty of these unspoilt surroundings. This unusually picturesque farmhouse, situated on 14,000 acres of hill farm, is four miles from the sea, one-and-a-half miles from the bus and has ample parking. Partially centrally heated accommodation in six rooms with washbasins, one bathroom, two toilets, lounge (without TV) and dining room. Open March to October. **Self catering** also available.
Mrs. M. Macaulay,
Dalilea House,
Acharacle.
Tel: Salen (096 785) 253.

36

INVERORAN HOTEL
Nr. Bridge of Orchy, Argyll
083 84 220

Now under new family management, this traditional Scottish Inn with eight bedrooms offers a cosy atmosphere, home cooking and a warm welcome. Salmon fishing on private 2 mile stretch of River Orchy, with seven named pools, which is not restricted to fly fishing, but has 4 rods only. Also fishing on Loch Tulla next to hotel with fly and boat only.

PEACE & QUIET AT ROCKHILL FARM

GOOD FISHING, FOOD & WINE

Rockhill Guest House is only 150 yards from Loch Awe with a farm road to the waters edge, boat & engine available. Also small private Lochan for Brown Trout. Plenty of good river fishing in the area. Rockhill is situated on the south-east shore of Loch Awe with Panoramic views of the Cruachan range of mountains and Priest Island, which is Rockhill property, and the bay between the island and our shore (Wire Bay) is one of the best spots for fishing on the loch. First class home cooking using produce from our large picturesque garden and farm (packed lunches with home cookies etc). We will cook your catch for your breakfast or freeze it for you to take home. Though the guesthouse dates back to 1630 it has been attractively modernised with every comfort and convenience: 6 double and family bedrooms all with H&C, electric blankets and fires, colour T.V., tea making facilities, shaver points etc. 2 bathrooms, 2 showers; 4 toilets. You have access to the house at all times of day. An ideal spot for those who enjoy peace and quiet. Good fishing and food in beautiful surroundings where guests return year after year.

Open Easter to October AA listed Residential Licence.
SAE for comprehensive brochure.
Mrs. Helena Hodge & Mr & Mrs B. Whalley, Rockhill Farm,
Guesthouse Ardbrecknish, by Dalmally, Argyll PA33 1BH.
Telephone: 086-63 218

ARDBRECKNISH, LOCH AWE
SELF CATERING HOLIDAYS WITH EXCELLENT TROUT & PIKE FISHING

Cottages and apartments for 2 to 12 in owner/architect's superb conversion of 17th century house in secluded lochside grounds, with truly spectacular views.

From £45 per week (£30 per weekend) for 2 in low season, with VAT, bed linen, TV's, library, laundry, barbecues, indoor and outdoor games facilities for all ages and loch fishing inclusive.

Loch fishing all inclusive throughout the year.

BOATS, ENGINES, RODS & GHILLIE SERVICE ALSO AVAILABLE

Donald & Beth Wilson, Ardbrecknish House,
By Dalmally, Argyll
Tel: (08663) 223

A
R
G
Y
L
L
S
H
I
R
E

STRATHECK INTERNATIONAL CARAVAN PARK

Loch Eck by Dunoon, Argyll PA23 8SG.
Telephone: Kilmun (0369 84) 472

AA   RAC   COMMENDATION

Seven miles from Dunoon on the A815 this fine, secluded and beautifully situated riverside park is bounded by Loch Eck and the famous Younger Botanic Garden. Ample room for 50 caravans and tents.
Luxury Caravans for hire and sale. Seasonal sites available. Also Tourers for hire.
Modern toilet block.
Launderette and Off Licence shop. Loch and river fishing permits may be granted. Boats and canoes for hire.
Sailing, pony-trekking, hill and forest walking, swimming and mountaineering close at hand.

Car essential. Write for brochure and details of hire caravans to:
Len and Margaret Dixon, Resident Proprietors.

ARGYLLSHIRE

GLENDARUEL HOTEL — RIVER RUEL

Sea Trout   ★   Salmon   ★   Brown Trout

Rates — dinner/bed/breakfast from £14 including fishing.

★ *Biggest sea trout 1985 over 19lb* ★

Day permits available at the hotel or Argyll Marine & Sports Centre (0369) 4722

Glendaruel Hotel, Clachan of Glendaruel Tel: (036982) 274

CLAONAIG ESTATE
Kintyre — Argyll

Holiday on an agricultural estate in one of our five cottages and flats. Situated on the East Coast of Kintyre, unspoiled area, safe beach, superb views to Arran and Bute. Excellent area for touring and nearby ferries to Arran, Gigha, Islay and Jura. Golf, sea, river and loch fishing and pony trekking locally available. Stalking can be arranged on the estate at suitable times. All houses have electrical equipment including immersers, fridges, cookers and fires. All have open fires. Sleep four to six people. Fibre glass dinghy included, except winter months, with rent.

DETAILS ON APPLICATION FROM MRS S. OAKES
CREGGAN, CLAONAIG, TARBERT, ARGYLL OR TELEPHONE (088 06) 225.

PORTSONACHAN HOTEL
South Lochaweside by Dalmally
Argyll   PA33 1BL
Tel: Kilchrenan (086 63) 224

Situated on the south side of Loch Awe, Portsonachan Hotel is perfectly situated for an angling holiday. We have 10 boats on the loch and are able to arrange beats on the Rivers Awe and Orchy. Sea and hill loch fishing is also available, as well as a ghillie service.

We aim to make the food at Portsonachan as memorable as the scenery and produce a different menu every day, using fresh local ingredients and where possible vegetables and herbs from the garden.

Portsonachan is an ideal centre for touring and visiting the West Highlands. Write to Christopher Trotter.

TRADES DESCRIPTION ACT

The accommodation mentioned in this holiday guide has not been inspected and the publishers rely on information provided. The publishers have every confidence in their advertisers but cannot be held responsible for the accuracy of the descriptions published.

Enjoy the famous

SEA LIFE EXPERIENCE

in the beautiful surroundings of Argyll

See seals from the underwater observatory and hundreds of other fascinating sea creatures displayed in ideal viewing conditions.

ATTRACTIONS FOR 1987 INCLUDE THE SUPERB NEW SHORELINE RESTAURANT

Delicious home baked fare & salad table. Lovely surroundings & wonderful views.

OPEN EVERY DAY, 9am–6pm (till 8pm July/August) ON THE A828 11 MILES NORTH OF OBAN NEW GIFT SHOP · FREE PARKING

Sea Life Centre

MORE THAN EVER THE WEST COAST'S LEADING ATTRACTION

INVERAWE FISHERIES

Taynuilt, Argyll   Tel. (08662) 446

THREE LOCHS STOCKED DAILY
WITH PRIME
HARD-FIGHTING
RAINBOW TROUT
FROM 1-16lbs   Best 1986 FISH — 14½lbs

One mile of salmon and sea trout fishing on the River Awe

Tackle Shop · Casting Tuition · Rod Hire

RING OR WRITE GRAHAM FUSCO FOR DETAILS

SPECIMEN HUNTING IN THE KYLES

There is a variety of good fish all year round in the Kyles of Bute and surrounding sea lochs. Two superb boats for parties of 12 or 8 with experienced skippers, or self hire 1–4 persons. Bed, breakfast, packed lunch, evening meal. Relax and enjoy the good fishing and the food and friendship of the Kames. Individual or freshwater lake and river by arrangement.
Send for brochure.

KAMES HOTEL Tighnabruaich, Argyll
Telephone: (0700) 811489
Under New Management

Please mention this Pastime Publications guide.

OCEANS OF FUN

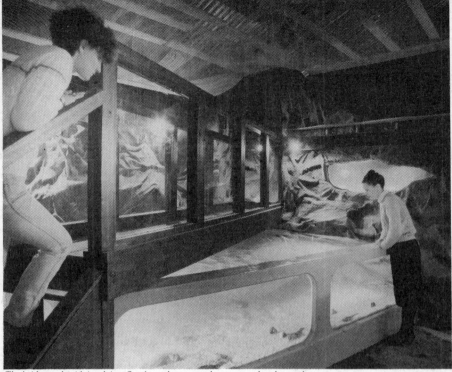

The bridge tank with its plaice, flouders, skate, rays, lesser spotted and spur-dogs.

Armed bullheads, spiny spider crabs, cuckoo rays – no it's not a plug for the Ministry of Defence, but some of the array of sea creatures on display at Seaworld. The variety of types of creatures and their colours will fascinate people of all levels of interest – yet every species in the exhibition has been caught locally in the Clyde or off the West Coast of Scotland.

The exhibition is housed in a Sandinavian-style building resting among the sand dunes in front of Beach Park, just south of the Harbourside at Irvine and overlooking the sea to the hills of Arran. On entering the building, there is a sharp contrast between the beach atmosphere of the reception area and the exhibition area where there is a wide variety of marine wildlife and fish to be seen and where the close encounter with such a variety of wildlife is dramatic indeed – it's like being underwater without needing a wetsuit! The sights and smells of the sea shore are all around – and you can pick up some of the sturdier shore animals from the rock pool and discover about starfish and crabs in more detail. The total experience is enhanced by the background sound effects of gulls and terns.

The animals in the Exhibition area are changed constantly for they are just visitors too, brought ashore to be accessible to all for the public's enjoyment and interest but as the seasons change

they will be replaced by other species that migrate along the coast.

The visitor can find out more about the creatures that they have seen, in the adjoining Creel Room – where they are all found, what eats what and how the rich coastal wildlife can be safeguarded.

Seaworld is an all-season, all-weather centre. The Exhibition is open 10am-9pm from May to September and 10am-5pm during the winter months. The Restaurant is open 10am-11pm seven days a week, summer and winter, for snacks, dinners, coffee and pastries, and there is a table licence.

Grey gurnard, spindle shell and the delicate red swimming crab in a corner of one of the community tanks.

Under the sea from
An Unforgettable Angle

SEAWORLD – a spectacular exhibition of marine wildlife from the Firth of Clyde and the coastal waters around the West Coast of Scotland.

Even experienced sea anglers and commercial fishermen are amazed at such a variety of sea creatures. The display of social groups of each species so that the enthusiast can study their interactions makes the SEAWORLD experience unique, so don't rush your visit. See them all living in naturalistic settings at close quarters.

Relax after your 'underwater safari' in the Beach Cafe/Licensed Restaurant.

SEAWORLD is open every day
10 a.m. – 9 p.m. May – September
10 a.m. – 5 p.m. October – April

BEACH · PARK · IRVINE
Next to the Magnum Leisure Centre
Telephone: 0294 311414

Please mention this Pastime Publications guide.

A Y R S H I R E

FISHING TACKLE

If you're in Ayrshire be sure to pop in and see us and have a browse round our extensive range of tackle, flies, fly dressing and rod building materials, and country clothing etc.

MAIL ORDER

If you would like a copy of our FREE catalogue packed with thousands of interesting items just send us your name, address and a 1st class stamp.

P. & R. TORBET,
Dept. F, 27 Portland Street,
Kilmarnock, Ayrshire, Scotland
Tel: (0563) 41734

We also stock camping, hill walking and back packing equipment.

B A N F F S H I R E

BANFF SPRINGS

Scotland. **HOTEL** Golden Knowes Road, Banff AB4 2JE. Telephone 02612-2881

B E R W I C K S H I R E

SELF CATERING HOLIDAYS ON THE BERWICKSHIRE COAST

Secluded Holiday Cottages and Chalets centred on private Trout Loch in wooded country estate close to sea. Shops and sandy beach 2 miles. An ideal centre for anglers, naturalists and walkers or for touring the Borders. Edinburgh and Northumberland.

Write or phone for brochure:

Dr and Mrs E. J. Wise

WEST LOCH HOUSE Coldingham, Berwickshire. Tel. (08907) 71270

The Black Bull Hotel Duns

Tel: Duns (0361) 83379   AA Listed

Surrounded by the beautiful Lammermuir and Cheviot Hills.

Fully Licensed family run hotel.
Varied cuisine in a relaxed atmosphere.
Real ale looked after by a qualified brewer.
Sing alongs Fri, Sat, and Sunday.

Fishing permits issued for local trout rivers.

Edinburgh Tattoo booking agent.

OPEN ALL YEAR.

42

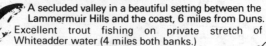

Abbey St Bathans
situated in the Scottish Borders

A secluded valley in a beautiful setting between the Lammermuir Hills and the coast, 6 miles from Duns. Excellent trout fishing on private stretch of Whiteadder water (4 miles both banks.)

Bankend House, sleeps 8;
Retreat Lodge, sleeps 6;
Priory and Whiteadder Cottages, sleep 4 each

Full particulars from: **Mrs J. J. Dobie, Abbey St Bathans, Duns Berwickshire. Tel: (036 14) 242;** or **Scottish Country Cottages, Suite 2d Churchill Way. Bishopbriggs Glasgow. Tel. (041-772) 5920.**

B E R W I C K S H I R E   C A I T H N E S S

SEE MAPS
ON
PAGES 71-83

WELCOME TO LADY JANET'S WOOD CARAVAN & CAMPING SITE

THURSO

Hard standings for caravans and caravanetes – showers, shop, recreation room with pool table. 4-6 berth caravans for hire.

Telephone Thurso (0847) 62611 or 64588

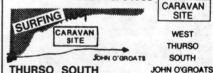

THURSO SOUTH

CARAVAN SITE
WEST THURSO SOUTH
JOHN O'GROATS

Ladbroke Mercury Motor Inn Wick

Riverside Wick Caithness KW1 4NL Tel: (0955) 3344

For anyone seeking far away, remote Scotland. Wick is about as far as you can go! This is the wild romantic side of Scotland, with the Orkneys a short, if somewhat rough, boat ride away. Sea loch and river fishing is excellent and reasonably priced here.

Visit the Caithness Glass Factory shop and the Caithness Leather Goods shop for attractive souvenirs. There's also the Wick Heritage Centre and the Dounreay Exhibition Centre, and the famous John O'Groats is just 17 miles away. But the main attraction is the beautiful lonely countryside of the far north of Scotland.

The Ladbroke Mercury Hotel overlooks Riverside Park and offers you a warm welcome, with food fit for a local hero in the Caithness Crofters Restaurant or enjoy a malt whisky from our extensive selection in the Wicker Bar.

D U M F R I E S S H I R E

FREE FISHING

For salmon, sea trout and brown trout when you stay at Warmanbie Hotel

A SMALL HOTEL WITH A BIG WELCOME

Warmanbie, a Georgian country house hotel is set in secluded woodland grounds overlooking the river Annan. Here you'll find an ideal place to relax and enjoy old fashioned service, fine wine and creative cooking. All our spacious bedrooms have private bathroom, telephone, colour T.V. and radio alarm. Fishing is free on the hotel's private stretch (only 100 yds away). Fishing on other stretches also arranged. Special rate for 3 or more nights or weekends - Sunday trout fishing can be arranged.

For futher details write to:—
Warmanbie Hotel, Annan DG12 5LL
or telephone Rod Duncan on Annan (046 12) 4015/6

CAIRNDALE HOTEL
English Street, Dumfries DG1 2DF
Tel: 0387 54111   Telex 777530

RAC★★★   Ashley Courtenay   Exec. Hotel

Privately owned and managed by the Wallace family this traditional hotel near the centre of town offers all the comforts normally expected from one of the region's leading 3 star hotels.

Fishing, shooting and golfing parties by arrangement.

Regular Scottish evenings throughout the summer. Weekend breaks available all year.

Dinner, Bed & Breakfast from £25 per person

The Dryfesdale Hotel   Lockerbie, Dumfriesshire.
Tel. Lockerbie (05762) 2427

Privately owned and managed hotel set in 7 acres. Comfortable bedrooms most with private bathrooms, all with TV and telephone. A la carte restaurants, also appetising bar meals. Ideal touring situation. Riding, shooting, fishing, golf available. Fishing on several beats on the Annan, also good coarse fishing in locality. Egon Ronay and Ashley Courtenay recommended.

RIVER AND LOCH
FISHING

Mid-Annandale, with easy access from the A74 or A75 in a country area. Salmon, Trout, Pike and Coarse fishing on River Annan and in stocked lochs. Terms on request for fishing on Nith and Cairn.

Contact Mrs. M. Vaughan.

Braehead Farmhouse, Heck, Lockerbie, Dumfriesshire Tel. Lochmaben (038 781) 444. Own meat, eggs, vegetables, home baking, parties up to six persons £98-£105 per person weekly, full board, including packed lunches, fishing & Scotpass discount card.

Three day break including all above except Scotpass £43-£47.

44

LIVE YOUR SPORTING DREAM

FISHING
Salmon, Sea Trout, Brown Trout, Grayling on 11 miles association water, & private beat.

SHOOTING
4000 acre rough shoot – rabbit, pigeon, hare, partridge, woodcock, pheasant, crow. Clay pigeon shoots arranged.

GOLF
9 hole golf course 300 yards from hotel. Also 30 courses within 30 miles.

SANQUHAR
DUMFRIESSHIRE DG4 6JJ
Tel: Sanquhar (06592) 270
Residents 8205

Blackaddie House Hotel

**HOLIDAY VILLAGE,
SOUTHERNESS
Nr DUMFRIES
tel: 038-788 256**

● MODERN CARAVANS ● CHALETS ● SEAVIEW CABINS
All either overlook the beach or are in close proximity.
● MODERN TOURING AND TENTING PARK.
WE ARE NOW A THISTLE AWARDED PARK.
S.A.E. FOR FREE COLOUR BROCHURE

COUNTRY SPORTS
Tel: Dunfermline 729546

Country Sports' comprehensive range includes tackle for game, sea and coarse fishing.

Fair & wet weather clothing, wellies, waders and accessories, all at competitive prices.

Fishing permits available.

ST. ANDREWS STREET · DUNFERMLINE

ALVIE
Kincraig, by Kingussie, Inverness-shire, PH21 1NE
(4 miles south of Aviemore)
SALMON, SEA TROUT, BROWN TROUT, PIKE

on
Loch INSH   River SPEY   Loch ALVIE
Self catering accommodation — 4 Cottages.
Camping, touring, seasonal and static caravans + caravans for hire on Dalraddy Caravan Park.
also
Shooting and many other recreational activities available locally.
Phone Kincraig (05404) 255 for details and brochure.

Alvie

DUMFRIESSHIRE

FIFE

INVERNESS-SHIRE

OSPREY FISHING SCHOOL

The Aviemore Centre, Aviemore
TELEPHONE AVIEMORE (0479) 810 911 or 810 132

The Osprey Fishing School is situated in the beautiful Spey Valley, in the Highlands of Scotland. Weekly, week-end, daily and private instructional courses are held throughout the year in wet and dry fly casting, and in spinning for game and coarse fish on the famous River Spey and on Highland lochs. Salmon courses and salmon holidays with Ghillie/Guide are available during the season on private waters.

Accommodation can be reserved on request. Unaccompanied children are welcome. Several 'all-in' packages are available in the Aviemore Centre, and in neighbouring villages. Experienced, novice, families and children are welcome, with reductions available for party reservations. The Osprey Fishing Tackle Shop is open throughout the year for advice, permit issues, tackle sales, fly tying materials and demonstrations.

For information on courses, fishing holidays and fishing waters in the Spey Valley, please contact: **THE OSPREY FISHING SCHOOL, The Fishing Centre, Aviemore, Inverness-shire. Telephone: Aviemore (0479) 810 911 or 810 132.**

Rothiemurchus Estate, By Aviemore, Inverness-shire

A wealth of angling opportunities are available to the expert and novice alike in this beautiful Estate which lies in the heart of the Cairngorms.

Salmon, Sea Trout, Brown Trout, on four beats of the River Spey, Lochs and Burn fishings, Char in the remote highland Lochs, predatory Pike in Loch An Eilein and Loch Pityoulish, or wilderness fishing for the angler preferring solitude.

At our Inverdruie Fishery the angler can try for the hard fighting Rainbow Trout. Here a policy of regular stocking ensures a chance of a double figure Trout.

At Inverdruie Fishery we offer tuition for the beginner or novice at our regular angling classes or private tuition is available by appointment. Here while the angler fishes, his family can enjoy a few hours at the Fish Farm feeding the fish, using the recreation and picnic areas of visiting the Farm Shop.

FISHING TACKLE FOR SALE. RODS ETC. FOR HIRE.
Ghillie/Guides available if required. Accommodation arranged on request.
Reductions for party reservations.
For information and bookings – contact **Ron Griffiths, Inverdruie Fisheries, By Aviemore, Inverness-shire. PH22 1QH. Tel. (0479) 810395 or 810703.**

MAINS OF AIGAS
BEAULY

Mains of Aigas is an old home farm in the most beautiful setting beside the River Beauly on the A831 five miles from Beauly village. A stone built cottage, standing in its own grounds offers complete privacy and comfort. Three spacious apartments, self contained, part of the farm courtyard, are tastefully equipped for all family comforts. Good loch and river fishing locally.

S.A.E. J. Masheter,
Mains of Aigas, Beauly, Inverness-shire IV4 7AD.
Tel: (0463) 782423.

GLENMORISTON ESTATES LTD.(P.T.F.)

GLENMORISTON ESTATES BY LOCH NESS.
Whether walking or stalking salmon/trout fishing or touring by car we offer ideal accommodation for your holiday. 21 fully equipped chalets & 5 cottage bungalows (18 units have colour TV) each sited to provide maximum peace and a nearby parking space. All are superbly equipped and furnished for a labour saving holiday. To provide a nice change for the cook the Glenmoriston Arms Hotel offers bar lunches/evening meals and the Estates' old farm whisky.

Glenmoriston Nr. Inverness IV3 6YA
Telephone (0320) 51202 Telex: 8954667 GME

Scottish Tourist Board
COMMENDED

CLAVA LODGE HOLIDAY HOMES
CULLODEN MOOR, INVERNESS IV1 2EJ
Telephone 0463 790228/790405

Enjoy your Highland holiday and the freedom of self-catering in one of our holiday homes (log cabin, chalets or cottages). All of our well-furnished units are very well appointed and coin operated meters supply electricity. These homes are ideally situated for a perfect family holiday. Salmon & Trout fishing on private stretch of the River Nairn, pony riding, children's play area, golf, swimming, sailing & cruising on Loch Ness, walking, touring or just relaxing and enjoying some of Scotland's grandest scenery and history. From £100-£180. Linen may be hired. Well behaved pets welcome.

S.A.E. please for brochure & further details:
Mis M. Skinner or Mrs. J. Smith, Clava Lodge Holiday Homes,
Culloden Moor, Inverness IV1 2EJ. Tel: (0463) 790228/790405

Fishing—Salmon, Brown Trout, Sea Trout, Sea Angling and Stalking can be made available.

LOCHAILORT INN
Lochailort, Inverness-shire PH38 4LZ
Tel. Lochailort 208 (STD Code 068 77)

Traditional Scottish Cooking from local meat, fish and game at modest prices.

On the road
to the Isles

Fully
Licensed

I N V E R N E S S - S H I R E

Please mention this Pastime Publications guide.

47

Morar Hotel

Morar, Inverness-shire PH40 4PA
Telephone: (0687) 2346

All holiday packages include free use of hotel boats on Loch Morar with salmon, brown trout and sea trout.

Family run hotel on the fabled "Road to the Isles". 42 miles from Fort William; 3 miles from Mallaig – the Southern Gateway to Skye.

33 rooms, many with private bathrooms and all with tea facilities, electric blankets. Fully licensed. Family atmosphere; children welcome. Abundant parking.

THE MOUNTVIEW HOTEL

**Nethy Bridge, PH25 3EB
Tel: 047-982 248/324**

The hotel is situated in Nethy Bridge and has outstanding views of the Spey Valley and Cairngorm Mountains. Fishing is available on the Rivers Spey and Nethy. Loch fishing is also available and private fishing can be arranged. Sea angling parties are also catered for.

You are assured of a warm welcome along with excellent food and friendly service. Twin, double and single rooms are offered. The hotel also has residents' TV lounge, dining room and lounge bar, offering bar meals with a wide selection of beers, wines and spirits. Complete fishing packages available or accommodation only.

Write or phone for brochure and details to:
Jim Wilson, Mountview Hotel, Nethy Bridge.

CARNOCH FARMHOUSE
STRATHGLASS

An exceptional recently renovated farmhouse beside the River Glass, Carnoch is available for self-catering holidays throughout the summer. Ideally situated for loch and river fishing, walking, birdwatching and touring the northern Highlands. Well equipped sunny kitchen, sitting room with log fires, sleeps 8.

Brochure available from: **Grange Estate Co.,
Aigas House, Beauly, Inverness-shire, IV4 7AD.
Tel: 0463 782443.**

TO ASSIST WITH YOUR BOOKINGS
OR ENQUIRIES
YOU WILL FIND IT HELPFUL TO MENTION THIS

Pastime Publications Guide.

Ask your bookshop
for
Pastime Publications
other Holiday Guides

Scotland for the
Motorist

Scotland Home of
Golf

200 years of tranquillity and good sport for the keen brown trout fly fisherman. A different hill loch each day: free fishing on the Lodge's four private lochs. Plus salmon in Loch Ness and nearby rivers. *Special packages available Spring and Autumn*

Knockie Lodge Hotel

Whitebridge, Inverness-shire IV1 2UP
Tel.: Gorthleck (04563) 276

Galloway for your 1987 Holiday.

High-quality self-catering accommodation.
Over 170 houses throughout South West Scotland.
*Peaceful Country Cottages
*Elegant Country Houses
*Convenient Town Houses
*Quiet Farm Houses
*Free fishing with some houses
SUPERB SCENERY, SANDY BEACHES, FRIENDLY PEOPLE, FISHING AVAILABLE

For free colour brochure, send 28p to: G.M. THOMSON & CO., 27 King Street, Castle Douglas, Kirkcudbrightshire DG7 1AB. Tel: Castle Douglas 2701.

Your Chalet in Bonnie Galloway
Only 1 hour from the M6 at Carlisle

Luxorious self-catering log houses in outstandingly beautiful countryside. So many amenities near your holiday home. Private fishing, golf courses, a riding school and pony-trekking. Also an excellent restaurant and two bars. Nearby (within walking distance) is Sandyhills beach. There are many places locally of historical interest to visit, too. Dogs welcome. Colour T.V., centrally-heated, continental quilt and all linen provided.

For details:
**Barend Properties Ltd.
Barend 25, Sandyhills, Dalbeattie,
Kircudbrightshire.**
Telephone Southwick 663/648 STD (0387 78)

KIRKCUDBRIGHTSHIRE LANARKSHIRE

Selkirk Arms Hotel

KIRKCUDBRIGHT   A Taste of Scotland Hotel

David & Esther Armstrong extend a specially warm welcome to all Fishing visitors. We can offer you private river fishing on the Dee. Break Rates available.

The Hotel is situated in the beautiful artist's town of Kirkcudbright in the heart of spectacular Galloway on the coast, and just five minutes walk from the harbour. Ideal for family touring holiday as well as for activities including golf, sailing, riding and bird watching, with sea angling, fishing and shooting available during season. 19 Bedrooms — Large secluded garden. Regular garden barbeques. Access, Visa, American Express and Diners Club credit cards welcome. Please write for your free colour leaflet or for further information and reservations telephone **Kirkcudbright (0557) 30402.**
A.A. ★★ R.A.C. ★★ Les Routiers, Ashley Courtenay, Good Pub Guide.

Gone Fishing

TACKLE DEALER & GUN DEALER

FULL RANGE OF SEA, GAME & COARSE TACKLE
LIVE RAGWORM & FROZEN BAITS, MAGGOTS & WORMS
GUNS, CARTRIDGES & ACCESSORIES
Salmon fishing on own private beat of River Earn, Perthshire, plus permits for all local waters.

Gone Fishing, 29 Main Street, The Village, East Kilbride.
Tel: East Kilbride 28952

GUNSMITH & FISHING TACKLE SPECIALISTS

New & Secondhand Fishing Tackle & Guns — All Makes • Goods Bought & Sold
• Advice, Tuition Given • All Accessories in Stock • Wide range of
Outdoor Clothing • Competitive Prices • Repair Service
• Open Mon-Sat 10am —5.30pm

 918 Pollokshaws Road, Glasgow G41
Telephone: 041-632 2733

THE ANGLERS' RENDEZVOUS

SCOTLAND'S FISHING TACKLE SHOP
– Huge Range of Tackle Game, Coarse and Sea Fishing –

ALL AT DISCOUNT PRICES

74-78 SALTMARKET, GLASGOW.
Tel: 041-552 4662

50

JAMES I. KENT

FISHING TACKLE

"WHERE SUCCESS BEGINS"

2380 DUMBARTON ROAD, GLASGOW G14

A choice of perfection in Tackle by:–
Hardy's Farlow's Sharp's, Bruce & Walker, Daiwa, Shakespeare, Sundridge, ABU, Olympic, Garcia, Etc.
A Full Range of Clothing by the Top Brand Names:– BARBOUR & KEEPERWEAR.
This is Scotland's most comprehensive selection of all that's best in Game Fishing, plus experienced helpful advice is your assurance of
THE COMPLETE SERVICE

Permits | Tackle-Hire | Casting Tuition

Telephone: 041-952 1629
L.L.A.I.A. MEMBER

NO PARKING PROBLEMS

GLASGOW'S

GAME FISHING SPECIALITY · HARDY'S MAIN STOCKIST – VERY LARGE SELECTION OF WATERPROOF CLOTHING, BREEKS, SHIRTS ETC.

Wm. Robertson & Co.

(Fishing Tackle) Ltd.,

27 WELLINGTON STREET, GLASGOW.
Phone 041-221 6687

OPEN ALL DAY SATURDAY

TROUT FISHING

in Lothian Regional Council Reservoirs

11 reservoirs within easy reach of Scotland's capital city. Each located in picturesque surroundings in the Pentland, Moorfoot or Lammermuir Hills. Wild trout and regular stocking with brown, rainbow and brook trout. 3 further reservoirs including the giant Megget in the Tweedsmuir Hills.
ENQUIRIES: Director of Planning, Lothian Regional Council, 12 St. Giles Street, Edinburgh 031-229 9292 Ext. 2559.
BOOKINGS: Director of Water and Drainage, Lothian Regional Council, Comiston Springs, 55 Buckstone Terrace, Edinburgh 031-445 4141.

Lothian Regional Council

"COUNTRYLIFE"

031-337 6230

SCOTLAND'S NO. 1 TACKLE SHOP

Game, coarse and sea angling equipment by Hardy, B. Walker, Diawa, Shakespeare etc.
Clothing by Barbour, Belstaff, Grenfell, Beaver etc.
Second hand tackle bought and sold.
Private salmon beats to let.

229 Balgreen Road
Edinburgh

Please mention this Pastime Publications guide.

LOTHIAN

MORTON FISHERIES

Offer excellent boat and bank angling for Brown and Rainbow

ON TWO RESERVOIRS OF 4 AND 22 ACRES SET IN BEAUTIFUL SURROUNDINGS WITHIN A FEW MILES OF EDINBURGH

Tel: Mid-Calder 882293

**MORTON
MID-CALDER
WEST LOTHIAN
SCOTLAND**

MORAYSHIRE

VISIT

THE MILL SHOP

NEWMILL ELGIN

Opening hours 9.00 a.m. to 5.30 p.m. Monday to Saturday
Credit cards accepted.

KNITWEAR IN CASHMERE, WOOL AND SHETLAND
KILTS, SKIRTS AND JACKETS
SCOTTISH CRAFTS AND SOUVENIRS
SHEEPSKIN PRODUCTS

FABRICS

TIES, SCARVES AND RUGS

Royal Hotel
TYTLER STREET, FORRES

Open all year the Hotel offers very comfortable accommodation with most rooms having either shower or shower/bath with toilet.

All bedrooms have tea, coffee making facilities, colour TV and Radio call. Continental quilts and electric blankets are on all beds.

The Hotel is centrally heated throughout.

The lounge offers comfort and extensive choice of drinks whilst in the public bar you can enjoy the homely atmosphere of a log and peat fire whilst chatting with the locals.

Forres is ideally placed in a central position for visiting the many attractions of the Highlands' Aviemore Ski Centre with all facilities including ski lift. Within easy reach of Forres.

Two for the price of one B.B., Fri-Sun: Children up to 15 free accommodation.

For further details and Bookings TEL: (0309) 72617

52

Ben Mhor Hotel

Grantown-on-Spey PH26 3EG
Tel: (0479) 2056

BEDROOMS: 4 Single, 3 Double, 15 Twin,
2 Family.
All Rooms with Private Bathroom.
OPEN: January to December.
PRICES: On application.

**Private Car Park at rear. Golf nearby. Licence. Children & pets welcome. Evening entertainment.
Reduced Rates for children. Parties welcome. Colour TV/Tea & Coffee facilities in all rooms.
Wide selection of menu available. Drying room available.**

Among the riches
of the Highlands . . .

Speyside spells superb scenery, touring, walks, fishing (and whisky!), but above all — the Grant Arms Hotel. The Grant Arms provides a warm welcome in the real tradition of Scottish hospitality. Only a short drive away are Aviemore Centre, Landmark Nature Trail and the sandy beaches of Moray Firth. Colour TV in all rooms.

GRANT ARMS HOTEL

Grantown-on-Spey   Tel: (0479) 2526

GREEN TREE HOTEL

41 Eastgate, Peebles
Tel: (0721) 20582

Comfortable small hotel conveniently situated 27 miles from Edinburgh. The hotel has 14 bedrooms, 10 en suite, colour TV in all rooms. Tea making facilities. Secluded gardens. Full central heating. Open all year.

COSHIEVILLE HOTEL
By Aberfeldy, Perthshire

Situated 3 miles from Kenmore and at the entrance to Glen Lyon, this small country hotel provides good food and comfortable accommodation. All our seven bedrooms have private bathrooms, tea and coffee making facilities and colour televisions, with central heating throughout. All forms of outdoor pursuits are available in this beautiful area of Perthshire. Trout and salmon fishing on River Lyon and River Tay.

Special rates for 3 Day and Weekly Stays throughout the year.

For full details and brochure contact Resident Proprietors,
Etive S. Brown and Alan D. Malone on **Kenmore (08873) 319**

M
O
R
A
Y
S
H
I
R
E

P
E
E
B
L
E
S
S
H
I
R
E

P
E
R
T
H
S
H
I
R
E

P
E
R
T
H
S
H
I
R
E

TROUT + SALMON FISHING AT THE

"BEN LAWERS HOTEL"
ABERFELDY

FOR £19.50 PER DAY BETWEEN 15 JAN & 15 OCT ENJOY
FISHING ON OUR OWN STRETCH ALONG THE TAY

PRICE INCLUDES 1 BOAT ENGINE AND EIGHT MILES OF FISHING

★ GHILLIES SUBJECT TO AVAILABILITY ★

PHONE MR. MACKAY ON (05672) 436 **NOW.**

Get away from the traffic and the crowds to the Braes o'Balquhidder. Our friendly looking white walled 18th century hideaway is tucked comfortably into the mountainside with a stunning view from its lawns over the heads of oak and ash to the glimmering expanse of Loch Voil, one of Scotland's most lovely lochs. The Loch was stocked many years ago and contains a variety of fish, including brown trout, char and the occasional salmon. Both boat and bank fishing are available. A warm welcome, with good food and fine wines, comfortable rooms and log fires, awaits you at . . .

LEDCREICH

**Braes o'Balquhidder, By Lochearnhead, Perthshire. FK19 8PQ
Telephone — Strathyre (08774) 230**

Egon Ronay recommended.

A haven of peace and tranquility 4 miles off the A84.

CRAIGHALL SAWMILL COTTAGES SELF CATERING

Many local rivers, lochs and reservoir. Boats for hire. Salmon, trout, perch, roach, pike. Excellent tackle & sports shops.

Large 3 bedroom cottage and 4 luxury apartments. Warm and very comfortable. Bed linen provided.

Putting green, games room, trout pool, gardens.

Ask for details and colour brochure. £110-£250 p.w.

**Mrs. M. Nicholson, Craighall Sawmill, Blairgowrie, Perthshire.
Tel: (0250) 3956**

IVYBANK HOUSE
Boat Brae, Rattray, Blairgowrie

Excellent accommodation and fine food. All rooms are centrally heated and have tea/coffee making facilities. Ample car parking. Fishing arranged. Free use of private floodlit tennis court. Parties of up to fourteen can be accommodated. Dinner, bed and breakfast at reasonable rates. Drying facilities available.

For bookings phone Monica Hadden (0250) 3056

TO ASSIST WITH
YOUR BOOKINGS
OR ENQUIRIES
YOU WILL FIND IT
HELPFUL TO MENTION
THIS

**Pastime
Publications Guide**

Guns bought and sold
Part exchange
Cartridges
Shooting equipment
Fishing tackle hire
Tackle and gun repairs
Sporting equipment
Waterproof clothing, etc.
Fishing and shooting rights handled

Jas. Crockart & Son
Established 1852

Allan Street, Blairgowrie
Telephone: Blairgowrie (0250) 2056
Visitors welcome.
Information and advice
freely given

Braco Hotel and Restaurant

**Braco, Perthshire.
Tel: (078688) 203**

Accommodation, Bistro Restaurant, two bars, bar meals all day. Packed lunches available. Live Scottish music Friday and Saturday nights. Situated midway between Stirling and Crieff on A822 with Rivers Allan and Earn and Lochs nearby.

INVERHERIVE HOUSE

Inverherive House (O.S. NN.369265) overlooks the River Fillan/Dochart. With these rivers and the nearby Loch Awe, Loch Lomond and Loch Tay, a full range of fishing can be expected. According to season salmon, brown trout, sea trout and pike are numerous in these waters. Boats and permits can be arranged.
Further details from:
ANDREW AND JOYCE RUSSELL,
Inverherive House, By Crianlarich, FK20 8RU.
Tel: (08383) 220.

PERTHSHIRE

CULTOQUHEY HOUSE HOTEL
by Crieff, Perthshire

Distant Hills, Log Fires, Wild Rhododendrons, Ancient Oaks, Stags Heads, Four-Post Beds, Family Home, Weathered Sandstone, Game Pie, Rhubard Fool, Woodland Walks, Bats at Dusk — Relax Bed & Breakfast Around £20. AA ★★ RAC "Taste of Scotland"

Scottish Tourist Board COMMENDED ♦♦♦

Phone Crieff (0764) 3253

THE KENMORE HOTEL

Scotland's oldest Inn
Established in 1572

B.T.A. Commended Country House Hotel
A.A. ★★★ R.A.C.   EGON RONAY

Beautifully situated in Kenmore, one of Scotland's loveliest villages, now a conservation area and surrounded by countryside listed for its outstanding natural beauty THE KENMORE HOTEL offers a unique combination of old world charm, elegance and comfort matched only by its excellent cuisine, cellar and personal service.

Reduced rates on our own Taymouth Castle Golf Course (Par 69)

Salmon and Trout Fishing on our own private beats on the Tay.

For Hotel brochure and reservations apply to:
Mr Ian Mackenzie, Manager
Telephone: Kenmore (08873) 205

KENMORE, PERTHSHIRE

SEE MAPS
ON
PAGES 71-83

KILLIN HOTEL
Main Street
Killin, Perthshire FK21 8TP
Tel: (056 72) 296/573

In the beautiful Perthshire countryside, situated on the banks of the River Lochay, you will find this fine Highland Hotel, offering eight miles of the finest salmon fishing on Loch Tay to the expert and novice alike. We have 30 bedrooms, most with private facilities, telephones and television, family suites, lift to all floors, log fires and central heating. We provide excellent Scottish cuisine and boast a well-stocked wine cellar. Enquire about our special fishing package.
Write or telephone — **Killin Hotel, Killin, Perthshire 05672 296 Telex 76660 (Coroak-"G")**

56

QUEEN'S COURT HOTEL
KILLIN
Tel: Killin (05672) 349
Proprietors: Bill & Isobel Patrick

Fully licensed hotel opposite caravan park at east end of Killin. Activities available in the area include trout and salmon fishing, golfing, hill-walking, sailing. Also convenient centre for touring. All bedrooms with H & C and tea/coffee making facilities. Ample car parking. Bed & Breakfast £10.00. Dinner optional. Bar meals available. Brochure and details on request.

Come to the central Highlands

THE DUNALASTAIR HOTEL
Kinloch Rannoch, North Perthshire

Situated amongst majestic mountain and lochland scenery that is without equal. Fishing 100 yards from hotel, freezer facilities, packed lunches and drying room available. **Wild brown trout fishing free to residents.**

For further details phone: 08822 323.

COTTAGES TO LET IN PERTHSHIRE

Four well-equipped holiday cottages on 250 acre arable/stock farm facing South between Crieff and Perth. Sleeps 4/5 persons, Elec. cooker, fridge, washing machine, immersion, TV, electric heaters and an open fire. Dogs allowed. Cot on request.

Contact: **Mrs. P. Mackenzie Smith, Newrow, Methven, Perthshire. Tel: (076483) 222.**

Grandtully Hotel

Grandtully, Strathtay, Pitlochry PH9 0PL

Telephone Strathtay (08874) 207
Booking Contact: A.R. & M. & C.C. Warren
Family run hotel overlooking River Tay, perfectly situated for touring, golfing, fishing, shooting, stalking, hill walking, etc. Free golf and trout fishing for residents. Food of the highest standard, excellent wine cellar. Coffee and tea making facilities in all rooms. Games room (pool, darts). Public Bar and Lounge Bar, Colour TV. Salmon fishing on hotel's private water.
Tariff details (include VAT and Service) Bed & Breakfast from £10.00. Bed, Breakfast & Evening Meal from £14.00.

Supplements Payable
Private Bathroom/Shower £3.50 per person per night   Booking Deposit Required £5 per adult per night

PERTHSHIRE

DALGUISE
SALMON FISHINGS

RIVER TAY   DALGUISE BEAT
1½ MILES DOUBLE BANK

£15 – £30/Rod/Day
TEL. 03502-593 or write SAE for details
THE ORCHARD, DALGUISE, BY DUNKELD

THE LAKE HOTEL

The hotel stands on the shore of Scotland's only lake amidst the tree-clad hills of western Perthshire. Close to the Trossachs and Rob Roy country. A perfect centre for tourists, being one hours run from Glasgow and within easy distance of places of scenic or historical interest such as Oban, Stirling and Callander. Ideal holiday base for golfing, pony-trekking and especially fishing. Please call for brochure. **Proprietors: D. Nisbet & Son, The Lake Hotel, Port of Menteith, Perthshire. Tel: (08775) 258**

Moor of Rannoch Hotel

Rannoch Station, Perthshire, PH17 2QA.
Telephone Bridge of Gaur (08823) 238.

This small fishing hotel is 1,000 feet above sea level in the centre of one of Scotland's wildest and least populated areas. It is approached by the West Highlands line to Rannoch station or by the Road to the Isles from Kinloch Rannoch.

Our food is of the highest standard with traditional fish and game dishes featuring frequently on the menu.

The hotel has fishing on Loch Laidon and the River Gaur, both of which have long been famed for their Ferox Brown Trout. Fishing is also available on the Dubh Lochan for native Brown Trout or stocked Canadian Brook Trout. Fishing is also available on Loch Rannoch & Loch Eigheach.

For further information contact: Mr PHILLIP TURNER.

ROSS-SHIRE

LOCH MAREE HOTEL by Achnasheen,
Ross-shire. Telephone (044 589) 200

Loch Maree Hotel famous for sea trout fishing. Salmon and brown trout
May/Mid-June, sea trout Mid-June/October.
Excellent catches. Boats and ghillies available.
Trout run up to 6 lbs on Loch Maree.
REMARKABLE SPORT.

CRAIGDARROCH Lodge

hotel

Ashley Courtenay, Egon Ronay and AA ★★ Recommended

Craigdarroch Lodge is a family run 2 Star Country House Hotel set in 12 acres of relaxing natural gardens and woodlands well known for its friendly atmosphere and log fires. There is a personal welcome awaiting you, and all that's best in Scottish cuisine and comfort. There are facilities for the young to the old which include tennis, grass bowls, full sized snooker table, salmon and trout fishing on our own beats.

Craigdarroch is the linkpin of Ross-shire for day trips to Wester-Ross, Sutherland, The Isle of Skye, Western Isles, Dornoch Firth, Black Isle, Inverness, Loch Ness and Moray Firth. Do not hesitate to ask for further information on our special interest package holidays, assistance in travel arrangements, and in house car hire facility.

Open all year round for residents and non residents, bar lunches and evening dinner.

CRAIGDARROCH LODGE HOTEL, Craigdarroch Drive, Contin, Ross-shire. Tel: Strathpeffer (0997) 21265.

AA ★★ RAC

Scottish Tourist Board COMMENDED

Balmacara Hotel

A family owned and run Lochside Hotel with 30 rooms. All private facilities. Special 3 day package £120.00 per person includes Dinner, Bed & Breakfast, Landrover transport to Hill Lochs (6). Brown/Rainbow Trout. Come and relax with us and enjoy our Highland Hospitility. For brochure and tariff contact **Balmacara Hotel, by Kyle of Lochalsh, Rosshire IV40 8DH. Tel: 059 986 283.**

TIGH AN EILEAN HOTEL

Situated on the shore of Loch Torridon. Tigh an Eilean makes a perfect centre of climbing the Torridon Mountains, touring the beautiful Applecross Peninsula or simply relaxing in a comfortable, friendly, family run hotel. Pony trekking and boat hire locally. Licensed and A.A. classified. SALMON and TROUT Fishing permits available.

Tigh an Eilean, Shieldaig, Strathcarron, Ross-shire Phone 05205-251

ROSS-SHIRE

HILLS, GLEN, FORESTS
RIVER AND LOCHS
ON YOUR DOORSTEP

THE SCOTLAND YOU
DREAM ABOUT. TROUT
FISHING - DAY PERMITS

THE HOTEL IN THE VERY HEART OF A SCENIC HIGHLAND GLEN

14 miles from Muir of Ord – 11 miles of picturesque driving from
Marybank on the main A832 road.
Bar meals – Dinner (by reservation) – Non residents welcome
Brochure on request from Resdient Proprietors Mr & Mrs S. W.
TOUGH. Telephone: Strathconon 09977 222.

RHIDORROCH LODGE ULLAPOOL

EARLY FISHING

West Coast spate river offers
exciting salmon & grilse runs from
the end May, June and July. Hill
lochs stocked with brown and
rainbow trout up to 3½ lbs.
Self catering lodge renowned for its
peace and beauty.
Ponytrekking, sea fishing & the
picturesque village of Ullapool
within easy reach.

Lochbroom Hardware
Ullapool

For all your hardware, camping
and fishing tackle requirements.

Salmon and Sea Trout fishing
permits available.

Tel: Ullapool (0854) 2356

INVERLAEL COTTAGES
LOCH BROOM, by ULLAPOOL, ROSS-SHIRE

**Salmon and sea trout fishing on River
Broom.**
Some trout loch fishing. Self-catering
cottages in mountainous National
Trust beauty area. Good food and
night life locally. Heating and TV
aerials available. *SAE please or
telephone (0854) 85262*

RODONO HOTEL

A charming Country Hotel and Restaurant situated in pleasant grounds overlooking St. Mary's Loch.
FREE FISHING FOR RESIDENTS AND ALL 11 BEDROOMS HAVE H & C, TEA AND COFFEE MAKING FACILITIES.
Bed and Breakfast with lunch and dinner optional. Special diets also catered for by arrangement. Liquor licence and residents' lounge. Central heating throughout.

ST. MARY'S LOCH SELKIRKSHIRE TD7 5LH
TEL: CAPPERCLEUCH (0750) 42232

WHITMUIR ESTATE, SELKIRK, SCOTLAND

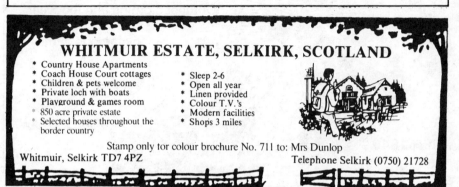

* Country House Apartments
* Coach House Court cottages
* Children & pets welcome
* Private loch with boats
* Playground & games room
* 850 acre private estate
* Selected houses throughout the border country

* Sleep 2-6
* Open all year
* Linen provided
* Colour T.V.'s
* Modern facilities
* Shops 3 miles

Stamp only for colour brochure No. 711 to: Mrs Dunlop

Whitmuir, Selkirk TD7 4PZ

Telephone Selkirk (0750) 21728

PHILIPBURN HOUSE HOTEL

For further details contact:
Jim and Anne Hill
at Philipburn House Hotel, Selkirk 7.
Telephone (0750) 20747.

The Tweed, the Ettrick and the Yarrow are names to quicken the pulse of fishermen everywhere. Names that conjure up the picture of Scotland's finest waters nestling deep in the tranquility of the Borders. Names that are spoken of in the same breath as nearby award-winning Philipburn House Hotel.

The country warmth of log and peat fires, the unmistakable glow of Scotland's finest whiskies, and a lively bar where talk of fishing is a not unfamiliar sound. Succulent food . . . fine wines . . . spacious rooms, poolside suites and a pine lodge. Drying rooms and a relaxing hot bath to soak in. Heated swimming pool and badminton for the energetic. Fishing permits, pony trekking and golf by arrangement.

Truly the complete hotel for the complete angler.

WALMER HOTEL
90 Henderson Street, Bridge of Allan

The Reids welcome you to their family run hotel, situated in an ideal position for salmon, sea and brown trout fishing on the rivers Annan, Forth & Teith. All rooms have colour TV and tea-making facilities. Entertainment at weekends. Central heating. Open all year. **SAE or phone for further details. Tel: (0786) 832967/832352.**

SELKIRKSHIRE

STIRLINGSHIRE

STIRLINGSHIRE

D. Crockart & Son

"THE FINEST RANGE OF FISHING TACKLE IN CENTRAL SCOTLAND"

15 KING STREET, STIRLING Tel. 73443

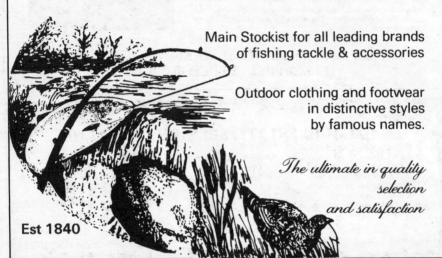

Main Stockist for all leading brands
of fishing tackle & accessories

Outdoor clothing and footwear
in distinctive styles
by famous names.

*The ultimate in quality
selection
and satisfaction*

Est 1840

SUTHERLAND

ALTNAHARRA HOTEL

by Lairg, Sutherland IV27 4UE
Tel: 054 981 222

In the heart of Sutherland, we
offer some of the best salmon
and sea trout fishing in the
north, with warmth, comfort and
friendliness to match.

Inchnadamph Hotel
Assynt, Sutherland

A family run hotel, delightfully situated at the
head of lovely Loch Assynt in the heart of the
majestic and inspiring beauty of the North West
Highlands. An ideal "anglers retreat" and a
restful and comfortable centre, perfect for
exploring a magical area of Scotland. Closed
December-February. Salmon and brown trout
fishing included. **Tel: (05712) 202.**

SUTHERLAND

THE ROYAL MARINE HOTEL
& CURLING RINK
BRORA, SUTHERLAND KW9 6QS.
"The North's Favourite Golfing & Fishing Hotel"

— Offers a friendly, relaxed atmosphere, good food and the opportunity to fish for salmon & trout amidst some of the most beautiful scenery in the North of Scotland. Golden beaches, bowling, tennis, golf, and curling. Brora can offer a holiday to suit all tastes. The hotel's swimming & leisure centre adds to your enjoyment after a day on the river.

Dinner, Bed and Breakfast from £28.00
Telephone: 0408-21252 for brochure and tariff.
2 Night Breaks from £65-£200 per week.

Rob Wilson

FOUNTAIN SQUARE · BRORA SUTHERLAND **(0408 21373)**

Rod maker, Retail Fishing Tackle, Guns, Rifles, Ammunition, Boats, Clothing, Repairs done and angling instruction given when possible. Permits for River Brora, and boat on Loch Brora. Advice freely given on all fishing in Sutherland.

cape wrath hotel

Durness, Sutherland, Scotland
Reservations: (097181) 274

Situated in one of the last truly unspoilt counties of Scotland, the Cape Wrath Hotel stands on a peninsula in the beautiful Kyle of Durness. You will marvel at picturesque lochs and rivers teeming with fish, including Salmon, Sea Trout & Brown Trout, and the rugged grandure of the mountains rising from glens originally gouged out by the ice-age and little changed since.

If you want a holiday with complete independence, then Cape Wrath Hotel is for you, we have 40,000 acres of freedom awaiting your pleasure.

SUTHERLAND

PEACEFUL, RELAXED FISHING HOLIDAY?

Come to the remoteness of Sutherland for a quiet friendly holiday at the Forsinard Hotel.
FULLY LICENSED A.A., R.A.C.**

Private fishing, trout on several lochs with boats, salmon when available, on the Upper Halladale.

Excellent food and accommodation, most rooms private shower/bath.

For further details, bookings or brochure: Norah & Gordon McKay Lyon.

FORSINARD HOTEL, FORSINARD, SUTHERLAND KW13 6YT.

Tel: HALLADALE (064 17) 221

LAIRG — FISHING TACKLE

Scottish-made Trout and Salmon Flies
and a Wide Range of Lures in Stock

R. ROSS Main Street, Lairg

Telephone: Lairg (0549) 2239

LOCH SHIN PERMITS · ROD HIRE · LOCAL ADVICE · WATERPROOF CLOTHING

THE MELVICH HOTEL

AA**   SUTHERLAND   RAC**

FOR SOME OF THE FINEST LOCH AND RIVER FISHING IN SCOTLAND

Overlooking the Pentland Firth the Melvich Hotel has been fully refurbished and now offers a friendly welcome from the new proprietors Ian and Betty MacGregor. Excellent food and comfort as expected of a first class hotel. Modern Bedrooms, some with en-suite facilities, all with tea/coffee making facilities & colour TV.

For futher particulars write or telephone:- 064 13 206

SCOURIE HOTEL

SCOURIE   SUTHERLAND

Set amidst the wild and majestic beauty of West Sutherland, your comfort and a happy holiday are assured in this hospitable hotel which enjoys a high reputation for the excellence of its cooking and table appointments. Fully licensed. A.A. and R.A.C. recommended.

Fishing for Brown Trout available in over 200 hill lochs. Four lochs with Salmon and Sea Trout. Close to the Island of Handa renowned as a bird sanctuary and its magnificent cliff scenery. Station, Lairg 40 miles.

Illustrated brochure gladly sent on request.

Telephone: Scourie (0971) 2396
Resident Proprietors: Mr & Mrs IAN A. S. HAY

64

DRUMLAMFORD ESTATE
SOUTH AYRSHIRE-WIGTOWNSHIRE

River Cree, three miles, salmon and trout

Loch Nahinny
Loch Drumlamford } — stocked brown, rainbow, brook trout at £8 per day.

Loch Marberry
Domal } — coarse fishing at £3 per day.

Boats at £4 on all lochs. Permits apply Keeper, Barrhill (046582) 256.

Self catering holiday cottages also available — apply Mrs. Beale, Barrhill (046582) 220

SPECIAL TERMS FOR FISHING PARTIES!

COARSE fishing on site on our 3 lochs (one stocked), and 3 miles of river. This spacious Thistle Award park offers facilities of the highest standard. Hire one of our luxury caravans, or bring your own. Sailing, windsurfing also available.

Three Lochs Caravan Park,
Balminoch, Kirkcowan, Wigtownshire DG8 0EP.
Tel: (067183) 304

THE CREEBRIDGE HOUSE HOTEL
Newton Stewart DG8 6NP

A Holiday in Scotland surely cannot be complete without a visit to South Western Galloway. Here the roads are never too busy and there is some of the most beautiful and varied scenery in Scotland. Within thirty miles of Newton Stewart you will find ancient battlegrounds, sub tropical gardens, the Galloway Forest Park, a wealth of hills to climb and tracks to explore, several nine hole golf courses, well stocked trout lochs, ancient relics of the first Christianity in Scotland and the newest RSPB reserve.

Run by The Oliver Family, the Creebridge House Hotel offers a comfortable base for a holiday. In winter log fires burn in the elegant drawing room, blue lounge and bar. We have seventeen individually appointed bedrooms, fourteen with private bathroom and colour television, tea and coffee making facilities, direct dial telephones and central heating.

The dining room overlooking the garden offers a daily changing "Taste of Scotland" menu cooked from the best local and fresh ingredients.

The hotel is rated two star by both the RAC and AA who also awarded us an "h" symbol. We are Egon Ronay recommended and members of the "Taste of Scotland" scheme.

Please call or write for a copy of our brochure and tariff.

Duncan Oliver
Newton Stewart (0671) 2121

WIGTOWNSHIRE

CORSEMALZIE HOUSE HOTEL

Port William

Newton Stewart
AA ★ ★ ★ RAC

Wigtownshire

Country House Hotel set in 40 acres of gardens and woodland privately owned and personally run. Total seclusion and peace. *Excellent food and wines.* Taste of Scotland and taste of Galloway food:
PRIVATE SALMON/TROUT FISHING & SHOOTING
ALSO FREE GOLF ON TWO LOCAL COURSES.
Write for brochure or tel: **098 886 254**
Resident Props: Mr & Mrs P. McDougall

S.W. SCOTLAND "Get away from it all" AT LUCE BAY

Cock Inn Caravan Park

**AUCHENMALG : NEWTON STEWART : WIGTOWNSHIRE
SCOTLAND**

Peaceful, select Caravan Park adjacent pleasant little beach and small Country Inn. Panoramic view across Luce Bay. Bathing, Sailing, Sea Angling, etc. Also Bungalow all year round.

★ GOLF ★ PONY TREKKING ★ FISHING NEARBY

Modern toilet block, showers, shaver points and all facilities.

Shop on site   Bar Meals available at the Inn

HOLIDAY CARAVANS FOR HIRE TOURERS WELCOME

Please send s.a.e. for brochure or telephone . . .

Auchenmalg (058-15) 227

ARRAN

the Isle of Arran

Scotland in miniature

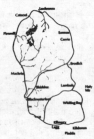

Sub-tropical palms grow in the open and pay tribute to the Gulf Stream's warm caress. Red deer roam, the golden eagle soars over the purple heather and the grey seal slips from grey rock.

There is so much to see and do for the lover of peace and beauty, the sportsman, the family, that the only problem is where to start.

Savour the Arran experience. Sail for an hour from busy, hustling West Central Scotland — and enter another world. Let the magic of the beautiful Isle of Arran cast its enchanting spell upon you.

**For free full colour brochure
Tel 0770 2140
(24 hours)**

Or write to the Isle of Arran Tourist Board,
Tourist Information Centre, Brodick, Isle of Arran.

CORRIE HOTEL
Corrie, Isle of Arran KA27 8JB

The ideal location for climbing, walking, fishing, pony-trekking, golfing and diving. Family hotel which provides good food and comfort at reasonable prices. Reduced rates and special facilities for families with children. Bar lunches and bar teas. Beer garden on sea front. Open all year round. Resident Proprietors: John and Anne Bruce.

Tel: (077081) 273

A R R A N

BUTE ENTERPRISES LTD
26 Bishop Street
Rothesay, Bute PA20 9DG

Superior self-catering flats — sleep 4. Furnished to a high standard, including colour TV and washing facilities. Bed linen and towels provided plus cleaning service. Situated five minutes from town centre and five minutes from Loch Fad for Brown Trout and Rainbow Trout.

Office staff available to arrange outings etc. and assure you of a happy holiday on our beautiful Island of Bute.

For further details contact: Miss Isabel Hay — (0700) 4754.

B U T E

PORT ASKAIG HOTEL
Isle of Islay, Argyll PA46 7RD
TELEPHONE: PORT ASKAIG 245 (STD 049 684-245)

The Port Askaig Hotel is situated on the beautiful Sound of Islay adjoining and overlooking the pier at which the daily car ferries arrive.

Some of the Island's finest trout lochs are close to the hotel and are easily accessible. The river Laggan offers good sea trout and salmon. Sea fishing may be had in the Sound itself, or several sea lochs around the coast.

Port Askaig Hotel is a genuine old Island Inn, providing warm, comfortable hospitality and good food. Colour T.V. All bedrooms have radio, colour T.V. and tea/coffee making facilities and are situated on the first floor — some with private bathrooms. Home garden produce. Brochure on request.

A.A., R.S.A.C., R.A.C., ** Ashley Courtenay Recommended

I S L A Y

MULL

QUINISH ESTATE ISLE OF MULL

One of the most attractive coastal estates on this lovely island. Six miles of Atlantic Coastline, amenity woodlands, sea lochs and a farm rising to heather hills with magnificent views of the Hebrides.

Facilities include own loch and river fishings – sea trout, salmon and brownies.

M/V KITTIWAKE – sails daily from the estate pier for some of the best sea angling on the W. Coast, or cruises to Staffa, Treshnish, Coll etc.

QUINISH HOUSE PRIVATE HOTEL – Large mansion house catering for small numbers only.

SELF CATERING – 7 very individual estate cottages. Sleeping 2-10.

Write or phone for our brochure and details of early season and long stay discounts.

Richard and Judy Fairbairns,
Quinish Estate,
Dervaig,
Isle of Mull. 06884 223

GLENGORM CASTLE by Tobermory, Isle of Mull

Very comfortable flats in Castle and four cottages on beautiful 5,000 acre estate. Spectacular setting overlooking Atlantic Ocean. Free bank fishing on three well-stocked lochs; brown, rainbow, sea trout and occasional salmon. Spinning available from the rocks around Glengorm's coast — boats avialable.

Brochure available contact:
J.R.E. Nelson,
Glengorm Castle, Tobermory,
Isle of Mull.
Telephone 0688-2321

A PASTIME PUBLICATION
will help you
to find a Happy Holiday for all

SCOTLAND HOME OF GOLF

SCOTLAND FOR FISHING

SCOTLAND FOR THE MOTORIST

See our Guides on Sale
at Your Local Newsagent
and Book Shop.

PASTIME PUBLICATIONS
LIMITED

BARONY HOTEL

BIRSAY, ORKNEY ISLES
Tel: 0856 72 327

BEDROOMS: 3 Single, 2 Double, 2 Twin,
1 Family, 3 Public Bathrooms.

OPEN: April-September.
PRICES: Single £11.50. Double/Twin £10.50
Dinner B & B £21.50

MERKISTER HOTEL
Loch Harray, Orkney KW17 2LF
Tel: 085-677-366

Open Mid-April to Mid-October

Boats – Gillie – Outboards available from own boathouse and pier.

Fishing under personal supervision of the owner.

5 double rooms, 5 twin-bedded rooms, 1 family room, 7 single rooms (4 rooms with private facilities), 3 public bathrooms.

**Prices £16.50 Bed & Breakfast
Dinner, Bed & Breakfast – £24.50**

STANDING STONES
HOTEL
Stenness, Orkney. KW16 3JX
Props: Bob and Linda Ross
Telephone 0856 850449

UNDER NEW MANAGEMENT

Bob and Linda Ross invite you to stay in one of Orkney's finest family run Hotels. Set on the shores of the Stenness Loch — only 11 miles from Kirkwall and 4 miles from the Ferry Terminal town of Stromness.

Free fishing — boats and ghillies for hire — with Jim on hand to give you the benefit of his lifetime's experience of fishing on the Orkney lochs.

Simply the best opportunities nearby for those interested in birds, cliffwalking, mediaeval monasteries, golf etc.

Relax in this peaceful country hotel and enjoy the first class cuisine and sample many local products. Reservations 0856 850449.

Prices: £14 single £12 Double/Twin £3 Private Facilities. Dinner from £7.

TRADES DESCRIPTION ACT

The accommodation mentioned in this holiday guide has not been inspected, and the publishers rely on information provided. The publishers have every confidence in their advertisers but cannot be held responsible for the accuracy of the descriptions published.

Enjoy Scotland for Fishing

C. W. MILLER

The charm of fishing in Scotland is not just catching fish but enjoying fishing in beautiful uncrowded surroundings for wild Atlantic salmon, sea trout and native brown trout, in natural clean water rivers and lochs. Many places have now supplemented stock by the introduction of rainbow trout. Much of the difficulty of planning a fishing holiday has been saved by 28 privately owned independent hotels in Scotland banding together several years ago as Inter Hotel Scotland and who have now pooled their experience to offer Stay and Enjoy Scotland fishing holidays designed to give quality accommodation at good value for money prices and at the same time, make booking easy. All that is required is one call on a 24 hour service, a letter or telex and a staff of experienced advisors are there to help you at no extra cost. Scotland, wherever you go, takes time to discover and to avoid the stress of living out of a suitcase Stay and Enjoy Scotland fishing holidays are primarily designed on a 3-5-7-night no rush basis with free advice and ideas on wherever you wish to go and want to do.

Fishing in Scotland is renowned throughout the world and Inter Hotel Scotland members will help, not only by looking after your comfort, but also advising on best times and arranging your fishing. Tackle hire, guides and tuition are available at some hotels by arrangement at certain times.

You can choose one or two centres for short breaks or as many as you wish for longer holidays, touring out each day to discover the area. Each hotel as well as offering welcome and hospitality will give you advice on places of interest, scenic routes, castles, gardens, shopping, crafts and activities including golf, riding, walking, birdwatching arts and many more as well as fishing.

Pre-booking arrangements are to be advised in Scotland even for increasingly popular off-season breaks. Stay and Enjoy Scotland holidays are all booked ensuring rooms with bath or shower and toilet en suite and most provide extras including tea and coffee tray, colour television, radio, telephone and hairdryers.

There are hundreds of miles of unspoilt coastline in Scotland which adds to the pleasure of sea fishing off our shores.

Lesser sought after species such as char and grayling as well as coarse fish including pike and perch are available, even if not listed.

Best times vary from area to area and time of year and Inter Hotel Scotland has a list of hotels specialising in fishing and others with fishing in the area.

A lot of care has gone into planning these no-rush holidays which offer more than touring, sightseeing and activities.

For the family there are special concession prices and children sharing with two adults have free accommodation.

Special occasions have been thought of and on arrival or for an anniversary during your holiday, a surprise welcome including champagne and flowers can be arranged at any of the hotels – ideal for honeymoons or birthdays.

Taste of Scotland Holidays are part of the scheme for those who enjoy good food and wish to savour a selection of local and traditional Scottish dishes.

Special terms have been arranged in the scheme for car-hire if required, together with air and rail travel link-up information for both home and overseas visitors. Insurance arrangements are also on hand at concession rates for UK residents.

These location holidays which begin with a minimum of three nights at any one centre can be extended as long as is wished. For instance you can make up a seven day holiday with three nights in one area and four in another, or stay at one hotel. The longer you stay at one hotel, the cheaper the rate becomes and the rates are adjusted for good value in both low and high season. High season dates are 14th May to 30th September.

The 1987 rates per person, per night sharing a twin or double room with bath include VAT. No service charge is made for any of these holidays and gratuities are purely at guests discretion.

	High Season	Low Season
3 Nights:	£32.75	£28.50
5 Nights:	£31.25	£27.75
7 Nights:	£29.75	£26.00

Even stop-over nights en route are offered at bed and breakfast rates for one or two nights.

All the hotels are privately owned and most of them are run by the owners themselves and their families. Although they have grouped together they do not belong to one large company controlled and supervised by a head office.

Inter Hotels in Scotland are individual, none of them are alike and this is one of their attractions.

When you stay in an Inter Hotel, whether by the sea or lochside, in the country or in the town, you will receive the welcome and hospitality for which Scotland is famous.

For further information and booking ring, write or telex and say you have read Scotland for Fishing.

Stay and Enjoy Scotland
Booking and Advise Service
Room M
2d Churchill Way
Bishopbriggs
Glasgow G64 2RH
Phone: 041 762 0838
Telex: 777205 INSCOT G

SCOTLAND

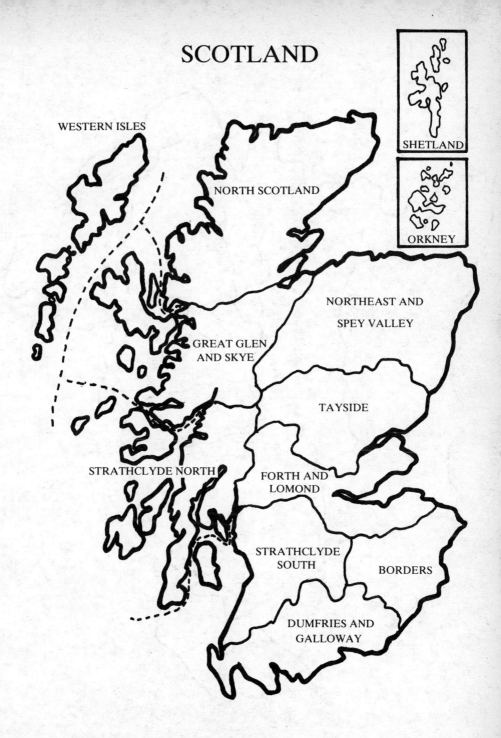

WESTERN ISLES

NORTH SCOTLAND

SHETLAND

ORKNEY

NORTHEAST AND
SPEY VALLEY

GREAT GLEN
AND SKYE

TAYSIDE

STRATHCLYDE NORTH

FORTH AND
LOMOND

STRATHCLYDE
SOUTH

BORDERS

DUMFRIES AND
GALLOWAY

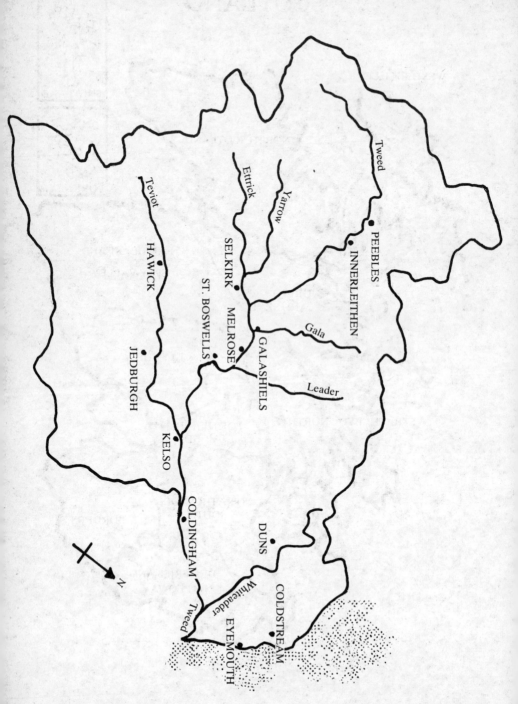

Tweed

Ettrick

Yarrow

Teviot

HAWICK

SELKIRK

ST. BOSWELLS

MELROSE

JEDBURGH

PEEBLES

INNERLEITHEN

GALASHIELS

Gala

Leader

KELSO

COLDINGHAM

Tweed

Whiteadder

DUNS

COLDSTREAM

EYEMOUTH

N

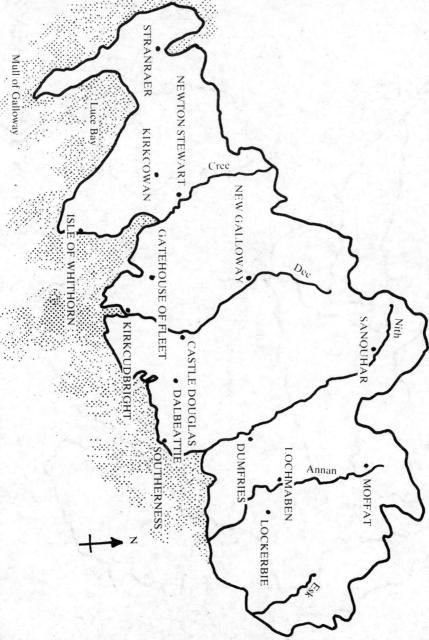

DUMFRIES AND GALLOWAY

Mull of Galloway

STRANRAER

Luce Bay

NEWTON STEWART

KIRKCOWAN

Cree

NEW GALLOWAY

ISLE OF WHITHORN

GATEHOUSE OF FLEET

Dee

Nith

SANQUHAR

KIRKCUDBRIGHT

CASTLE DOUGLAS

DALBEATTIE

SOUTHERNESS

DUMFRIES

Annan

LOCHMABEN

MOFFAT

LOCKERBIE

Esk

N

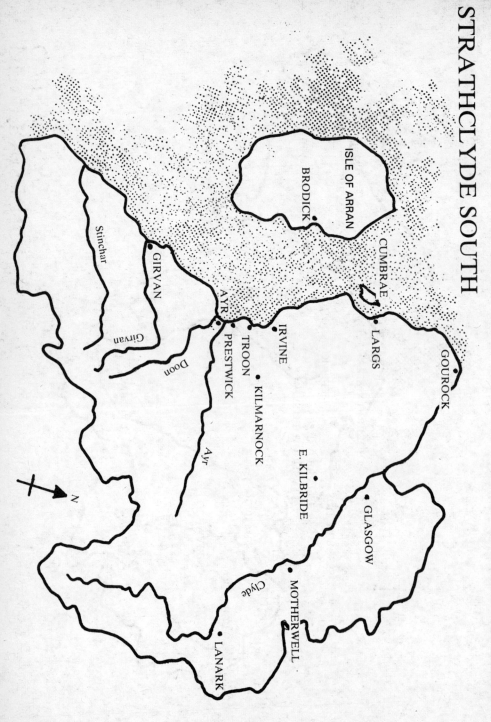

STRATHCLYDE SOUTH

ISLE OF ARRAN

BRODICK

CUMBRAE

GIRVAN

Stinchar

Girvan

Doon

AYR

PRESTWICK

TROON

IRVINE

LARGS

GOUROCK

KILMARNOCK

Ayr

E. KILBRIDE

GLASGOW

Clyde

MOTHERWELL

LANARK

N

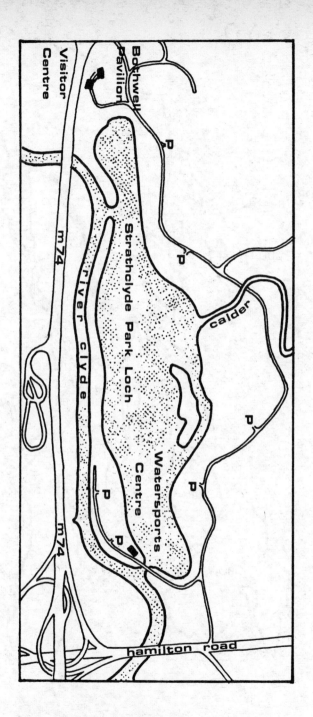

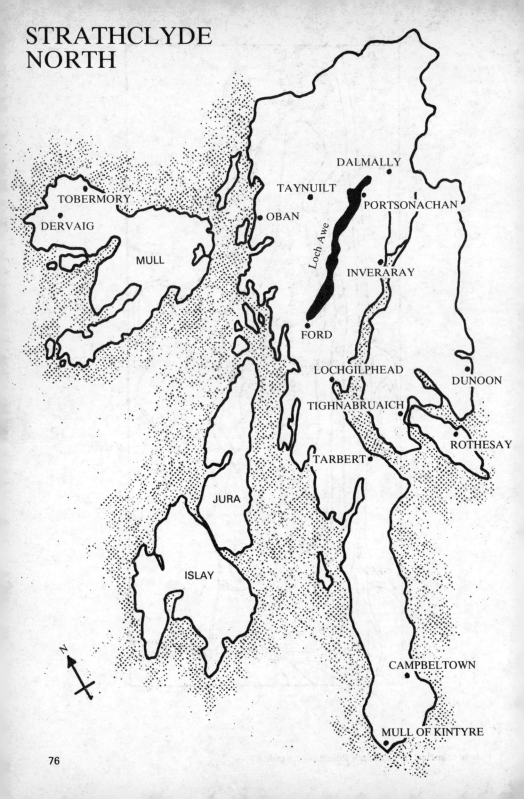

STRATHCLYDE
NORTH

DALMALLY

TAYNUILT

PORTSONACHAN

OBAN

Loch Awe

TOBERMORY

DERVAIG

MULL

INVERARAY

FORD

LOCHGILPHEAD

DUNOON

TIGHNABRUAICH

TARBERT

ROTHESAY

JURA

ISLAY

N

CAMPBELTOWN

MULL OF KINTYRE

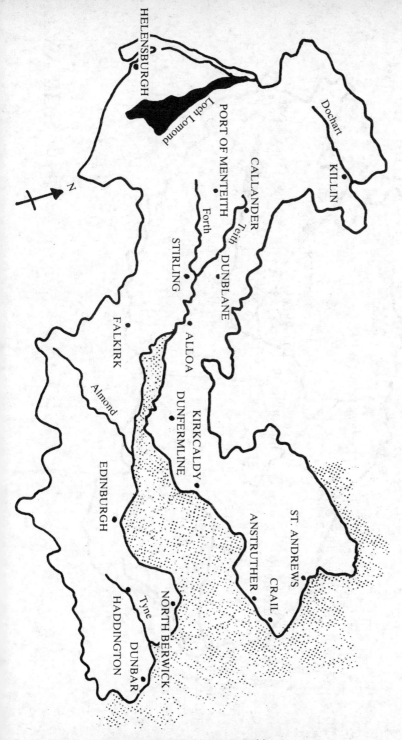

FORTH AND LOMOND

TAYSIDE

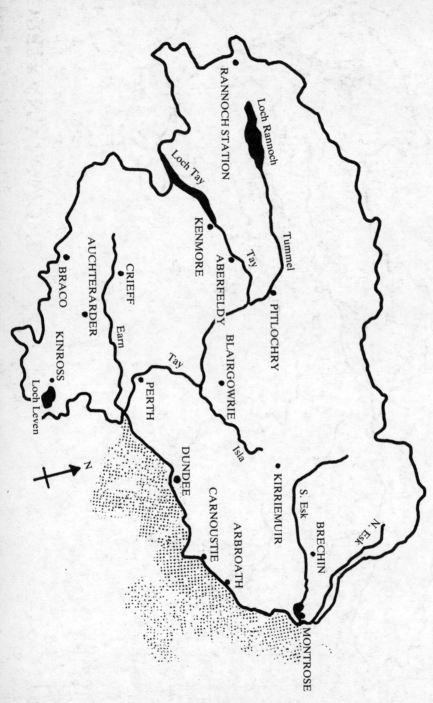

RANNOCH STATION

Loch Rannoch

Loch Tay

KENMORE

Tummel

Tay

AUCHTERARDER

CRIEFF

BRACO

ABERFELDY

PITLOCHRY

Earn

KINROSS

Tay

Earn

BLAIRGOWRIE

PERTH

Loch Leven

N

DUNDEE

CARNOUSTIE

Isla

ARBROATH

KIRRIEMUIR

S. Esk

BRECHIN

N. Esk

MONTROSE

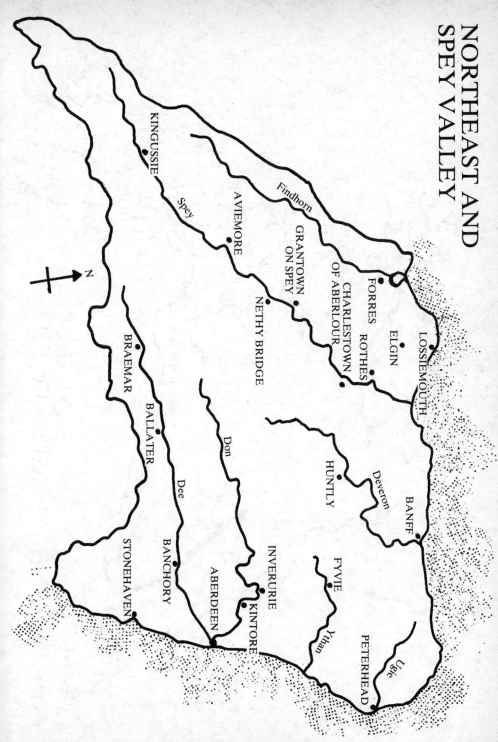

NORTHEAST AND SPEY VALLEY

N

KINGUSSIE

Spey

Findhorn

AVIEMORE

GRANTOWN ON SPEY

CHARLESTOWN OF ABERLOUR

FORRES

ROTHES

ELGIN

LOSSIEMOUTH

NETHY BRIDGE

BRAEMAR

BALLATER

Don

Dee

HUNTLY

Deveron

BANFF

STONEHAVEN

BANCHORY

ABERDEEN

INVERURIE

KINTORE

FYVIE

Ythan

PETERHEAD

Ugie

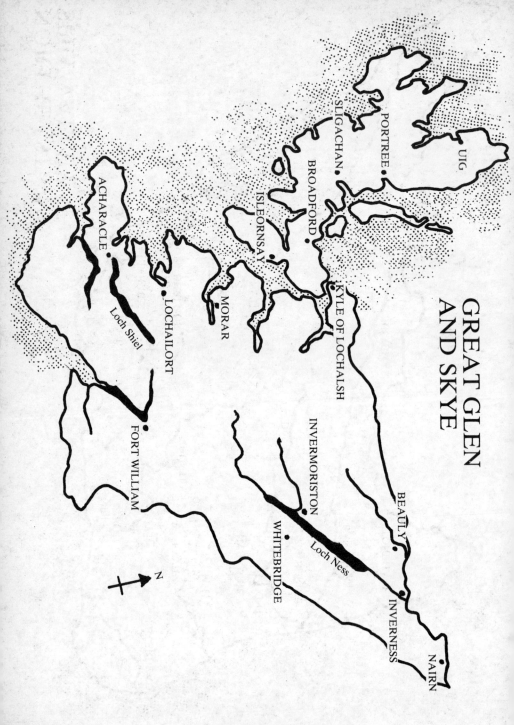

GREAT GLEN
AND SKYE

UIG

PORTREE

SLIGACHAN

BROADFORD

ISLEORNSAY

KYLE OF LOCHALSH

ACHARACLE

Loch Shiel

LOCHAILORT

MORAR

INVERMORISTON

BEAULY

FORT WILLIAM

WHITEBRIDGE

Loch Ness

INVERNESS

NAIRN

N

NORTH SCOTLAND

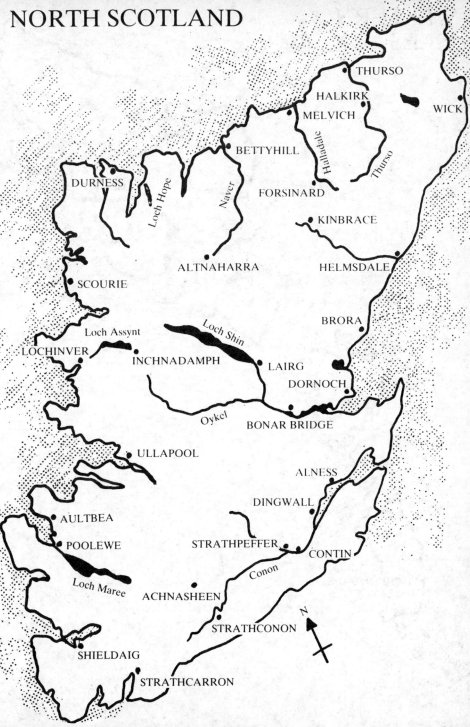

THURSO

HALKIRK

MELVICH

WICK

BETTYHILL

DURNESS

Loch Hope

Naver

FORSINARD

Halladale

Thurso

KINBRACE

ALTNAHARRA

HELMSDALE

SCOURIE

BRORA

Loch Shin

Loch Assynt

LOCHINVER

INCHNADAMPH

LAIRG

DORNOCH

Oykel

BONAR BRIDGE

ULLAPOOL

ALNESS

DINGWALL

AULTBEA

POOLEWE

STRATHPEFFER

CONTIN

Conon

Loch Maree

ACHNASHEEN

N

STRATHCONON

SHIELDAIG

STRATHCARRON

WESTERN
ISLES

LEWIS

STORNOWAY

KEOSE

TARBERT

HARRIS

LOCHMADDY

NORTH UIST

CREAGORRY

SOUTH UIST

LOCHBOISDALE

N

BARRA

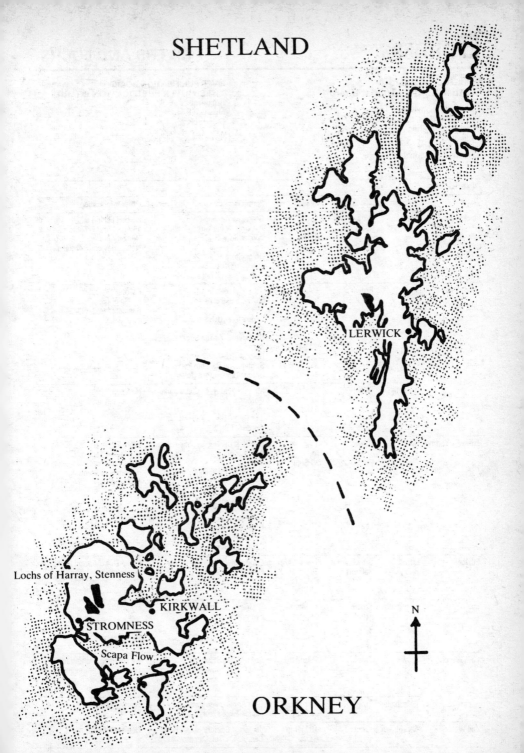

SHETLAND

LERWICK

Lochs of Harray, Stenness

KIRKWALL

STROMNESS

Scapa Flow

N

ORKNEY

Area Tourist Board
Scottish Borders Tourist Board

Director of Tourism
Scottish Borders Tourist Board
Municipal Buildings
High Street
Selkirk TD7 4JX
Tel: Selkirk (0750) 2055

RIVER PURIFICATION BOARD
TWEED RIVER PURIFICATION BOARD
Burnbrae
Mossilee Road
Galashiels
Tel: Galashiels 2425

RIVERS

Water	Location	Species	Season	Permit available from	Other Information
Blackadder	Greenlaw	Brown Trout	1 Apr to 6 Oct	Greenlaw Angling Club A. Lamb, Waterford Wester Row, Greenlaw Doigs Store The Cafe Greenlaw Post Office. All Hotels	No bait fishing till 15 Apr. Sunday fishing No spinning. No Sunday competitions.
Eden Water	Kelso	Brown Trout	1 Apr to 30 Sept	J. Dickson & Son 35 The Square, Kelso Redpath & Co, Horsemarket Kelso Sportswise, 43 The Square Kelso. River Watchers Springwood Caravan Park Border Temperance Hotel	Fly only No Spinning Restricted to 3 rods
	Gordon	Brown Trout	15 Mar to 6 Oct	Mr. W. Halliday, 46 Glebe Park, Gordon J.H. Fairgrieve, Burnbank Gordon. Tel: 357	No Spinning No Sunday fishing
Ettrick & Yarrow	Selkirk	Brown Trout	1 Apr to 30 Sept	Selkirk & District Angling Association. A. Murray, 40 Raeburn Meadow, Selkirk D. & H. MacDonald, 9-11 High Street, Selkirk, Tel: 21398 Gordon Arms Hotel Tushielaw Hotel Cross Keys Hotel P.O.'s at Ettrick, Yarrowford, Yarrow, Ettrickbridge	Night Fishing. 15 May-14 Sept. Week ticket only. No minnows or Spinning No Sundays.
Ettrick	Ettrick Bridge	Brown Trout Salmon	Trout 1 Apr-30 Sept Sal. 1 Feb-30 Nov	Ettrickshaws Hotel (0750) 52229	Packed lunches and flasks for residents. Permits also available for other waters.
Eye Water	Eyemouth	Brown Trout	15 Mar to 6 Oct	R. Grieve, 21 High Street, Eyemouth	Fly only No Spinning No Sundays Catch limit 6.
Gala Water	Stow	Trout	1 April to 30 Sept	Royal Hotel, Stow Post Office, Stow	No spinning. Fishing to cease 1 hour after sunset until 1 hour before sunrise.
	Galashiels	Trout	1 Apr to 30 Sept	Gala Angling Association (as for Tweed entry)	Sunday fishing
Jed Water	Camptown	Trout	15 Mar to 6 Oct	Jedforest Country House Hotel Camptown. Tel: Camptown 274	Hotel residents only

Water	Location	Species	Season	Permit available from	Other Information
Jed/Oxnam Waters	Jedburgh	Trout	1 Apr to 30 Sept	Jedforest Angling Association First & Last Shop, Kenmore Toll, Jedburgh W. Shaw, Cannongate, Jedburgh	1 Apr-30 Apr fly only. 1-30 Sept no Spinning no spinning reels, no floats, no minnows Minimum size 9in. No Sundays
Kale Water	Eckford	Trout Grayling	15 Mar to 30 Sept	Gamekeeper No.4 Eckford	No Sundays
	Morebattle	Trout Grayling	1 Apr to 30 Sep	Mr. H. Fox Orchard Cottage Morebattle	No ground baiting No Sunday fishing
Leader Water	Lauderdale	Trout	15 Mar to 6 Oct	Lauderdale Angling Association D.M. Millgan, 41 High Street, Haddington. Lauder P.O. Tower Hotel, Oxton A. Hogarth, 20 Market Place, Lauder Lauderdale Hotel The Chip Shop Anglers Choice, High Street. Melrose. Committee members	No Spinning. Sunday fishing. No Grayling fishing.
Leader Water/ Tweed	Earlston	Trout	15 Mar to 30 Sept	Earlston Angling Association P. Hessett 2 Arnot Place Earlston Tel: 577 J. McQuillan, Newsagent, Earlston L. Wilson, Newsagent, Earlston G. Birbeck Grocers Earlston Hotels in Earlston Tweed Permits J. Yule Huntspool, Eastgreen Earlston. Tel: 216	No Sundays Other Restrictions as per permit
Leet	Coldstream	Trout Grayling Dace Gudgeon	15 Mar to 6 Oct	Coldstream Angling Association Market Square, Coldstream Tel: 2719	Fly only. No Spinning
Liddle Water	Newcastleton	Salmon Sea trout Brown trout	Salmon 1 Feb to 31 Oct Sea trout 1 May to 30 Sept Brown trout 15 Apr to 30 Sept	R. J. B. Hill, Solicitor, Langholm Tel: Langholm 80428 J. D. Ewart, Drapers, Newcastleton. Tel: Liddlesdale 257 Mrs. B. Elliott, Thistlesyke, Newcastleton. Tel: Liddlesdale 200	Spinning allowed when water is above markers at Newcastleton and Kershopfoot Bridge. Tickets also available for Esk, Liddle & tributaries. Full details on association pamphlet available from Mr. Hill, Bank of Scotland Buildings, Langholm.
Lyne Water	Tweed Junction to Flemington Bridge	Trout Grayling	1 Apr to 30 Sept	Peebleshire Trout Fishing Association D.G. Fyfe, 39 High Street Peebles. Tel: 20131. I. Fraser, Northgate Peebles, Tel: 20979 Tweed Valley Hotel, Walkerburn. J. Dickson & Son, 1 Frederick Street, Edinburgh Post Office, Stobo The Luckenbooth,	No Sundays. No Spinning. No bait fishing April and Sept Tickets also cover Tweed.

Water	Location	Species	Season	Permit available from	Other Information
Leader Water/ Tweed contd.				High Street, Innerleithen. Crook Inn, Tweedsmuir. Sonnys Sports Shop, 29 High Street, Innerleithen.	
Teviot	Kelso	Trout Grayling	1 Apr to 30 Sept	Kelso Angling Association C. Hutchison, 53 Abbotseat Kelso Tel: Kelso 23340 J. Dickson & Son, 35 The Square, Kelso Redpath & Co, Horsemarket, Kelso. Tel: Kelso 24578 Sportswise, 43 The Square, Kelso Border Temperance Hotel Springwood Caravan Park	Fly only 1 Apr to 30 Apr. No Sundays. Restrictions on spinning. No maggots or ground bait, Size limit 9in.
	Eckford	Salmon Sea Trout Brown Trout	Salmon 1 Feb to 30 Nov Trout 15 Mar to 6 Oct.	Gamekeeper, No 4, Eckford	No Sundays Limited to 4 day permits Bait and Spinning 15 Feb-15 Sept only. Spinning for Trout and Grayling prohibited
	Jedforest	Salmon Trout Grayling	Salmon 1 Feb to 31 Nov Trout 1 Apr to 30 Sept	Jedforest Angling Association A. Whitecross, 42 Howden Road, Jedburgh. First & Last Shoop, Kenmore Toll, Jedburgh (Trout permits only) W. Shaw, Cannongate, Jedburgh.	No Sundays. Salmon: 3 rods per day only Spinning allowed from 15 Feb to 14 Sept Fly only 15 Sept to 30 nov. No spinning for trout Salmon day permits n/a on Saturdays.
Teviot (and Ale Slitrig Borthwick Rule)	Hawick	Brown trout Salmon Grayling	15 Mar to 30 Sep 1 Feb to 30 Nov 1 Jan to 30 Sep	Stotharts, 6 High Street, Hawick Tel: 72231 Pet Shop, 1 Union Street, Hawick Club Premises, 5 Sandbed, Dickman (Saddler), Denholm.	All rules and regulations on ticket.
Teviot	Above Chesters	Salmon Sea trout	1 Feb to 30 Nov	Stotharts, Tackle Shop, 6 High Street, Hawick Tel: 72234	All rules and regulations on ticket. Limited to 4 rods/day. Visitors only if vacancy.
Tweed	Tweedsmuir	Salmon	1 Oct to 30 Nov	Crook Inn. Tweedsmuir Tel: Tweedsmuir (08997) 272	Regulations as Peebleshire Salmon Fishing Association.
	Peebleshire (30 miles of river)	Trout Grayling	1 Apr 30 Sept	Peebleshire Trout Fishing Association D.G. Fyfe, 39 High Street, Peebles Tel: 20131 Post Office, Stobo I. Fraser, Tackle Dealer Northgate, Peebles Tweed Valley Hotel, Walkerburn Tel: 220 The Luckenbooth, High Street Innerleithen Sonny's Sport Shop, 29 High Street Innerleithen John Dickson & Son 21 Frederick Street, Edinburgh Crook Inn, Tweedsmuir	No spinning. No bait fishing Apr and Sept. No Sunday fishing. Tickets also cover Lyne Water. Waders desirable. Fly only on Tweed from Lynefoot upstream.
	Peebles (Wire Bridge Pool to Nutwood Pool — excluding Kailzie)	Salmon	21 Feb to 30 Nov	Peebleshire Salmon Fishing Association Seasons: Blackwood & Smith, W.S., 39 High Street, Tel: 20131 Days: I. Fraser, Northgate, Peebles. Tel: 20979	Fly fishing only. No Sundays. No double or treble hooks above size 4. No single hooks above size 4/0. No waders or swivels. No loaded flies exceeding ¾oz

Water	Location	Species	Season	Permit available from	Other Information
Tweed contd.					including tube and hook. No wire cast or bubble float. No gaffs. No lead cored line.
	Peebles	Salmon	21 Feb to 30 Nov	Residents: Tweeddale District permit applies. Visitors: I. Fraser Northgate, Peebles. Tel: 20979	Restricted to 20/day No seasons for visitors Advance booking advisable. Sept to Nov. No Sundays. No Swivels. Other regulations as Peebleshire Salmon Fishing Association.
	Walkerburn	Trout Sea Trout Salmon	Salmon 1 Feb to 30 Nov Trout 1 Apr to 30 Sept	Tweed Valley Hotel Walkerburn. Tel: 089687 220 Telex: 946240 Ref: 15014620	Salmon tickets hotel guests only after 14 Sept. Special salmon and trout weeks, tuition. Trout and Grayling permits available to all.
	Fairnilee	Salmon Sea Trout	1 Oct to 30 Nov	Tweed Valley Hotel Walkerburn. Tel: 089687 220 Telex: 94620 Ref: 19014620	3½ miles single bank, private beat. 17 named pools, ghillie, hut, rod room.
	Peel	Salmon Sea Trout	15 Sept to 30 Nov 1 Feb to 31 Aug	Tweed Valley Hotel Walkerburn. Tel: 089687 220 Telex: 946240 Ref: 19014620	Private 2-rod salmon beat South Bank.
	Nest	Salmon Sea Trout	1 Feb to 14 Sept 15 Sept 30 Nov	Tweed Valley Hotel, Walkerburn. Tel: 089687 220 Telex: 946240 Ref: 19014620	Private salmon/sea trout beat approx. 1¾ miles, 4 rods. Fly only 15 Sept to 30 Nov m Tel: Langholm 80428
	Ashiesteel to Elwyn	Trout	1 Apr to 30 Sept	Tweed Valley Hotel, Walkerburn. Tel: 089687 220 Telex: 946240 Ref: 19014620	Angling course for both trout and salmon fishing spring and autumn both fly and bait casting, single handed, two handed and spinning rods.
	Galashiels	Trout	1 Apr to 30 Sept	Gala Angling Association Messrs. J. & A. Turnbull, 30 Bank Street, Galashiels. Tel: 3191 Tweed Valley Hotel, Walkerburn. Tel: 220. Kingsknowes Hotel. Galashiels. Tel: 3478 Clovenfords Hotel, Clovenfords. Tel: 203	No Sundays. Day tickets available on Saturdays. No Spinning.
	Boleside	Salmon	1 Feb to 10 Sept	N. Fell, Fisherman's Cottage, Boleside. Tel: Galashiels 2972.	Fly only 1-14 Feb. Any legal lures till 14 Sept. No Sundays. After 10 Sept Fully booked.
	Melrose	Trout Grayling	1 Apr to 6 Oct 7 Oct-15 Mar	Melrose & District Angling Association. Anglers Choice, High Street, Melrose. Telo: 3070.	No Spinning. No ground baiting. No Sundays. Minnow fishing not permitted. Spinning reels of all types prohibited.
	Melrose	Brown Trout	1 Apr to 6 Oct	The Brother Superior, St. Aidans, Gattonside, Melrose.	No Spinning. Bait and fly only. Sunday Fishing Restrictions on number of rods. See permit for full details.
	Melrose (Ravenswood Tweedswood)	Brown Trout	1 Apr to 30 Sept	Anglers Choice, High Street, Melrose Tel: 3070	Fly Only. No Sundays. Limit of 10 trout per day per angler. Limit of 6 anglers at any time.

Water	Location	Species	Season	Permit available from	Other information
	Melrose (Pavilion)	Salmon Sea Trout	1 Feb to 30 Nov	Anglers Choice, High Street, Melrose Tel: 3070	Fly only — 1 to 15 Feb and 15 Sept to 30 Nov. Feb 16-Sept 14 fly and spinning.
	St Boswells	Brown Trout	1 Apr to 30 Sept	St. Boswells Angling Association Mr. Law, Main Street, St. Boswells G. MacLaren Rowanbrae Tweedside Road, Newton, St. Boswells Tel: 22568. C.D. Grant, Newsagent, Newton St. Boswells Mr. Geddes, Fishermans House, Mertoun Mill. Dryburgh. Dryburgh Abbey Hotel. Anglers Choice, Melrose Miss. A. Laing, Newsagent Newton St. Boswells.	Fly only 1 Apr to 1 May. No bait fishing until May 1. No Sundays. No spinning tackle. No coarse fishing allowed outside season. Full details of local rules on permit. Access to restricted beats by special permits only Full details shown on permit.
	St. Boswells	Trout	1 Apr to 30 Sept	Dryburgh Abbey Hotel. St. Boswells. Tel: 0835 22261.	No Sundays. No spinning. No ground baiting.
Tweed (and Teviot)	Kelso	Trout	1 Apr to 30 Sept	Kelso Angling Association C. Hutchison, 53 Abbotseat, Kelso.	No Sundays. Size limit 9in. Fly only 1-30 Apr. Spinning restrictions. No maggots or ground bait.
		Grayling and Roach	1 May-31 Aug and 1 Dec-31 jan	J. Dickson & Son, 36 The Square, Kelso Redpath & Co, Horsemarket, Kelso. Sportswise, 43 The Square, Kelso, River Watchers, Border Temperance Hotel Springwood Caravan Park.	
Tweed	Kelso	Salmon Brown Trout Coarse Fish	1 Feb-30 Nov 1 Apr-30 Sept	J. Dickson & Son 36 The Square, Kelso.	
	Coldstream	Brown Trout Grayling Roach Dace Gudgeon	Varies according to best. Details on permit.	Coldstream Angling Association Market Square, Coldstream. Tel: 2719 Tourist Information Centre, Coldstream.	Fly only. No Sunday or night fishing. No Spinning.
		Brown trout	15 Mar to 6 Oct	The Manager, Milne Garden, Coldstream	No Sunday fishing. No night fishing. Fly only
	Cornhill	Salmon Sea Trout Brown Trout	Salmon 1 Feb to 30 Nov	Tillmouth Park Hotel, Tel: Coldstream 2255.	No Sundays. No Worming, Boats available. Ghillie available. Special terms for residents.
	Ladykirk	Brown Trout	15 Mar to 8 Oct	Ladykirk and Norham Angling Association Masons Arms, Norham, Tel: (0289) 82326 Victoria Hotel, Norham Tel: (0289) 82237.	No Spinning. No ground baiting. Fly only above Norham Bridge to West Ford. No Sundays.
	Horncliffe (Tidal)	Trout, Grayling, Roach, Dace	15 Mar-6 Oct.	No permit required	
Whiteadder & Dye & Tributeries	30 miles	Brown trout Rainbow trout	15 Mar to 30 Sept	Whiteadder Angling Association Mr. Cowan, Crumstane Duns. (Bailiff). R. Welsh, Abbey St. Bathans Duns. Peter Grzeszuk Whitchester, Ellemford.	No Sundays. Fly only before 15 Apr Worm from 15 Apr only. Minnow from 1 May only. Tickets in advance, size limit 8 inches. River stocked annually.

Water	Location	Species	Season	Permit available from	Other Information
Whiteadder	Allanton	Trout	15 Mar to 30 Sept	Berwick & District Angling Association per J. Moody, Hon. Secy. 12 Hillcrest, East Ord, Berwick. Bus Parties limited in numbers and prior arrangement only with Hon. Secretary. Messrs. Jobson, Marygate, Berwick Messrs. Game Fair, Berwick Red Lion, Allanton.	Fly only before May. No Spinning (rod and/or reel). No threadline. No maggot fishing. No ground bating. 8in. minimum Maximum bag of 20 fish per day. No Sundays. Permits must be obtained beforre commencing to fish.

LOCHS AND RESERVOIRS

Water	Location	Species	Season	Permit available from	Other Information
Acreknowe Reservoir	Hawick	Brown trout	15 Mar to end Sept	Stotharts, 6 High Street, Hawick. Pet Shop, 1 Union Street, Hawick. I. Rennie, 10 Bourtree Place, Hawick, Club Premises, 5 Sandbed, Hawick	Ticket covers al other trout waters managed by Hawick Angling Club.
Alermoor Loch	Hawick	Brown trout		As Acreknowe.	Bank fishing only.
Alermoor Loch	Hawick	Brown trout Perch Pike		As Acreknowe Mr. Speirs, Alemoor.	
Coldingham Loch	Coldingham	Brown trout Rainbow trout	15 mar to 30 Oct	Dr. E.J. Wise West Loch House, Coldingham, Tel:270	Fly only. 6 Boats (max. 12 rods) 6 Bank rods. Sunday fishing. 10 a.m. to Dusk. Bag limit 5 per rod full day. Min size 12in. Frequent stocking throughout season. Full details on leaflet.
Fruid Reservoir	Tweedsmuir	Brown trout	1 Apr to 30 Sept	Boat and bank permits from Reservoir Superintendent. Tel: Tweedsmuir 225.	Sunday fishing. Two boats to be booked in advance. Bus parties can be accommodated. Prior notice to water keeper preferred. Tel: Tweedsmuir 225.
Heatherhope Reservoir	Morebattle	Trout	1 Apr to 30 Sep	Mr. H. Fox, Orchard Cottage Morebattle	No ground bating No Sunday fishing.
Hellmoor Loch	Hawick	Brown Trout		As Acreknowe.	No boat.
Lindean Reservoir	Selkirk	Brown trout Rainbow trout	1 Apr to 31 Oct	D. & H. McDonald, 9-11 High Street, Selkirk, Tel: 21398	Fly only. No bank fishing. Bag limit, 4/Rod. Min. size 10in.
Loch of the Lowes and St. Mary's Loch	Selkirk	Trout	1 Apr to 30 Sept	St. Mary's A.C., per Secretary, J. Miller, 8/5 Craighouse Gardens, Edinburgh, Tel: 031-447 0024	Spinning & Bait after 1 May only. Club fishing-apply in advance to Secretary. Sunday fishing allowed. Weekly permits are obtain-able from the keepers. Permits must be obtained before commencing to fish. No float fishing. Boats from keepers only. River Tweed Protection Order applies.
		Pike Perch Eels	1 May-30 Sept	The Glen Cafe, Cappercleuch,. Gordon Arms Hotel, Yarrow. Tibbiesheils Hotel. (Loch side) Anglers Choice, High Street Melrose. Crook Inn, Tweedsmuir. Keeper, Henderland East Cottage, Cappercleuch Tel: Cappercleuch 42243 Rodono Hotel (Loch Side) Sonnys Sports Shop, 29 High Street, Innerleithen.	

Water	Location	Species	Season	Permit available from	Other Information
Megget Reservoir	Selkirk	Brown trout	1 Apr to 30 Sept	Boat and bank permits from Mrs. Baigrie 2 Gillwood Cappercleuch Tel: 0750 42265	Sunday Fishing. Fly only 6 boats & bank fishing.
Peebleshire Lochs	Tweed Valley	Brown trout Rainbow trout	Apr-Oct	Tweed Valley Hotel, Walkerburn. Tel: 089687 220 Telex: 946240 Ref: 15014620	Stocked Private Lochans
Talla Reservoir	Tweedsmuir	Brown trout	1 Apr to 30 Sept	Boat and Bank permits from Reservoir Superintendent, Tel: Tweedsmuir 209.	Sunday fishing, fly only. Two boats may be booked in advance. Bus parties can be accommodated. Prior notice to water keeper preferred. Tel: Tweedsmuir 209
Watch Reservoir	Longform-acus.	Brown trout Rainbow trout	15 Mar to 30 Sept	Whiteadder A.A. G. Amos Tel: (03617) 278/230.	Sunday fishing.
Whiteadder Reservoir	Cranshaws	Brown trout	Boat fishing 1 Apr to 30 Sept. Bank fishing 1 Jun to 30 Sept	Boat and Bank permits from waterkeeper — Tel: Longformacus 257.	Sunday fishing. Fly only. 3 boats may be booked in advance. Bus parties can be accommodated. Prior notice to waterkeeper preferred.
Willestruther Loch	Hawick	Brown trout		As Acreknowe	No boat.
Wooden Loch	Eckford	Brown trout Rainbow Trout	1 Apr to 30 Sept 1 Apr until 31 Oct.	Gamekeeper, No.4 Eckford	One boat. No bank fishing. Only Rainbow trout after 30 Sept. Only 3 rods at any time. Advance booking necessary.

BORDERS
Sea Angling

The Scottish Borders provide some of the best sea angling in the UK. Based on Eyemouth, which has the largest fishing fleet in the South of Scotland, and the smaller fishing villages of Burnmouth and St. Abbs, the clear unpolluted waters are well stocked with a wide variety of sea fish. So clear is the water that one of the first Marine Reservations has been established off Eyemouth.

The rugged coastline with its unique fauna make a spectacular background to your day's fishing. It should be noted that sea angling is not permitted off St. Abbs Head National Reserve (Petticowick – Long Carr).

Eyemouth is only nine miles north of Berwick-upon-Tweed, just off the A.1. Its colourful boats, fish auction and sandy beach make it a popular resort during the summer. Well known for its excellent rock fishing, the town is also a useful point of access to shoreline to the north and south. Boat fishing has developed over the years due to the efforts of Eyemouth Sea Angling Club who now run a number of shore and boat competitions throughout the season.

The club operates the coast from Burnmouth harbour in the south to the harbour at St. Abbs in the north.

Types of fish: Shore – cod, mackerel, coalfish, flounder, plaice, sole, haddock, whiting, catfish, ling and wrasse. Boat – the same species can be caught as on shore but larger specimens.

Boats: A large number of fishing boats are usually available from Eyemouth, St. Abbs and Burnmouth for parties of anglers at weekends. For bookings and further information write, c/o F.M.A., Harbour Road, Eyemouth or J. Weatherhead and Sons, Harbour Road, Eyemouth. (50382).

Area Tourist Board
Dumfries and Galloway Tourist Board

Director of Tourism
Dumfries and Galloway Tourist Board
Douglas House,
Newton Stewart
Wigtownshire DG8 6DQ
Tel: Newton Stewart (0671) 2549

RIVER PURIFICATION BOARD
SOLWAY RIVER PURIFICATION BOARD
Rivers House, Irongray Road,
Dumfries DG2 0JE
Tel: Dumfries 720502.

RIVERS

Water	Location	Species	Season	Permit available from	Other information
Annan	Newbie Estate	Salmon Sea Trout	25 Feb to 15 Nov	Mr. Bailey, Newbie Mill, Annan, Tel: Annan 2608	Fly fishing all season. Spinning when above mark on Galabank Bridge. Worm fishing in flood.
	Hoddom Estate Ecclefechan	Salmon Sea trout	10 Feb to 15 Nov	Mrs. Cruikshank, Ecclefehan Hotel, Ecclefechan.	
	Halleaths Estate Lockerbie	Salmon Sea Trout	25 Feb to 31 oct	Messrs. McJerrow & Stevenson, Solicitors, Lockerbie, Dumfrieshire. Tel: Lockerbie 2123.	Limited number of tickets.
	Royal Four Towns Water Lockerbie	Salmon Sea trout	25 Feb to 15 Nov	Castle Milk Estate Office, Norwood, Lockerbie, Dumfrieshire, Tel: Kettleholm 203/4	Boats prohibited. Fly and Spinning Only.
	St. Mungo's Parish	Salmon Sea trout Brown trout	25 Feb to 15 Nov 15 Mar-6 Oct.	Castle Milk Estates Office, Norwood, Lockerbie. Tel: Kettleholm 203/4	Fly fishing only. No Sunday fishing.
	Kinmount Estate Lockerbie	Salmon Sea trout	10 Feb to 15 Nov	Factor, Kinmount Estates, Lockerbie.	
	Moffat	Salmon Sea trout Brown trout	25 Feb to 15 Nov 1 Apr to 15 Sept	Upper Annandale Angling Association A. Black, 1 Rosshill, Grange Road, Moffat. Tel: Moffat 20104.	Limited number of seasons available.
	Lockerbie	Grayling Chub		Clerk & Commissioners of Royal Four Towns Fishing, K. Ratcliffe, 'Jay-Ar' Hightae, Lockerbie Tel: Lochmaben 220	
Bladnoch	Newton Stewart	Salmon	1 Mar to 30 Sept	Newton Stewart Angling Association Galloway Guns and Tackle, Albert Street, Newton Stewart.	
Cairn	Dumfries	Salmon Sea trout Brown trout	25 Feb to 31 Oct 15 Mar to 31 Aug	Dumfries and Galloway Angling Association Secretary, D.G. Conchie, 46 Barrie Avenue, Cresswell, Dumfries. Tel: 56223 D. McMillan, 6 Friars Vennel, Dumfries. Tel: Dumfries 52075.	Limited number of permits. No Sunday fishing. Restrictions depend on water level.
Cree (and Pencill Burn Palnure Burn)	Newton Stewart	Salmon Sea trout	1 Mar to 30 Sept	Newton Stewart Angling Association Galloway Guns and Tackle, Albert Street, Newton Stewart.	

Water	Location	Species	Season	Permit available from	Other information
Cross Water of Luce	New Luce	Salmon Sea Trout	1 May to 31 Oct	Stranraer and District Angling Association. McDiarmid Sports Shop, 90 George Street, Stranraer. Tel: (0776) 2705 And local Hotels	
Black Water of Dee	Mossdale	Salmon	11 Feb to 31 Oct	New Galloway Angling Association Secretary, N. Birch, Galloway View, Balmaclellan, Castle Douglas Tel: New Galloway 404 Local Hotels.	
		Trout Pike Perch	15 Mar to 30 Sept		
Esk **Liddle and Tributaries** **Ewes, Wauchope, Tarras**	Langholm Canonbie Newcastleton (All waters ticket)	Salmon Sea trout Brown trout	1 Feb to 31 Oct 1 May to 30 Sept 15 Apr to 30 Sept	Esk and Liddle Fisheries Association Secretary, R.J.B. Hill, Solicitor, Bank of Scotland Buildings, Langholm. Dumfriesshire. Tel: Langholm 80428 J.I. Wylie, Byreburnfoot, Canonbie, Dumfriesshire. Tel: Canonbie 279. P. Little, 19 Rowanburn, Canonbie. Tel: Canonbie 224.	Spinning allowed until 14 Apr and from 1 Oct, otherwise only when water is above markers at Willow Pool, Canonbie Bridge, Skippers Bridge and River Little markers. No Sunday Fishing.
	Canonbie Ticket			Secretary	No Sunday fishing
	Langholm Ticket			Secretary and J.I. Whyte, Byreburnfoot, Canonbie	Spinning allowed until 14 Apr and from 1 Oct, otherwise only when water is above marker at Skippers Bridge. No Sunday fishing.
	Canonbie Lower Liddle Ticket			Secretary and J.I. Wylie, Byreburnfoot, Canonbie	Spinning allowed until 14 Apr and 1 Oct otherwise only when water is above marker at Canonbie Bridge. No Sundays fishing.
	Newcastleton Ticket	Salmon Sea trout Brown trout	15 Apr-31 Oct 1 May-30 Sept 15 Apr-30 Sept	Secretary and J.D. Ewart, Drapers, Newcastleton. Tel: Liddlesdale 257	Spinning allowed when water is above markets at Newcastleton and Kershopelfoot Bridges. No Sunday fishing.
	Langholm Area Tributaries Ticket	Salmon Sea trout Brown trout	15 Apr to 30 Sept	Secretary and J.I. Wylie, Byreburnfoot, Canonbie. P. Lillie, 15 Rowanburn, Canonbie.	No Spinning. No Sunday fishing.
	River and Tributaries	Coarse fishing	1 Nov to 31 Jan	R.J.B. Hill, Bank of Scotland Buildings, Langholm.	Club applications.
Fleet	Gatehouse of Fleet	Salmon Sea trout Brown trout	25 Feb to 31 Oct 15 Mar-6 Oct	Cally Estates Office, Gatehouse of Fleet.	
	Gatehouse of Fleet	Salmon Sea trout Brown trout	25 Feb to 31 Oct 15 Mar-6 Oct.	Murray Arms Hotel, Gatehouse of Fleet (05574) 207 On application.	
Ken	New Galloway	Salmon Sea trout Brown trout	11 Feb to 31 Oct 15 Mar to 3 Sept	New Galloway Angling Association N. Birch, Galloway View Balmaclellan Castle Douglas Tel: New Galloway 404. Local Hotels	
	Dalry	Salmon Sea trout Brown trout	11 Feb to 31 Oct 15 Mar-6 Oct	Dalry Angling Association J. Kentley, Glenkens Cafe, Dalry.	
Milk	Above Scrogg Bridge	Sea trout Brown trout	1 Apr to 30 Sept	Castle Milk Estates Office Norwood, Lockerbie Tel: Kettleholm 203/4	Fly fishing only. No sunday Fishing.

Water	Location	Species	Season	Permit available from	Other Information
Nith	Dumfries	Salmon Sea trout Brown trout	25 Feb to 30 Nov .15 Mar to 6 Oct	Director of Finance Nithsdale Direct Council Municipal Chambers, Dumfries, Tel: Dumfries 53166.	
	Dumfries	Salmon Sea trout Brown trout	25 Feb to 30 Nov 15 Mar to 6 Oct	Dumfries and Galloway Angling Association Secretary D.G. Conchie 46 Barrie Avenue, Cresswell, Dumfries. Tel: 56223 D. McMillan, 6 Friar's Vennel, Dumfries.	Limited number of permits. Weekly permits from Mon-Fri. Advance booking possible. Spinning restrictions.
	Thornhill	Salmon Sea Trout Brown Trout	25 Feb to 30 Nov 1 Apr to 15 Sept	Mid-Nithsdale Angling Association Pollok & Oag, 1 West Morton Street, Thornhill.	No day permits on Saturdays. Spinning and worming allowed, only in flood conditions.
	Thornhill	Salmon Sea trout Brown trout	April to 30 Nov	Buccleuch Estates Ltd, Drumlanrig Mains, Thornhill Tel: (08486) 283	Three beats — weekly lets two rods per beat One beat-daily let-three rods. Two trout lochs.
Nith (and Tributeries Kello Crawick Euchan Mennock)	Sanquhar	Salmon Sea trout Brown trout	15 Mar to 30 Nov	Upper Nithsdale Angling Association. W. Forsyth, Solicitor, 100 High Street, Sanquhar, Dumfrieshire. Tel: Sanquhar 241.	No visitors day tickets on Sats. No Sunday fishing. Visitors must stay in district Visitors must have letter of introduction from Secretary of own angling club.
Nith	New Cumnock	Brown trout	15 Mar to 6 Oct	New Cumnock Angling Association, A. Lockhart, 79 Dalhanna Drive, New Cumnock.	
Tarf	Kirkcowan	Sea trout Brown trout	Easter- 30 Sept	B, Stevens, Three Lochs Caravan Park, Kirkcowan, Newton Stewart, Wigtownshire. Tel: Kirkcowan 304.	No Sunday fishing
	Kirkcowan	Salmon Brown trout Pike	18 Feb- 31 Oct	Derek Lynch Torwood House Hotel Glenluce, Newton Stewart. Tel: 05813 463.	Sunday fishing for Pike only. Salmon best 1 Sep-31 Oct.
Urr	Dalbeattie	Salmon Sea trout Brown trout	25 Feb to 29 Nov 1 Apr to 6 Oct	Castle Douglas and District Angling Association Tommy's Sport Shop, King Street, Castle Douglas. Tel: (0556) 2861.	No Sunday fishing.
	Dalbeattie	Salmon Sea trout Brown trout	25 Feb to 29 Nov 1 Apr to 6 Oct	Dalbeattie Angling Association, N. Parker, High Street, Dalbeattie. Tel: (0556) 610448	
White Esk	Eskdalemuir	Salmon Sea trout	15 Apr to 30 Sept	Hart Manor Hotel, Eskdalemuir, by Langholm Tel: Eskdalemuir 217.	Fly and Spinner only.

LOCHS AND RESERVOIRS

Water	Location	Species	Season	Permit available from	Other Information
Barnbarroch Loch	Whauphill	Bream Carp Roach Tench Rudd	No close season	Derek Lynch, Torwood House Hotel Glenluce, Newton Stewart, Tel: (05813) 469	Day tickets. Available to matches. Up to 20 pegs.
Barscobe Loch	Balmaclellan	Brown trout Rainbow trout	15 Mar to 6 Oct	Sir Hugh Wontner, Barscobe Balmaclellan, Castle Douglas, Tel: (064 42) 245/294.	
Black Esk Reservoir	Eskdalemuir	Brown trout	1 Apr to 30 Sept	Hart Manor Hotel, Eskdalemuir. Tel: Eskdalemuir 217.	Fly and Spinner only.

Water	Location	Species	Season	Permit available from	Other Information
Black Loch	Newton Stewart	Brown trout (stocked)	15 Apr to 30 Sept	Forestry Commission, Creebridge. Tel: (0671) 2420 Galloway Deer Museum, New Galloway. Tel: (064 42) 285.	Fly only until 1 July.
Brack Loch	Dalry	Brown trout Rainbow trout	1 Apr to 30 Sept	Milton Park Hotel Dalry Tel: (064 43) 286.	1 Boat. Sunday fishing
Bruntis Loch	Newton Stewart	Brown trout Rainbow trout	15 Mar to 30 Sept	Newton Stewart Angling Association. Galloway Guns and Tackle, Albert Street, Newton Stewart.	Bank fishing only. Sunday fishing.
Castle Loch	Lochmaben	Bream Perch	No Close Season	Mr. Armstrong, Lochside Cottage Lochmaben. Tel: Lochmaben 340	
Clattering-shaws Loch	New Galloway	Brown trout Pike Perch	15 Mar to 6 Oct	Newton Stewart Angling Association Galloway Guns and Tackle, Albert Street, Newton Stewart. New Galloway Angling Association, Secretary, N. Birch, Galloway View, Balmaclellan Castle Douglas Tel: New Galloway 404 Local Hotels	Bank fishing only. Sunday fishing. Fly, Spinner and bait.
Dalbeattie Reservoir	Dalbeattie	Brown trout Rainbow trout	16 Apr to 30 Sept	Dalbeattie Angling Association N. Parker, High Street, Dalbeattie. Tel: (0556) 610446	Bank fishing. Fly only.
Loch Dee	New Galloway	Brown trout (stocked)	15 Mar to 6 Oct	Forestry Commission, Creebridge, Tel: (0671) 2420 Galloway Deer Museum, New Galloway. Tel: (064 42) 285.	Fly only. Bank fishing. Sunday fishing only.
Dernagler Loch	Glenluce	Pike Perch	No Close Season	Derek Lynch, Torwood House Hotel, Glenluce, Newton Stewart. Tel: (05813) 469.	
Dindinnie Reservoir	Stranraer	Brown trout	15 Mar to 30 Sept	Stranraer and District Angling Association, McDiarmid, Sports Shop, 90 George Street, Stranraer. Tel: (0776) 2705 & Local Hotels.	Bank fishing only. Sunday fishing.
Ervie Estate Fishings	Castle Douglas	Brown trout Rainbow trout	1 Apr to 30 Sept	G.M. Thomson & Co Ltd, 27 King Street, Castle Douglas, Tel: (0556) 2701.	Bank fishing only. Limited rods. Sunday fishing. Bag limit-6 fish.
Glenkiln Reservoir	Dumfries	Brown trout Rainbow trout (stocked)	1 Apr to 30 Sept	Director of Water and Sewerage, Dumfries and Galloway Regional Council, 70 Terregles Street, Dumfries. Tel: (0387) 63011.	
Hightae Mill Loch	Lochmaben	Bream Carp Tench Rudd Chub Roach		J. Wildman, Annandale Cottage, Greenhill, Lockerbie. Tel: Lochmaben 478.	Fishing by boat only. No restrictions.
Jericho Loch	Dumfries	Brown trout Rainbow trout Brook trout	1 Apr to 30 Sept	Pattie's of Dumfries 103 Queensberry Street, Dumfries. Tel: (0387) 52891. Baird and Stephenson. Locharbriggs. Tel: (0387) 710237.	Bank fishing only. Fly fishing only. Sunday fishing.
Loch Ken	Parton	Pike	All year	G.M. Thomson & Co Ltd, 27 King Street, Castle Douglas, Tel: Castle Douglas 2701/2973.	Self catering accom. available throughout Galloway.
	Aird's Lodge	Trout	15 Mar to 6 Oct	New Galloway Angling Association, Secretary, N. Birch,	

Water	Location	Species	Season	Permit available from	Other Information
		Pike Perch	All Year.	Galloway View, Balmaclellan, Castle Douglas, Tel: New Galloway 404. Local Hotels.	
Kirriereoch Loch	Newton Stewart	Brown trout	15 mar to 6 Oct	Newton Stewart Angling Association, Galloway Guns and Tackle, Albert Street, Newton Stewart.	Bank fishing only. Fly fishing only. Sunday fishing.
Knockquassen Reservoir	Stranraer	Brown trout	15 Mar to 30 Sept	Stranraer and District Angling Association, McDiarmid Sports Shop, 90 George Street, Stranraer. Tel: (0776) 2705. Local Hotels	Bank fishing only. Fly and Spinner. Sunday fishing.
Lairdmannoch Loch	Twynholm	Brown trout	1 Apr to 30 Sept	G.M. Thomson & Co Ltd, 27 King Street, Castle Douglas Tel: (0556) 2701	Boat fishing only. Limited rods. Limited days. 2 boats included in house rent.
Lillies Loch	New Galloway	Brown trout	15 Mar to 6 Oct	Forestry Commission, Creebridge. Tel: (0671) 2420. Galloway Deer Museum, New Galloway. Tel: (06442) 285.	Bank fishing only. Any legal method. Sunday fishing.
Lochenbrack Loch	Lauriston	Brown trout	1 Apr to 30 Sept	Watson McKinnel, 15 St. Cuthbert Street, Kincudbright. Tel: (0557) 30693 Twiname Newsagents, Gatehouse of Fleet.	8.30am to 10pm Bank fishing. Four boats. Sunday fishing.
Lochinvar Loch	Dalry	Brown trout	1 Apr to 30 Sept	Mr. Armour, Lochinvar Lodge, Dalry Tel: (06443) 355.	Sunrise to Sunset. Bank fishing. Two boats. Fly fishing only.
Loch of the Lowes	Newton Stewart	Brown trout (stocked)	15 Mar to 6 Oct	Forestry Commission, Creebridge. Tel: (0671) 2420.	Fly only. Sunday fishing.
Lochmaben	Lochmaben	Bream Roach Tench Vendace	No close season	The Warden, Lochfield, Lochmaben. Tel: Lochmaben 340.	Matches can be arranged.
Loch Ochiltree	Newton Stewart	Brown trout Brook trout Pike	15 Mar to 6 Oct All year	Newton Stewart Angling Association.	Fly, Spinning and belt. Bank fishing and two boats. Sunday fishing. No live belt.
Penwhirn Reservoir	Stranraer	Brown trout	15 Mar to 30 Sept	Stranraer and District Angling Association, McDiarmid, Sports Shop, 90 George Street, Stranraer. Tel: (0774) 2706 & local hotels.	Fly fishing and Spinning. Bank fishing and one boat. Sunday fishing.
Loch Roan	Castle Douglas	Brown trout Rainbow trout	1 Apr to 6 Oct	Tommy's Sports Shop, King Street, Castle Douglas, Tel: (0556) 2851.	Fly fishing only. Four boats.
Soulseat Loch	Stranraer	Brown trout Rainbow trout	15 Mar to 30 Sept	Stranraer and District Angling Association, McDiarmid, Sports Shop, 90 George Street, Stranraer. Tel: (0776) 2705 & local hotels	Fly, Spinning and bait. Bank fishing and two boats. Sunday fishing.
Loch Stroan	Castle Douglas	Pike Perch		Forestry Commission, 21 King Street, Castle Douglas, Tel: (0556) 3262.	

Water	Location	Species	Season	Permit available from		Other Information
Torwood Lochs	Glenluce	Trout Bream Tench Carp Roach Rudd Perch	No close season	Derek Lynch, Torwood House Hotel, Glenluce Newton Stewart. Tel: (05813) 469		
Loch Whinyson	Gatehouse of Fleet	Brown trout Rainbow trout	1 Apr to 30 Sept	Murray Arms Hotel, Gatehouse of Fleet. Tel: (055 74) 207.		8am to 10pm Four boats and bank fishing. Fly fishing. Spinning from bank. Sunday fishing.
Whitefield Loch	Glenluce	Pike Perch	No Close Season	Derek Lynch Torwood House Hotel, Glenluce, Newton Stewart. Tel: (05813) 469.		

DUMFRIES AND GALLOWAY
Sea Angling

Solway Firth to Mull of Galloway and Loch Ryan
The Solway Firth area is noted for its many fine shore marks, many of which produce species such as bass, bullhuss and tope in far greater numbers than marks further north. Shore marks on the Kirkcudbrightshire coast regularly produce large cod during the winter months.

Kippford by Dalbeattie
Kippford is a well known yachting centre on the Solway Firth which offers some very good fishing, especially for flatfish.
Types of fish: Cod, flounder, plaice from the shore. Flatfish (including turbot), cod, tope, mackerel, and pollack from boats.
Tackle: Available from Kippford Slipway Ltd., Kippford. M. McCowan and Son, 43 High Street, Dalbeattie. M. Pattie, Dumfries, Dumfriesshire.
Bait: Lugworm can be dug locally. Cockles and mussels from the shore at low water. M. McCowan and Son can supply prepack baits.
Season for fishing: Best May-October. Some winter fishing for cod to 30lb.
Further information and boat details from: J. Moran, Hon. Sec., Dalbeattie & District S.A.C., 12 Church Crescent, Dalbeattie. Tel: Dalbeattie (0556) 610270

Kirkcudbright
Kirkcudbright is a picturesque town with a very good but tidal harbour. It is approximately three miles from fishing grounds, which offer excellent tope as well as good general fishing. The coast is rugged and not recommended for dinghy or small boat fishing.
Types of fish: Cod, coalfish, conger, bass, plaice, flounders, pollack and dogfish from the shore. Cod, coalfish, conger, dogfish, mackerel, haddock, tope, pollack, all types of flatfish and whiting from the boats. Local sea angling clubs hold regular outings and competitions, where visitors are welcome. Information in Harbour Square.
Boats: H. Williams, 10 The Crofts, Kirkcudbright. Tel: 0557 30367. Gordon House Hotel, 116 High Street, Kirkcudbright. Tel: 0557 30670. S. Unsworth, Merse Avenue, Kirkcudbright. Tel: 0557 30337.
Tackle: Available from W. McKinnel, 15 St. Cuthbert Street, Kirkcudbright. M. McCowan, Castle Douglas and Dalbeattie and Patties, 109 Queensferry Street, Dumfries, Dumfriesshire. Castle Douglas Guns & Tackle, 9 St. Andrews Street, Castle Douglas.
Bait: Lugworm can be dug locally. Mussels available at low water.
Season for fishing: May- October. Some winter fishing.
Further information from: Tourist Information Centre, Tel: Kirkcudbright (0557) 30494.

Garlieston
Garlieston has a potentially good but undeveloped tidal harbour on the east side of the Machars Peninsula in Wigtownshire with several square miles of water, sheltered by the land from prevailing winds and therefore suitable for trailed and car-top dinghies.
Types of fish: Mackerel, cod, pollack and coalfish from the shore. Mackerel, cod, pollack, ray, plaice, dab, flounder and coalfish from boats.
Bait: Lugworm may be dug and mussels gathered from the foreshore.
Season for fishing: June-September.
Further information from: Mr A. Houston, The Crescent, Garlieston, Newton Stewart. Tel: Garlieston (098-86) 238.

Isle of Whithorn
This picturesque old seaport on the souht-west corner of Wigtown Bay has an excellent redesigned harbour with a flourishing local sailing club. It tends to be busy in summer and is a port for 'Queenie' boats. The Isle Bay itself offers nearly a mile of sheltered water in all but severe weather conditions. There are many good rock fishing marks.
Types of fish: Cod, coalfish, dogfish, conger, pollack, mackerel, wrasse from the shore. Cod, rays, flatfish, spurdog, dogfish, mackerel, conger and tope from boats.
Boats: K. Lonsdale, Main Street, Isle of Whithorn. Tel: 098 85 393 W.F. McCreadie, 1 Barrhill Avenue, Newton Stewart, Tel: 0671 2466. A. Johnston, 64 Main Street, Isle of Whithorn. Tel: 098 85 358.
Tackle: Available from 'The Flotsam', Harbour Road, Isle of Whithorn. J. McWilliam, Grocer, Main Street, Isle of Whithorn.

Tel: (098-85) 246. A. McGhie, Radio Shop, George Street, Whithorn, R. McDowell, George Street, Whithorn. The Shop, Burrow-Head, Holiday Farm, Cutcloy, Isle of Whithorn. 'Redeemed' – Skipper, c/o Harbour Master, Isle of Whithorn.
Bait: Lugworm and ragworm, mussels and limpets can be gathered on the shore. Bait can also be bought from E. McGuire, Burnside Cottage, Isle of Whithorn, at a reasonable price (order in advance).
Season for fishing: June-September.
Further information from: Mr. E.C. McGuire, Burnside Cottage, Isle of Whithorn, Wigtownshire DG8 8LN. Tel: Whithorn (098-85) 468.

Luce Bay
There are some good shore marks, namely Sandhead Sands for Flatfish, Dogfish and Bass in season, Terrally Bay for these species plus Codling, Whiting, Spurdogfish.
Around East and West Tarbet bays at the Mull of Galloway good rock fishing may be had for Lesser Spotted Dogfish, Bull Huss, Spurdogfish, Conger Eels, Wrasse, Whiting, Pollack, Coalfish, Flatfish and Mackerel in season, normally from late April to December.
Boats: W. Carter, Castle Daly Angling Centre, Auchenmalg, Glenluce. Tel: 058 18 250. (Self drive boats for hire).

Port William
Port William is the starting point for many anglers wishing to fish the lower part of Luce Bay. The once famous shore mark of Monreith Bay, still a good bass beach, lies just to the south of Port William.
Types of fish: Tope, spurdog, rays, cod, pollack, flatfish from boats. Bass, wrasse, codling and pollack from the shore.
Boats: J. Lockwood, 24 South Street, Port William, Tel: 098 87 364.
Tackle: Available in village.
Bait: Lugworm, shellfish and molluscs along beach. Mackerel in bay.
Season for fishing: May- October.

Drummore
Drummore, the main port for anglers wishing to fish the western side of Luce Bay lies 5 miles north of the Mull of Galloway. Hotels and guest houses cater for anglers. There are many good shore marks on sandy beaches north of Drummore, while the Mull of Galloway provides excellent shore fishing over rocky ground. The Mull, the most southerly part of Scotland, is an area of very strong tides and is not recommended as a fishing area to anglers with small boats incapable of at least 10 knots, especially during ebb tides.
Types of fish: Pollack, wrasse from rocky shores, flatfish, bass, mullet, porbeagle shark and rays from sandy beaches. Pollack, coalfish, cod, whiting, wrasse, lesser, spotted dogfish, bullhuss, spurdog, tope, rays, conger from boats.
Boats: S. Woods, Clachanmore House, Ardwell, Drummore, Tel: 0776 89 297. S. Ilett, Bryces Corner, Drummore. Tel: 0776 89 337.
Bait: All types available on shore at low tide. Mackerel from Mull of Galloway shore marks.

Port Logan
An area with many good shore marks both to the north and south of the village. It is one of the few relatively easy launching sites on this coastline south of Portpatrick. A good alternative for the angler with his own boat when easterly winds prevent fishing in Luce Bay.
Types of fish: as for the southern part of Luce Bay with occasional haddock. Herring in June and July.

Portpatrick
There is good shore fishing from the many rocky points north and south of the resort, the best known being the Yellow Isle, ½ mile north of the harbour. Sandeel Bay, a little further north, and Killintringan Lighthouse are also worth fishing.
Types of fish: Pollack, coalfish, plaice, flounder, codling, mackerel, dogfish, conger, wrasse, and tope occasionally.
Boats: B. Watson, 1 Blair Terrace, Portpatrick. Tel: 0776 81 468, P. & M. Green, Hawthorn View, Lochans, Portpatrick. Tel: 0776 81 534, M. Wood, The

Knowe, 1 North Crescent, Portpatrick. Tel: 0776 81 441, B. Graham, 10 Merrick Crescent, Portpatrick, Tel: 0776 81 405. F3Tackle: Available from the Sports Shop, Stranraer.
Bait: None sold locally. Lugworm and some ragworm can be dug east of the railway pier, Stranraer.
Season for fishing: May-December.
Further information from: Mr D. McDiarmid, 90 George Street, Stranraer (no letters). Mr R. Smith, 24 Millbank Road, Stranraer. Tel: Stranraer (0776) 3691.

Stranraer & Loch Ryan
Stranraer, at the head of Loch Ryan, offers the angler, as a rail and bus terminal, a good stepping off point for many sea angling marks and areas in this part of Scotland, with Sandhead on Luce Bay (8 miles) to the south, Portpatrick (8 miles) to the west and Lady Bay (8 miles) on the west side of Loch Ryan with Cairnryan (6 miles) and Finnart Bay (10 miles) on the opposite side of the loch. Best Shore marks being Cairnryan Village, South of Townsend Thoreson ferry terminal. Old House Point and Conrete Barges north of Cairnryan Village, Finnart Bay on East Mouth of Loch, Wig Bay, Jamiesons Point and Lady Bay on west side of Loch Ryan. Boats may be launched at Wig Bay Slipway, Lady Bay and at Stranraer Market Street.
Types of fish: Cod, pollack, mackerel, whiting, flatfish, (Gurnard, conger, dogfish and occasional tope.
Boats: A.R. Miller, 5 Clifton Terrace, Stranraer. Tel: 0776 3325, C.C.M. Stewart, Craigencallie, London Road, Stranraer, Tel: 0776 2541, D. Scott, 52 Fisher Street, Stranraer, Tel: 0776 5968 or H. McDonald 0776 2207.
Tackle: The Sports Shop, George Street, Stranraer.
Bait: Excellent lugworms can be dug at low tide from the sands exposed to the east side of the railway pier at low tide.
Further information from: Mr D. McDiarmid, 90 George Street, Stranraer (no letters). Stranraer (0776) 2705. Mr. R. Smith, 24 Millbank Road, Stranraer, Tel: Stranraer (0776) 3691.

STRATHCLYDE (SOUTH)

CLYDE AND AYRSHIRE RIVERS AND LOCHS

Constituent Area Tourist Boards

Ayrshire and Burns Country Tourist Board
Tourist Officer
Ayrshire and Burns Country Tourist Board
39 Sandgate, Ayr KA7 1BG
Tel: Ayr (0292) 283196.

Ayrshire Valleys Tourist Board
Tourist Officer
Ayrshire Valleys Tourist Board
PO Box 13
Civic Centre, Kilmarnock,
Ayrshire KA1 1BY
Tel: Kilmarnock (0563) 21140

Clyde Valley Tourist Board
Tourism Officer
South Vennel,
Lanark ML11 7JT
Tel: Lanark (0555) 2544

Cunninghame District Council
Director
Deparment of Leisure and Recreation
Cunninghame District Council
Cunninghame House,
Irvine, Ayrshire, KA12 8EE
Tel: Irvine (0294) 74166

Isle of Arran Tourist Board
Area Tourist Officer
Isle of Arran Tourist Board
Information Centre, The Pier,
Brodick, Isle of Arran KA27 8AU
Tel: Brodick (0770) 2140/2401

Greater Glasgow Tourist Board
Chief Executive
Greater Glasgow Tourist Board
City Chambers, George Square
Glasgow G2 1DU
Tel: 041-221 5238

Other Tourist Organisations

CUMBERNAULD AND KILSTH
INVERCLYDE
MONKLANDS
EAST KILBRIDE
EASTWOOD

RIVER PURIFICATION BOARD
CLYDE RIVER PURIFICATION BOARD
River House, Murray Road East Kilbride
Tel: East Kilbride 38181

RIVERS

Water	Location	Species	Season	Permit available from	Other information
Annick (and Irvine)	Irvine	Salmon Sea trout Brown trout	15 Mar to 30 Oct 15 Mar to 6 Oct	Irvine and District Angling Club, Secretary, A. Sim, 51 Rubie Crescent, Irvine. Currie Sports, 32 High Street, Irvine. Tel: Irvine 78603	
Annick	Irvine	Salmon Sea trout Brown trout	15 Mar to 31 Oct 15 mar to 6 Oct	Dreghorn Angling Club, Dr. D.D. Muir 6 Pladda Avenue, Broomlands Irvine Ayrshire. Alexanderes, Fishmongers, 10 Bank St. Irvine (Tue-Sat)	
Annick (and Glazert)	Kilmaurs	Brown trout	15 Mar to 6 Oct	Kilmaurs Angling Club, J. Watson, 7 Four Acres Drive, Kilmaurs	
Avon	Strathaven	Brown trout Grayling	15 Mar to 6 Oct	Avon Angling Club, Local tackle shops, J.C. Tait, Stonehouse. R. & K. Sports, Strathaven DIY Shop, Strathaven.	
Ayr	Ayr	Salmon Sea trout Brown trout	11 Feb to 31 Oct 15 Mar to 6 Oct	Director of Finance, Kyle & Carrick District Council, Town Buildings, Ayr James Kirk, Union Arcade, Burns Statue Square, Ayr Gamesport, 60 Sandgate, Ayr.	
Ayr (Cessnock Lugar)	Mauchline	Salmon Sea trout Brown trout	11 Feb to 31 Oct 15 May-6 Oct	Mauchline Ballochmyle Angling Club, J.F. McCall, Post Office, High Street, Mauchline.	

Water	Location	Species	Season	Permit available from	Other information
Ayr (Lugar)	Auchinleck	Salmon Sea trout Brown trout	15 Mar to 30 Oct 15 Mar to 15 Sept	Auchinleck Angling Association. J. McColm, 21 Milne Avenue, Auchinleck.	
Cessnock	Mauchline	Brown trout	15 Mar to 6 Oct	Mauchline Ballochmyle Angling Club Linwood and Johnston, The Cross, Mauchline Post Office, Main Street, Ochiltree	
Clyde (and Douglas)	Motherwell and Lanark Carstairs Roberton & Crawford	Brown trout Grayling	15 Mar to 30 Sept All year	United Clyde Angling Protective Association, Secretary, Joseph Quigley, 39 Hillfoot Avenue, Wishaw. Permits widely available in tackle shops in Glasgow and Lanarkshire.	
Clyde	Lanark	Brown trout Grayling	15 Mar to 6 Oct	Lanark and District Angling Club William Frood 82 Rhyber Avenue (SAE Please)	
	Thankerton & Roberton	Brown trout Grayling	15 Mar to 6 Oct All year	Lamington and District Angling Association Secretary, B.F. Dexter 18 Boghall Park, Biggar. Bryden, Newsagent, Biggar or Bailiffs.	No Sunday fishing.
Doon	Patna	Salmon Sea trout Brown trout	15 May to 31 Oct 15 Mar to 6 Oct	Drumgrange and Keir's Angling Club, Mr. MacDonald, Palace Bar Waterside Stores, Dunaskin, Ayrshire. Tel: Patna 204.	No Sunday fishing.
Douglas (and Clyde)	Douglas Water	Brown trout Grayling	15 Mar to 30 Sept	United Clyde Angling Protective Association. Secretary, Joseph Quigley, 39 Hillfoot Avenue, Wishaw. Permits widely available in tackle shops in Glasgow and Lanarkshire.	
Fenwick (and local waters)	Kilmarnock	Brown trout	15 Mar to 6 Oct	Kilmarnock Angling Club, Messrs McCuricks, 39 John Finnie Street, Kilmarnock.	
Forth and Clyde Canal	Whole canal (excluding Club stretches)	Pike Perch Roach Tench Carp	No close Season	British Waterways Board, Canal House, Applecross St. Glasgow. Tel: 041-332 6936.	
	Wyndford	Pike Perch Roach Ternch Carp	No close Season	Central Match Anglers C. Palmer, 64 Dawson Place, Bo'ness. Tel: Bo'ness 823953.	
Garrell Burn	Kilsyth	Brown trout	15 Mar to 6 Oct	Kilsyth Fish Protection Association P. Brown, Colzium Sales and Service Station, Stirling Road, Kilsyth. Coachman Hotel, Kilsyth	
Garnock	Kilbirnie	Brown trout	15 Mar to 6 Oct	Kilbirnie Angling Club, I. Johnstone, 95 Dalry Road, Kilbirnie	

Water	Location	Species	Season	Permit available from	Other information
Garnock	Dalry	Brown trout	15 Mar to 6 Oct	Dalry Garnock Angling Club David Morton, Newsagent, Main Street, Dalry.	
Garnock (and Lugton)	Kilwinning	Salmon Sea trout Brown trout	26 Feb to 31 Oct 15 Mar to 6 Oct	Kilwinning Eginton Angling Club. M. Tudhope, 15 Viaduct Circle, Kilwinning. L. McCrorie, 60 Main Street, Kilwinning	
Girvan	Girvan	Salmon Sea trout Brown trout	25 Feb to 31 Oct	Carrick Angling Club, T.L. Wilson, 1 Church Square, Girvan.	
Glenrosa (and other waters)	Arran	Sea trout Brown trout		Arran Angling Club, A.J. Andrews, Park House, Corriecravie, Arran, Shops, Post Offices on island.	
Gryfe	Bridge of Weir	Brown trout	15 mar to 6 Oct	Bridge of Weir Angling Club, J. Milne, 8 Beach Avenue, Bridge of Weir.	
Gryfe	Kilmacolm	Brown trout	15 Mar to 6 Oct	Strathgryfe Angling Association, Mr. K. Wood 6 Beauly Crescent, Kilmacolm, and Cross Cafe, Kilmacolm.	
Irvine (and Annick)	Irvine	Salmon Sea trout Brown trout	15 Mar to 6 Oct 15 Mar to 6 Oct	Irvine and District Angling Club, Secretary. A Sim, 51 Rubie Crescent, Irvine Currie Sports, 32 High Street, Irvine.	
Irvine (and Annick)	Dreghorn	Salmon Sea trout Brown trout	15 Mar to 31 Oct 15 Mar to 6 Oct	Dreghorn Angling Club Dr. D.D. Muir 6 Pladda Avenue Broomlands Irvine Alexander's Fishmongers, 10 Bank Street, Irvine (Tue-Sat)	
Machrie	Arran	Salmon Sea trout	1 Jun to 15 Oct	Strathtay Estate Office, Strathtay Aberfeldy, Perthshire Tel: (0887) 20496	No Sunday fishing. Booking: Jan-Feb.
Stinchar	Colmonell	Salmon Sea trout	25 Feb to 31 Oct	Boars Head Hotel Colmonell Tel: (046588) 272 Queens Hotel, Colmoneli	

LOCHS AND RESERVOIRS

Water	Location	Species	Season	Permit available from	Other information
Banton Loch	Kilsyth	Brown trout	15 Mar to 6 Oct	Kilsyth Fish Protection Association, P. Brown, Colzium Sales and Services Station, Stirling Rd, Kilsyth Boats from: Coachman Hotel. Kilsyth	Boat session: 9am-5pm 6pm-midnight
Loch Bradan	Straiton	Brown trout (stocked)	15 Mar to 6 Oct	Forestry Commission, Straiton. Tel: (065 57) 637 Mr. R. Heany, Talaminnoch, Straiton. Tel: (065 57) 617.	Five boats.
Loch Breckbowie	Straiton	Brown trout	15 Mar to 6 Oct	Forestry Commission, Straiton Tel: (065 57) 637 Mr. R. Heaney, Talaminnoch, Straiton. Tel: (065 57) 617	One boat.

Water	Location	Species	Season	Permit available from	Other information
Castle Semple Loch	Lochwinnoch	Pike Perch Roach Eels	No close Season	St. Winnochs Angling Club 19 Glenpark Rd, Lochwinnoch, Chemists Shop, Lochwinnoch, Ranger Centre at the Loch.	Day permits for bank fishing. North shore only.
Daer Reservoir	Crawford	Brown trout	Easter to 6 Oct	Kilbryde Angling Club, John Mills, Mills McGraw & Co 1 Orchard Street, Motherwell Tel: (0698) 68511 D.T. Cormie, 6 Macadam Place, East Kilbride	Four boats. Fly fishing only.
Loch Doon	Dalmellington	Brown trout Char	15 Mar to 6 Oct	No permit required.	Bank fishing only. Sunday fishing.
Hillend Reservoir	Caldercruix	Brown trout Rainbow trout	15 Mar to 6 Oct	Airdrie Angling Club, Roy Burgess, 21 Elswick Dr. Caldercruix, Lanarkshire. Tel: (0236) 842050	All legal methods. Bag limit-6 trout. Bank fishing only. No ground bait. Sunday fishing.
Kilbirnie Loch	Kilbirnie	Brown trout	15 Mar to 6 Oct	Kilbirnie Angling Club I. Johnston, 95 Dalry Road Kilbirnie	
Lanark Loch	Lanark	Carp	No close Season	Clydesdale District Council, Lanark Moor Country Park.	
Loch Lure	Straiton	Brown trout	15 Mar to 6 Oct	Forestry Commission, Straiton. Tel: (065 57) 637 Mr. R. Heaney, Talaminnoch, Straiton. Tel: (065 57) 617	
Strathclyde Country Park Loch (and adjacent River Clyde)	Motherwell	Carp Bream Roach Pike Perch Dace Grayling Trout	17 Jan to 13 Mar

15 Mar to 29 Sept | Booking Office, Strathclyde Country Park, 366 Hamilton Road, Motherwell Tel: Motherwell 66155 | Regulations on permit. No fly fishing. |
| **Loch Thom and compensations 6,7, & 8** | Greenock | Brown trout | 15 Mar to 6 Oct | Greenock and District Angling Club Secretary, J. McMurthie, 45 Whinhill Court Greenock. Tel: (0475) 27551. Finlay & Co. 36 West Stewart Stret, Greenock. Ranger Centre, Cornalees | Fly fishing only. Bank fishing only. |

STRATHCLYDE SOUTH
Sea Angling

Loch Ryan to Ardrossan
The angling potential of much of the coast between Loch Ryan and Girvan remains unknown, the many rocky shores, small headlands and sandy beaches probably only attracting the anglers in an exploratory mood, or those seeking solitude in pursuit of their hobby.

Girvan
Girvan has a sheltered port and is a family holiday resort. From the end of the pier good fishing can be had for fair-sized plaice and flounders. Night fishing is good for rock cod. Just one mile to the south of the town and close to the Haven Hotel lies the noted 'Horse Rock', only about 50 yards from the main Stranraer road. Access to the rock may be gained from about half-tide. Except during very high tides and during storms it is a good shore mark providing access to water of about 20 feet on the sea-side even at low tide.

Types of fish: Haddock, plaice, hake, codling, rays, flounder, whiting, and gurnard (mostly from boat).

Tackle: Available from J.H. Murray, 3 Dalrymple Street, Girvan. Also from Johnsons (Ironmonger), and T. Gibson, 55 Dalrymple Street.

Boats: 'Leonora V' – T. Harrison. 'Carole Denise' – B. Nunn (can be booked at harbour). 'Dainty Lady' – A. Ingram. 'Morning Tide' – W. Coul. 'Ailsa Lady' –D. Robinson. MV 'Adelaide', 'Chimes' – K. Burns, 'Ealoner K' – S. McHendry. Maidens Marine and Leisure Centre, 27 Ardlochan Road, Maidens, by Girvan. Girvan Harbour, T. Harrison, 19 Penkill Road, Girvan. Tel: Girvan (0465) 2631. A. Ingram, 5 Shalloch Square, Girvan. Tel: Girvan (0465) 2320.

Ayr
Ayr is a popular holiday town on the estuaries of the Rivers Ayr

and Doon, 32 miles south-west of Glasgow. Good shore fishing can be had on the Newton Shore, north of the harbour, from the harbour jetty and from the rocky coastline at the Heads of Ayr. Boat fishing in the bay can be very productive with good catches of cod, haddock, thornbacks, spurdogs and flatfish. Tope have also been taken from around the Lady Isle.

Types of fish: Flounder, dab, cod, dogfish and conger from the shore. Spurdog, cod, pollack, whiting, dogfish, thornback, ray and conger from boats.

Boats: Available from Mrs M. Johnston, 59 Woodlands Crescent, Ayr. Tel: Ayr 81638. T. Medina, 44 Fort Street, Ayr. Tel: Ayr 85297.

Tackle: Available from James Kirk Ltd., 25 Kyle Street, Ayr. Games Sport, 60 Sandgate, Ayr.

Bait: Lugworm and ragworm from Ayr and Newton shore. Mrs M. Johnston, 59 Woodlands Crescent, Ayr. Tel: Ayr 81638, can supply herring, mussels and mackerel.

Prestwick
Prestwick is a pleasant seaside holiday town on the coast between Troon and Ayr. Shore fishing is best after dark. Temporary membership of Prestwick SAC can be obtained.

Types of fish: Shore – cod, flounder, plaice, dab, coalfish, dogfish and mullet. Boat – as above plus tope and rays, thornbacks and mackerel, except mullet.

Boats: 14ft skippered boat available from Prestwick Sea Angling Club and boats can also be chartered from Troon and Ayr. J. Wilson, 27 Wallace Avenue, Barassie, Troon, Ayrshire.

Tackle: T.G. Morrison, 117 Main Street, Prestwick, Ayrshire.

Bait: Lugworm and ragworm can be dug on Prestwick shore.

Season for fishing: Shore – October-March. Boat – all year.

Further information from: Mrs Templeton, Prestwick Sea Angling Club, 'Trebor', 15 Teviot Street, Ayr. Tel: Ayr 68072.

Troon
Troon is a popular holiday town between Ayr and Irvine with good public transport for coastal

fishing points. There is good pier fishing from the harbour. Cod and flatfish can be taken at low tide from Barassie shore. Local skippers have many good marks out on the bay, with a small wreck off the Lady Isle.

Type of fish: Shore – cod, plaice, flounder, coalfish, rays, dogfish, conger, whiting, pollack. Boat – as above plus thornback, and gurnard.

Boats: There are numerous boats available. 'Dusky Maid' – Mr J. Wilson, 27 Wallace Avenue, Barassie, Troon, Ayrshire. Tel: Troon 313161. M. V. Talisman. Tel: Prestwick 76543.

Tackle: P. & R. Torbet, 27 Portland Street, Kilmarnock. McCririck & Sons, 38 John Finnie Street, Kilmarnock, Ayrshire.

Bait: Lugworm, ragworm and mussels from shore only. Lugworm from the Barassie shore at low tide.

Season for fishing: All year.

Further information from: Glacier Angling Club, Mr N. Lindsay, 5 Ayr Road, Kilmarnock, Ayrshire.

Irvine
Irvine on the Ayrshire coast, is a rapidly developing New Town on the River Irvine. The sea is relatively shallow, with long sandy beaches. It is a good boat fishing area. Irvine was previously a very busy port, but now the river anchorage is used by a greater number of small craft. The estuary has, in the past two years come up trumps for flatfish, dabs, flounders and plaice. South of Irvine Estuary is a small island called 'The Lady Isle'. In the past year the pollack have increased not only in number but also in size. Just off this Isle pollack can be taken with ragworm on a long flowing trace. Pollack to 10 lbs., are not an unusual sight at some club matches. For cod, close inshore is best and small coloured beads are preferred to spoon and lures. The best bait by far is a cocktail of lugworm and cockle or ragworm and cockle, all of which can be obtained locally.

Types of fish: Flounder and cod from the shore. Cod, flounder, plaice, conger, haddock, ling, whiting, and coalfish.

Boats: Irvine Water Sports Club, 126 Montgomery Street, Irvine, J. Wilson. Tel: Troon (0292)

313161. J. Wass, 22 Templeland Road, Dalry. Tel: Dalry (029-483) 3724.

Tackle: Irvine Water Sports Club; Sports Shop, High Street, Irvine; Gilmour Sports, Bridgegate, Irvine; J.W. Fishing Shop, Seagate, Irvine.

Bait: Lugworm can be dug from foreshore at low tide and mussels under wharves.

Season for fishing: All year.

Further information from: Irvine SAC, Hon. Sec., W.R. Findlay, 40 Frew Terrace, Irvine. Tel: Irvine 79582.

Saltcoats & Ardrossan
Saltcoats with the neighbouring towns of Stevenston and Ardrossan, is situated on the Ayrshire coast 30 miles south-west of Glasgow. Shore fishing is possible in the South Bay and around the harbours. Approximately 3 miles north is Ardneil Bay which is prolific cod ground.

Types of fish: Cod, rays, flounder, coalfish, dogfish, conger, whiting and pollack from shore, plus haddock, dab, gurnard and thornback from boats.

Boats: Available from G. Dickie, 27 Braes Road, Saltcoats, Tel: 0294 61867. Mr A.S. Wass, 22 Templeland Road, Dalry, Ayrshire. Tel: Dalry (029-483) 3724. There are no professional hirers at Ardrossan but private owners are willing to help.

Tackle: Available from Woolworth, Dockhead Street, Saltcoats and Leisure Time, 42 Hamilton Street, Saltcoats. Also from Sports Centre, Chapelwell Street, Saltcoats, Ayrshire.

Bait: Limited supplies of ragworm, lugworm, sandgapers and crab are available at the tanker berth, while lugworm can be found on the north and south shores. N. Gibson can supply fresh or preserved bait.

Season for fishing: All year round from shore. March-October from boats.

Further information from: Mr. W.L. Currie, 6 McNay Crescent, Saltcoats. (Ardrossan) Bud McClymont, Hon. Sec. Ardrossan and District SAC, 1 Hill Street, Ardrossan.

Largs
Largs is within easy reach of several good fishing banks,

including the Piat Shoal, the Skelmorlie Patch and the east shore of Cumbrae.

Types of fish: Dogfish, flounders, gurnard, grey sole, haddock, hake, pollack, mackerel, plaice.

Boats: Are readily available from local hirers. Joe Smith (0475) 674496; P. Hamilton (0475) 675587; McIntyre Brothers (0475) 530566.

Tackle: Clyde Sports, 128 Main Street, Largs.

Bait: Mussels are available from Fairlie Flats.

Gourock

The coastline from Largs to Greenock is probably the most popular area in Scotland for shore angling, with many anglers from the Midlands of England and beyond making regular trips north. At Wemyss Bay, angling is not permitted from the pier, but good catches can be had to the south, and the Red Rocks, about a mile to the north, are noted for codling and other species. At Inverkip there is a sandy beach around the entrance to the marina where large flounders and other flatfish can be taken. Cloch Point, where the Firth turns east, is well known for its fishing potential, although the current can be fierce, and because of the rough bottom, relatively heavy lines are necessary. The coastline along Cloch along Gourock Promenade to the swimming pool car park provides good fishing and is easily accessible. Further inland, at Greenock Esplanade, codling and flatfish are among the species available, although the water here is shallower, and this area is more productive at night. This stretch of coastline provides the dinghy angler with easy access to many of the Clyde marks, including the Gantocks, where outsize cod and coalfish have been taken, mainly on pirks. The bay beside the power station holds large flatfish and the ground off Greenock Esplanade is popular for codling. Dinghy owners should note that no anchoring is permitted in the main navigation channels, and several other regulations must also be adhered to. Full details are given in 'The Small Boat Owner's Guide to Clydeport' which may be obtained, free of charge, from: Clyde Port Authority, Greenock.

Types of fish: Codling, whiting, pouting, conger, flatfish, mackerel and rays from boat and shore.

Tackle: Seasports, 61 Shore Street, Gourock; K.A. Binnie, 29 Kempock Street, Gourock.

Bait: Lug, rag, mussels, cockles and crabs are easily obtainable from the shoreline.

Boats: J. Crowther, Inverclyde Boat Owners Association, 164 Burns Road, Greenock. Tel: (0475) 34341 can advise.

Isle of Arran

The island of Arran, lying in the outer Firth of Clyde, may be reached from the mainland by ferries running from Ardrossan to Brodick, the largest community on the island. Good shore fishing is found around the whole of the island, much of which remains unexplored.

Lamlash

Lamlash is the main centre for sea angling on the island, probably because of its situation on the shores of Lamlash Bay, the large horse-shoe shaped bay which is almost landlocked by the Holy Isle. This gives excellent protection to the bay from easterly winds. Lamlash is also the starting point for boat trips to the excellent fishing grounds off Whiting Bay and those around Pladda to the south.

Types of fish: Cod, haddock, whiting, coalfish, pollack, conger, rays, flatfish, mackerel, dogfish.

Boats: Dinghies are available from the Arran Sea Angling Centre, Brodick (Tel: Brodick (0770) 2192); N.C. McLean, Torlin Villa, Kilmory (Tel: Sliddery (077 087) 240); Johnston Bros, Old Pier Shop, Lamlash (Tel: Lamlash (07706) 333). Mr Ambler, Kilmory Post Office, (Tel: Sliddery (077 087) 237.

Tackle: Available from Johnstone Bros, Pierhead Shop, Lamlash.

Bait: Obtainable from many beaches. May also be purchased from N.C. McLean.

Season for fishing: March-November.

Further information from: Mr N.C. McLean, Torlin Villa, Kilmory, Tel: Sliddery (077 087) 240.

Corrie

Corrie is situated on north east coast of the island.

Types of fish: Cod, haddock, conger, skate, dogfish, tope, turbot, ling, pollack, gurnard and garfish.

Whiting Bay

This bay, which takes its name from the whiting, is very open to the sea. There are excellent fishing banks from Largiebeg Point to King's Cross Point.

Boats: Dinghies can be hired from the Stanford Guest House and at the Jetty, Whiting Bay, Tel: Whiting Bay (07707) 313.

Bait: Cockles, mussels, lugworm, ragworm, limpets and crabs are abundant on the banks from half-tide.

Lochranza

Lochranza is situated at the northern end of the island. The loch is surrounded by hills opening out on to Kilbrennan Sound.

Types of fish: Cod, conger, and haddock from the shore. Cod, conger, haddock from boats.

Tackle: Available from boat hirers.

Bait: Mussels, cockles, lugworm and ragworm obtainable; scallops from Mr F. Murchie.

Brodick

Good fishing in Brodick Bay from Markland Point to Clauchlands Point.

Types of fish: Codling, plaice and other flatfish, conger, wrasse and pollack, can be had from the shore while cod, haddock, conger, skate, dogfish, tope, turbot, ling, pollack, gurnard, garfish and other round fish can be fished from boats.

Boats: Boats can be hired from Arran Sea Angling Centre, The Beach, Brodick. Tel: (0770) 2192. Bait, tackle and freezer facilities.

Bait: Mussels are obtainable from the rocks around Brodick Pier or may be purchased from boat hirers.

Isle of Cumbrae Millport

There is good fishing at a bank between the South East Point of Millport Bay (Farland Point) and Keppel Pier. Fintry Bay and Piat Shoal provide good sport. West of Portachur Point in about 15/20 fathoms and in Dunagoil Bay, S.W. Bute are good. Fairlie Channel directly seaward of Kelburn Castle is about 12/15 fathoms. East shore northwards about 10 fathoms line.

Types of fish: Saithe, conger, coalfish, haddock, dogfish and mackerel.
Boats: Mr W.S. McIntyre, Tel: Millport (0475) 530566. Mr Wright, Tel: Millport (0475) 530692. Mr A. Roberts, Tel: Millport (0475) 530465 or 530723.

Tackle: Available locally from boat hirers.

Bait: Mussels, worms, etc. on shore. Boat hirers and local shops provide bait.

STRATHCLYDE (NORTH)

ARGYLL AND BUTE RIVERS AND LOCHS

Constituent Area Tourist Boards

Dunoon and Cowal Tourist Board
Area Tourist Officer
Dunoon and Cowal Tourist Board,
Information Centre
Pier Esplanade
Dunoon, Argyll, PA23 7HL
Tel: Dunoon (0369) 3755

Oban, Mull and District Tourist Board
Area Tourist Officer
Oban, Mull and District Tourist Board
Boswell House, Argyll Square.
Oban, Argyll PA34 4AN
Tel: Oban (0631) 63122/63551

Mid Argyll, Kintyre and Islay Tourist Board
Area Tourist Officer
Mid Argyll, Kintyre and Islay Tourist Board
The Pier, Campbeltown
Argyll PA28 6EF
Tel: Campbeltown (0586) 52056

Rothesay and Isle of Bute Tourist Board
Area Tourist Officer
Rothesay and Isle of Bute Tourist Board
the Pier
Rothesay, Isle of Bute PA20 2AQ
Tel: Rothesay (0700) 2151

RIVER PURIFICATION BOARD
CLYDE RIVER PURIFICATION BOARD
Rivers House,
Murray Road,
East Kilbride
Tel: East Kilbride 38181

RIVERS

Water	Location	Species	Season	Permit available from	Other information
Add	Kilmartin	Salmon Sea trout	14 Feb to 31 Oct	Poltalloch Estate Office, Kilmartin.	
Aray	Inverary	Salmon Sea trout Brown trout	May to mid-Oct	Argyll Estates Office, Cherry Park, Inverary. Tel: Inverary 2203.	No Sunday fishing. Fly fishing only.
Awe	Taynuilt	Salmon Sea trout	Jun to Sept	Inverawe/Taynuilt Fisheries. Argyll. Tel: (08662) 262.	Rod hire Casting tuition.
Bellart	Mull	Salmon Sea trout		Tackle and Books, Main Street. Tobermory, Isle of Mull Tel: (0688) 2336.	
Coil	Ardgarton	Salmon Sea trout		Forestry Commision, Ardgartan Arrochar. Tel: Ardgartan 243	
Crinan Canal	Lochgilphead	Trout		Lochgilphead and District Angling Club.	No permit required.
Douglas	Inverary	Salmon Sea trout	May to mid-oct	Battlefield Caravan Park, Inverary, Argyll. Tel: (0499) 2285.	No Sunday fishing. Fly fishing only.
Euchar	Kilninver	Salmon Sea trout Brown trout	1 Jun to 15 Oct	Mrs. Mary McCorkindale, 'Glenann' Kilninver by Oban, Argyll.	No Sunday fishing.
	Kilninver	Salmon Sea trout	Mid Jul to Mid Oct	J.T.P. Mellor, Barncromin Farm, Knipoch by Oban, Argyll Tel: Kilninver 273.	3 days per week.
	Kilninver (Lagganmore)	Salmon Sea trout Brown trout	Jun to 14 Oct	Lt. Col. P.S. Sandilands, Lagganmore, Kilninver by Oban. Tel: Kilninver 200.	Not more than 3 rods per day. Fly fishing only. No Sunday fishing.

Water	Location	Species	Season	Permit available from	Other Information
Finnart	Ardentinny	Salmon Sea trout	11 Feb to 31 Oct	Forestry Commission, Cowal District Office Kilmun, Dunoon. Tel: (036 984) 422	
Forsa	Mull	Salmon Sea trout	mid-Jun to mid-Oct	Tackle and Books, Main Street, Tobermory Tel: (0688) 2336.	
	Mull	Salmon Sea trout	Early July to mid-Oct	Glenforsa Hotel by Salen, Tel: (06803) 377	No Sunday fishing.
Liever	Ford	Salmon		Forestry Commission, Mrs. Cameron Ford Post Office, Ford	
Machrie	Islay	Salmon Sea trout	25 Feb to 31 Oct	Machrie Hotel, Post Ellen, Islay	
Orchy	Dalmally	Salmon	11 Feb to 18 Oct	W.A. Church, Croggan Crafts, Dalmally, Argyll. Tel: Dalmally 201.	
Ruel	Glendaruel	Salmon Sea trout		Glendaruel Hotel, Glendaruel.	
Shira	Inverary	Salmon Sea trout	May to mid-Oct	Argyll Estates office, Cherry Park, Inverary, Argyll. Tel: Inverary 2203	Fly fishing only. No Sunday fishing.

LOCHS AND RESERVOIRS

Water	Location	Species	Season	Permit available from	Other Information
Loch Ascog	Tighnabruaich	Brown trout Rainbow trout	15 Mar to 5 oct	Kyles of Bute Angling Club R. Newton, Viewfield Cottage, Tighnabruaich. from several shops in Kames and Tighnabruaich.	Fly only.
Loch Ascog	Isle of Bute	Pike Perch Roach		Bute Estate Office Rothesay, Tel: Rothesay 2627	
Loch Assopol	Mull	Salmon Sea trout	Apr to beg. Oct	Argyll Arms Hotel, Bunessan, Isle of Mull Tel: Fionnphort 240.	Fly and Spinner only. No Sunday fishing.
Loch Avich	Taynuilt	Brown trout	15 Mar to 6 Oct	S. Davren, 40 Dalavich, by Taynuilt, Argyll Tel: Lochavich 216.	
Loch Awe	Taynuilt	Salmon Sea trout Brown trout Rainbow trout	12 Feb to 15 Oct 15 Mar to 6 Oct	S. Davren, 40 Dalavich, by Taynuilt, Argyll Tel: Lochavich 216.	
	Taynuilt	Sea trout Brown trout	12 Feb-15 Oct 15 Mar-6 Oct	Forestry Commission Manageress, Lochaweside Cabins, Dalauich Tel: Lochavich 211.	
	Ford	Brown trout	15 Mar-6 Oct	Ford Hotel, Ford, Argyll Tel: (054 681) 273	
	Dalmally	Salmon Brown trout	15 Mar-15 Oct 15 Mar-6 Oct	Portsonachan Hotel by Dalmally, Argyll. Tel: Kilchrenan 224.	
	Dalmally	Salmon Brown trout Rainbow trout	15 Mar to 6 Oct	Carraig Thurra Hotel, Lochawe Village, by Dalmally Tel: Dalmally 210.	
	Dalmally	Brown trout Rainbow trout Pike	15 Mar to 6 Oct All year	Ardbrecknish House, by Dalmally Argyll. Tel: 08663 223	Self Catering flats Rods, Tackle & Ghillie available.
	Dalmally	Salmon Brown trout Rainbow trout	15 Mar to 6 Oct	Dalmally Hotel, Dalmally	

Please mention this Pastime Publications guide.

Water	Location	Species	Season	Permit available from	Other Information
	Kilchrennan	Salmon Brown trout Rainbow trout		Taychreggan Hotel Kilchrennan	
Barnluasgan Loch	Lochgilphead	Brown trout	15 Mar to 6 Oct	Forest District Office Whitegates, Lochgilphead Tel: Lochgilphead 2518. Mrs. Robertson, Barnluasgan Lochgilphead.	
Coll Estate Lochs	Coll	Brown trout	1 Apr to 30 Sept	Factor, Coll Estate House, Aringour, Isle of Coll. Tel: Coll 367.	
Coille Bhar	Lochgilphead	Brown trout	1 Apr to 6 Oct	Forest District Office Whitegates, Lochgilphead, Tel: Lochgilphead 2518 Mrs. Robertson, Barnlusgan Lochgilphead.	Four boats.
Dubh Loch	Inverary	Salmon Sea trout Brown trout	15 Apr to 6 Oct	Argyll Estates Office, Cherry Park, Inverary, Tel: Inverary 2203.	
	Kilninver	Loch Leven trout Brown trout	Apr to mid-Oct	J.T.P. Mellor, Barndromin Farm, Knipoch, by Oban Tel: Kilninver 273	
Loch Eck	Dunoon	Salmon Sea trout Brown trout Char Powan	16 Mar to 31 Oct	The Whistlefield Inn, Loch Eck, by Dunoon, Argyll. Tel: (036 986) 250.	
Loch Fad	Bute	Brown trout Rainbow trout	1 Apr-6 Oct 1 Apr-1 Nov	Baliff in attendance at the Loch. Tel: (0700) 4871.	Bank fishing and ten boats. Fly methods from boats. All legal methods from bank. Double sessions: 8am to 5pm. 5pm to 10pm.
Loch Finlaggan	Islay	Brown trout		Brian Wiles, Islay House, Bridgend Tel: Bowmore 293.	Two boats.
Loch Gleann A'Bhaerradch	Lerags by Oban	Brown trout	15 Mar to 6 Oct	Cologin Homes Ltd, Lerags, by Oban, Argyll Tel: Oban 64501. The Barn Bar, Cologin, Lerags.	One boat available
Glen Dubh Reservoir	Connel	Brown trout Rainbow trout	15 Mar to 6 Oct	J. Lyon, Appin View, Barcaldine.	Fly only
Loch Gorm	Islay	Brown trout	15 Mar to 6 Oct	Brian Wiles, Islay House, Bridgend. Tel: Bowmire 293.	Boat and Bank fishing.
Inverawe Fisheries	Taynuilt	Rainbow trout	Mar to Nov	Inverawe Fisheries, Taynuilt, Argyll. Tel: (08662) 262.	Three lochs. Stocked daily with rainbow trout from 1 to 16 pounds, Rod hire. Tackle shop. Casting tuition. Salmon & sea trout on River Awe.
Kilmelford Lochs	Kilmelford	Brown trout		Oban and Lorn Angling Club.	Numerous Lochs.
Lochgilphead Lochs	Lochgilphead	Brown trout	15 Mar to 6 Oct	Lochgilphead and District Angling Club, H. MacArthur, The Tackle Shop, Lochnell Street, Lochgilphead.	Numerous Lochs.
Loch Lussa	Campbeltown	Brown trout	15 May to 6 Oct	McCrory & Co, Main Street, Campbeltown.	
Mishnish & Aros Lochs	Mull	Brown trout	15 Mar to 30 Sept	Tobermory Angling Association Brown's Shop, Tobermory. Tel: (0688) 2020.	No Sunday fishing.

Water	Location	Species	Season	Permit available from	Other Information
Loch Nant	Kilchrenan	Brown trout	15 Mar to 8 Oct	Kilchrennan Trading Post, Kilchrennan.	
Loch Nell	Oban	Brown trout	15 Mar to 6 Oct	Oban and Lorn Angling Club.	
Powderworks Reservoir	Argyll	Brown trout Rainbow trout	15 Mar to 5 Oct	Kyles of Bute Angling Club. From several shops in Kames and Tighnabruisch.	Fly and bait only. No Spinning.
Lochquien	Bute	Brown trout	1 Apr to 6 Oct	Bute Estate Office, Rothesay, Isle of Bute Tel: Rothesay 2627.	Fly only. Salmon and trout fishing in sea around Bute.
Loch Scammadale	Kilninver	Salmon Sea trout Brown trout	1 Jun to 15 Oct 15 Mar to 6 Oct	Mrs. McCorkindale 'Glenann', Kilninver, by Oban, Argyll. Tel: Kilninver 282.	No Sunday fishing.
Loch Seil	Kilninver	Sea trout Brown trout	Apr to mid-Oct	J.T.P. Mellor, Barndromin Farm, Knipoch, by Oban, Argyll. Tel: Kilninver 273.	
Loch Squabain	Mull	Salmon Sea trout Brown trout		Tackle and Books, Main St, Tobermory, Mull. Tel: (0688) 2336.	Boat fishing only.
Loch Tarsan	Dunoon	Brown trout	1 Apr to 30 Sept	Dunoon and District Angling Club, Local tackle shops.	No Sunday fishing.
Tighnabruaich Reservoir	Tighnabruaich	Brown trout	15 Mar to 5 Oct	Kyles of Bute Angling Club, From several shops in Kames and Tighnabruaich, Mull, Argyll.	
Torr Loch	Mull	Sea trout Brown trout Rainbow trout		Tackle and Books, Main St, Tobermory, Mull, Argyll. Tel: (0688) 2336.	Fly only.
Loch Tulla	Tyndrum	Brown trout		Royal Hotel, Tyndrum.	

STRATHCLYDE NORTH
Sea Angling

Isle of Bute Rothesay
The holiday resort of Rothesay, situated on the island of Bute, only a 30 minute crossing by roll-on/ roll-off ferry from Wemyss Bay, is sheltered from the prevailing south- westerly winds. Several boat hirers cater for sea anglers. There are also many excellent shore marks. The deep water marks at Garroch Head can be productive for both shore and boat anglers.
Types of fish: Shore – cod, pollack, plaice, mackerel, wrasse. Boat – cod, pollack, plaice, mackerel, conger, spurdog, thornback, coalfish, wrasse and whiting.
Boats: Peter McIntyre (Clyde) Ltd., Port Bannatyne (0700) 3171. MacLeod Marines, Montague Steet, Rothesay Pier (0700) 3044. Keith Todd, Carleol,

Alma Terrace, 1 fishing cruiser and boarding house. Advance booking necessary. *'Girl Irene'.* 28ft twin diesel, Skipper E. Pellegrotti, The Harbour (0700) 3625.
Tackle: Available from Bute Tools, Montague Street, Rothesay; MacLeod Marines, Montague Street, Rothesay; Roberton's, East Princes Street, Rothesay.
Bait: Low water at Port Bannatyne for mussels. Lugworm and ragworm from Rothesay harbour. Herring is also useful bait. Mussel bait can be obtained on shore.
Season for fishing: May-October.

Kilchattan Bay
Sheltered bay waters at the south end of the Isle of Bute renowned for its good all year round fishing.
Types of fish: Cod, pollack, plaice, mackerel, conger, dogfish, wrasse, whiting.
Boats: Mr C. Kay, St. Blanes

Hotel, Kilchattan Bay, Isle of Bute (070 083) 224.
Tackle: Mr C. Kay, St. Blanes Hotel, Kilchattan Bay, Isle of Bute.
Bait: Worm, fresh cockle available locally.
Season for fishing: All year.

Mainland Ardentinny
Ardentinny is a small unspoiled village picturesquely situated on the west shore of Loch Long, 12 miles from Dunoon by car.
Types of fish: Cod, mackerel, from the shore. Cod, conger, haddock, ray, plaice, flounder, whiting, coalfish and mackerel from boats.
Bait: Cockles, mussels, lug and ragworm easily dug in bay.
Season for fishing: All year, winter for large cod.

Dunoon
Types of fish:
Most of the shoreline around Dunoon provides catches of cod, coalfish, pollack, flounder,

mackerel, plaice. Using ragworm & lugworm, cockle, mussel, razorfish & Peeler crab. Boat fishing takes mostly cod, pollack, coalfish, dogfish, dabs, plaice, flounder. Also conger over wrecks or rough ground at night.
Winter fishing: Also produces fair sized cod. Also haddock and whiting. So anglers can fish all year round from boat or shore.
Boats: Rowing boats can be hired from A. Waddel, Sandbank, by Dunoon. Phone: (0369) 6374. Also does fishing parties on motor boat (advanced booking). Gourock skippers also fish Dunoon waters. Approx. 3 miles from Dunoon is Holy Loch.
Tackle: Argyll Marine Sports, 60 Argyll Street, Dunoon; Purdies Fishing Tackle & Sports, 112 Argyll Street, Dunoon. Tel: Dunoon (0369) 3232.
Bait: Can be bought at these shops most of the year or obtained in East Bay shore.
Further information from: Mr. W. Wilson, Sec. D.S.A.C., 35 Spence Court, Queen Street, Dunoon, PA23 8EZ.

Tighnabruaich
Tighnabruaich, on the Kyles of Bute, is famed for its beauty and typical Highland scenery. Access is possible to some good fishing banks on the west side of the Bute and around Inchmarnock.
Types of fish: Mackerel and coalfish from the shore, plus cod, haddock, flatfish, whiting and dogfish from boats.
Bait: Mussels can be gathered on the piers and shore; cockles and lugworm from the shore.
Season for fishing: May-September.
Contact: Graham Fusco, Kames Hotel. Tel: (0700) 811489.

Loch Fyne
This is the longest sea-loch in Scotland, penetrating into the Highlands from the lower Firth of Clyde. The depth of the water within the loch varies enormously with depth of around 100 fathoms being found not only at the seaward end but also at the head of the loch of Inveraray. Much of the shore angling potential remains unknown although access to both shores is made relatively easy by roads running down each side. Boat launching facilities are less easy to

find because of the rugged shoreline. Best side is Inveraray to Furnace. Quarry is now out of bounds.
Types of fish: Mackerel, cod, pollack, flatfish, conger (at night).

Inveraray
Inveraray stands on the west side near the head of Loch Fyne.
Types of fish: Cod, mackerel, pollack, coalfish, ling, dogfish, conger eel, hake and plaice.
Boats: Contact D. McKay, Charters, Inveraray; Battlefield Caravan Park, Inveraray. Tel: (0499) 2284.
Tackle: Available from Ironmonger Store, Inveraray.
Bait: Mussels and worms available from shore at low tide.
Season for fishing: June-September.

Tarbert (Loch Fyne)
The sheltered harbour and the adjacent coast of the loch near the lower end of the loch on the west shore are good fishing grounds for the sea angler.
Types of fish: Cod, mackerel, coalfish, and sea trout from the shore. Mackerel, cod, coalfish, rays, haddock and whiting from boats.
Boats: Evening out with the boats of the herring fleet can be arranged. Boats available from Dugald Cameron, McCulloch Buildings, Lochgilphead, Argyll (Tel: Lochgilphead 2773).
Tackle: Available from Alex Mackay & Son, Ironmonger, Tarbert; and other local shops.
Bait: There is an abundance of shellfish and worms on the mud flats.
Season for fishing: June, July and August.
Further information from: Mr. A. MacKay, Barmore Road, Tarbert.

Oban
Good catches can be occasionally taken in Kerrera Sound near the Cutter Rock and the Ferry Rocks. Fishing is much better off the south and west coasts of Kerrera Island, particularly near the Bach Island and Shepherds Hat, Maiden Island and Oban Bay give good mackerel fishing in July and August. These places are very exposed and should only be

attempted in good settled weather.
Types of fish: Boat – mackerel, dogfish, rays, pollack and occasionally cod and haddock. Heavy catches (mainly dogfish) have been taken in the entry to Loch Feochan during the past two seasons.
Tackle: The Tackle Shop, 6 Airds Place, Oban; David Graham, 9 Combie Street, Oban.
Bait: Mussels and lugworm, etc. can be dug from the Kerrera beaches.
Season for fishing: May-November. Contact: J. Williams, Oban (0631) 63662.

Sea Life Centre
11 miles north of Oban on A828. Underwater observatory for seals and other fascinating sea creatures and fish. Ideal viewing conditions. Restaurant.

Isle of Islay
This is the southernmost of the islands. Several of the larger communities like Port Ellen and Port Askaig have good harbours. With the exception of a small area much remains unexplored.
Types of fish: Boat – cod, haddock, whiting, coalfish, pollack, mackerel, gurnard, dogfish, spurdog, plaice, flounder, tope, ling, conger, skate and rays.
Boats: A 20 ft. motor boat from Port Charlotte Hotel, organised fishing parties catered for.
Tackle: A limited amount available from D. McNab, Port Ellen; Mr. Hodkinson, Bowmore; Mini-market, Bruichladdich.
Bait: Lugworm plentiful on most beaches. Clam skirts from fish factory waste. No bait for sale.
Season for fishing: July, August and September.

Isle of Mull (Salen)
Salen is situated on the east coast of Mull facing the Sound of Mull in a central position, 11 miles from Craignure and 10 miles from Tobermory. The village is sited between Aros River and a headland forming Salen Bay. The Sound of Mull is on the main skate marks in the Argyll area. Over twenty 100 lbs., plus skate have now been taken. One of the contributing factors is the sheltered nature of the Sound,

which can allow practically uninterrupted angling. This area has also yielded a number of fine tope, the largest of which was a specimen of 50 lbs. It is worth noting that cod and haddock seldom frequent the sound and should not be expected. This is an area recommended for dinghy owners.

Types of fish: Coalfish, pollack, cod, wrasse, flounder, mullet sea trout, and mackerel from the shore. Ray, skate, ling, pollack, coalfish, cod, spurdog, tope, conger and gurnard from boats.
Tackle: Available from the Tackle and Books, Main Street, Tobermory, 10 miles away.
Bait: Easily obtainable from shoreline. Mackerel bait from Tackle and Books.
Season for fishing: March-November.
Further information from: Mr. Duncan Swinbanks, Tackle and Books, 10 Main Street, Tobermory. Tel: Tobermory 2336.

Isle of Mull (Tobermory)
The principal town on Mull, it is situated on a very sheltered bay at the north eastern tip of the island. Apart from hitting the headlines in the national press with its treasure, Tobermory has been extensively covered in the angling press. It is the undisputed centre for skate fishing in 1985 and 86 claims for both British and World

records were made. The largest fish captured was a giant of 227 lbs. Every year an average of 50 ton-up specimens are caught, tagged and returned alive. It is this thoughtful conservation that has maintained the quality of fishing in the area. Large tope of between 35 lbs., and 45 lbs., can be numerous. Nine Scottish records, red gurnard, grey gurnard, blonde ray, spotted ray, spurdogfish, angler fish, turbot and two wrasse, have come from these Mull waters. Every year dramatic catches of migratory fish can be made. Coalfish, whiting, haddock and cod may be encountered on a vast scale.

Types of fish: Tope, skate, rays, pollack, coalfish, ling, conger, gurnard, spurdog, cod, haddock, flatfish (plaice, dabs, and turbot) and whiting from boats. Coalfish, pollack, cod, wrasse, flounder, grey mullet, sea trout, conger, thornback and mackerel from the shore.

Boats: Mr. Brian Swinbanks, 8 Main Street, Tobermory, has a purpose built 38 ft. sea angling boat for fishing parties with boat rods and reel available. There are 14-16 ft. dinghies for hire for fishing in and around the bay.

Tackle: A tackle shop, with a complete range of stock is on the Main Street.
Bait: Herring and mackerel

available from Tackle and Books, Tobermory. Mussels and lugworms are easily obtainable from the shoreline.
Season for fishing: May-November.
Further information from: Mr. Duncan Swinbanks, Tackle and Books, 10 Main Street, Tobermory. Tel: Tobermory 2336.

Isle of Coll
Coll is one of the smaller islands seaward of Mull. Fishing vessels concentrate on the Atlantic side, but good sport can be had on the Mull side and even at the mouth of Arinagour Bay where the village and hotel lie and the mail steamer calls. Fishing from rocks at several spots round the island can give good results.
Types of fish: Mackerel, coalfish, pollack, cod, conger, haddock, skate and flounder.
Boats: Dinghies with or without outboard engines can be hired from local lobster fishermen.
Tackle: Visitors are advised to bring their own.
Bait: Mussels, worms and small crabs can readily be obtained at low tide in Arinagour Bay.
Season for fishing: May to September and later depending on weather.
Further information from: Mr. Alistair Oliphant of Coll Hotel, Tel: Coll 334.

FORTH and LOMOND   RIVERS AND LOCHS

Constituent Area Tourist Organisations

City of Edinburgh District Council
Director
Department of Public Relations and Tourism
The City of Edinburgh District Council
9 Cockburn Street
Edinbrugh EH1 1BR
Tel: 031-226 6591

Forth Valley Tourist Board
Tourist Officer
Forth Valley Tourist Board
Burgh Hall, The Cross
Linlithgow
West Lothian EH49 7AH
Tel: Linlithgow (0506) 84 3306

Kirkcaldy District Council
Tourist Officer
Kirkcaldy District Council
Information Centre
South Street, Leven
Fife KY8 4PF
Tel: Leven (0333) 29464

East Lothian Tourist Board
Tourism Director
East Lothian Tourist Board
Brunton Hall
Musselburgh EH21 6AF
Tel: 031-665 3711.

Loch Lomond, Stirling and Trossachs
  Tourist Board
Tourism Manager
Loch Lomond, Stirling and Trossachs
Tourist Board
Beechwood House
St Ninians Road
Stirling FK8 2HU
Tel: Stirling (0786) 70945

St Andrews and North East Fife Tourist Board
Tourism Manager
St Andrews and North East Fife Tourist Board
2 Queens Gardens, St Andrews
Fife KY16 9TE
Tel: St. Andrews (0334) 74609

Other Tourist Organisation
MIDLOTHIAN

RIVER PURIFICATION BOARD
FORTH RIVER PURIFICATION BOARD
Colinton Dell House
West Mill Road, Colinton
Edinburgh EH11 0PH
Tel: 031-441 4691.

RIVERS

Water	Location	Species	Season	Permit available from	Other information
Allan	Bridge of Allan	Salmon Sea trout Brown trout	15 Mar to 31 Oct 15 Mar to 6 Oct	D. Crockart & Son, King Street, Stirling Allanbank Hotel. Greenloaning, McLaren Fishing Tackle & Sports Equipment, Bridge of Allan.	
Almond	Cramond	Salmon Sea trout Brown trout	1 Feb to 31 Oct 15 Mar to 6 Oct	Cramond Angling Club Post Office, Cramond Post Office, Davidsons Mains 'Shooting Lines' Roseburn	Mouth to Old Cramond Brig. East bank only.
	West Lothian	Salmon Sea trout Brown trout	1 Feb to 31 Oct 15 Mar to 6 Oct	River Almond Angling Association, Secretary, H. Meikle, 23 Glen Terrace, Deans Livingston. Tel: Livingston 411813.	20 miles of river.
Devon	Dollar	Salmon Sea trout Brown trout	15 Mar to 31 Oct 15 Mar to 6 Oct	Devon Angling Association, R. Breingan, 33 Redwell Place, Alloa Tel: Alloa 215185. Scobbie Sports, Primrose St. Alloa. D.W. Black, Hobby Shop 10 New Row, Dumferline.	No Sunday fishing Devonside Bridge upstream with excluded stretches. Fly fishing only from 15 Mar-12 Apr.
Eden (and Ceres Burn)	Cupar	Salmon Sea trout Brown trout	15 Mar to 6 Oct	Eden Angling Association Secretary, 21 New Town, Cupar. Tel: Cupar 54842 J. Gow & Sons, Union Street, Dundee.	No Sunday fishing.
Endrick	Drymen	Salmon Sea trout Brown trout	11 Feb to 31 Oct 15 Mar to 6 Oct	Loch Lomond Angling Improvement Association Messrs R.D. Clement & Co, 224 Ingram St, Glasgow	Members may fish all Association waters. No Sunday fishing. No worm fishing. Spinning restricted.
Esk	Mussel-burgh	Salmon Sea trout Brown trout	1 Feb to 31 Oct 1 Apr to 6 Oct	Musselburgh and District Angling Association T. Mealyou, Sports Shop, 11 Newbiggin, Musselburgh.	No Sunday fishing. Regulations on permit.
Esk	Mussel-burgh	Salmon Sea trout Brown trout	1 Feb to 31 Oct 15 Mar to 6 Oct	Musselburgh and District Angling Association T. Mealyou, Sports Shop, 11 Newbiggin, Musselburgh.	No Sunday fishing. Regulations on permit.

Water	Location	Species	Season	Permit available from	Other Information
Esk (North)	Midlothian	Brown trout	15 Mar to 6 Oct	Esk Valley Angling Improvement Association Kevin Burns, 53 Fernieside Crescent, Edinburgh Tel: 031-664 4685 Local shops. Officials on water.	Fly rod and reel only to be used. Regulations on permit.
Forth	Stirling	Salmon Brown trout	1 Feb-31 Oct 15 Mar to 6 Oct	Messrs. D. Crockart & Son, 15 King St. Stirling. Tel: Stirling 73443	
Forth and Clyde Canal	Castlecary	Perch Pike Carp Roach Tench Bream	No close Season	Edinburgh Coarse Anglers Secretary, R. Stephens, 68 Meadowhouse Rd, Edinburgh Tel: 031-334 7787 British Waterways Board Canal House, Applecross St. Glasgow Tel: 041-332 6936.	
Fruin	Helensburgh	Salmon Sea trout Brown trout	11 Feb to 31 Oct 1 Mar to 6 Oct	Loch Lomond Angling Improvement Association Messrs. R. A. Clement & Co. C.A. 24 Ingram Street, Glasgow.	Members only. Members may fish all Association waters. Fly fishing only.
Water of Leith	Edinburgh	Brown trout	1 Apr to 30 Sept	Lothian Regional Council Reception, George IV Bridge, Edinburgh. Tel: 031-229 9292 ext. 2355 Post Office, Balemo. Post Office, Currie. Post Office, Juniper Green.	Fly fishing above Slateford Road Bridge. No Spinning at any time. Regulations on permit.
Leven	Dumbarton	Salmon Sea trout Brown trout	11 Feb to 31 oct 15 Mar to 6 Oct	Loch Lomond Angling Improvement Association Messrs. R.A. Clement & Co. C.A. 24 Ingram Street, Glasegow. Various local tackle shops.	members may fish all Association waters. No Sunday Fishing.
Teith	Callander	Salmon	1 Feb to 31 Oct	J. Bayne, Main St. Callander. Tel: (0877) 30218.	
	Stirling (Blue Banks)	Salmon Sea trout	1 Feb to 31 Oct	D. Crocket & Son 15 King Street Stirling Tel: Stirling 73443	
Tyne	Haddington	Brown trout	15 Mar to 6 Oct	East Lothian Angling Association, J.S. Main, Saddlers, 87 High Street, Haddington Major Edinburgh tackle shops.	Twenty miles of river. No Sunday fishing. No threadlines. No Spinning.
Union Canal	Edinburgh To Falkirk	Pike Perch Roach Carp Tench	No close Season	Lothian Regional Council, George IV Bridge, Edinburgh. Tourist Office, Linthligow Ranger, Muiravonside Country Park Ranger, Union Canal, B.W.B. Broxburn.	Regulations on permit.

LOCHS AND RESERVOIRS

Water	Location	Species	Season	Permit available from	Other Information
Lochachray	Callander	Brown trout Perch Pike	15 Mar to 6 Oct	Forestry Commissiion, David Marshall Lodge, Aberfoyle. Loch Achray Hotel. Trossachs.	Bank fishing only.
Loch Ard	Aberfoyle	Brown trout	15 Mar to 6 Oct	Alskeath Hotel, Kinlochard. Post Office, Kinlochard.	

Please mention this Pastime Publications guide.

Water	Location	Species	Season	Permit available from	Other information
Ballo Reservoir	Leslie	Brown trout	1 Apr to 30 Sept	Water Section, Fife Regional Council, Craig Mitchell House, Flemington Road, Glenrothes. Tel: 0592 76541	Fly fishing only. No Sunday fishing.
Bonaly Reservoir	Edinburgh	Brown trout Rainbow trout	1 Apr to 30 Sept	None required	
Beecraigs Loch	Linlithgow	Brown trout Rainbow trout	15 Mar to 15 Oct	Beecraigs Country Park Tel: Linlithgow 844516	Fly fishing only.
Bowden Springs	Linlithgow	Rainbow trout	7 Mar to 11 Nov	W. Martin, Bowden Springs Fishery Linlithgow. Tel: Linlithgow 847269	Bank and boat fishing. Bag limit 3-5 fish.
Cameron Reservoir	St. Andrews	Brown trout	12 Apr to 27 Sept	St. Andrews Angling Club Secretary, 54 St. Nicholas St. Andrews. Tel: St. Andrews 76347 Fishing Hut Tel: Peat Inn 236.	No Sunday fishing. Three rods per boat. Pre-season bookings to Secretary.
Carron Valley Reservoir	Denny	Brown trout	Apr to Sept	Director of Finance, Central Regional Council Viewforth, Stirling. Tel: Stirling 73111.	Boat fishing only.
Loch Chon	Aberfoyle	Brown trout Pike	15 Mar to 6 Oct	Mr. McNair, Frenich Farm, Aberfoyle	Boats available
Clatto Loch	Cupar	Brown trout	1 Apr to 30 Sept	Crawford Priory Estate Mr. Colombo, West Lodge, Crawford Priory Estate, Cupar. Tel: Cupar 2678	No Sunday fishing
Clubbiedean Reservoir	Edinburgh	Brown trout Rainbow trout	1 Apr to 30 Sept	Lothian Regional Council Department of Water and Drainage, Comiston Spring, Buckstone Terr., Edinburgh Tel: 031-445 4141	Three boats. Bag limit-6 trout Fly fishing only Sessions May to Aug
Loch Coulter	Larbert	Brown trout Rainbow trout	1 Apr to 30 Sept	Larbert & Stenhousemuir Angling Club, Andrew Paterson, 6 Wheatlands Avenue Bonnybridge, Stirlingshire Tel: Bonnybridge 812693.	No Sunday fishing. Fly fishing only. Sessions: Day 9am-Dusk Evenings 6pm-Dusk
Crosswood Reservoir	West Calder	Brown trout Brook trout Rainbow trout	1 Apr to 30 Sept	Lothian Regional Council Department of Water and Drainage, Comiston Springs, Buckstone Terr. Edinburgh Tel: 031-445 4141 Department of Water and Drainage Lomond House, Livingston Tel: Livingston 414004	Two boats. Fly fishing only.
Danskine Loch	Gifford	Roach Carp Crucian Carp	(under review)	Edinburgh Coarse Anglers R. Stephens, 68 Meadowhouse Road, Edinburgh Tel: 031-334 7787	Members only
Loch Doine	Balquhidder	Salmon Brown trout	15 Mar-6 Oct	Mrs I.T. Ferguson Muirlaggan Farm, Balquhidder Tel: (087 74) 219	Two caravans to let free fishing to occupants.
Donolly Reservoir	Gifford	Brown trout	1 Apr to 30 Sept	Lothian Regional Council Department of Water and Drainage, Alderston House, Haddington. Tel: Haddington 4131	One boat. Collect key from Goblin Ha' Hotel, Gifford Fly fishing only.
Loch Drunkie	Aberfoyle	Brown trout	15 Mar to 6 Oct	Forestry Commission David Marshall Lodge Aberfoyle	Bank fishing only.

Water	Location	Species	Season	Permit available from	Other information
Duddingston Loch	Edinburgh	Carp Perch Roach Tench	No close season	Scottish Development Dept. 3-11 Melville Street, Edinburgh. Tel: 031-226 2570	Bird Sanctuary. Bank fishing. Restricted area. No lead weights
Loch Fitty	Dunfermline	Brown trout Rainbow trout	1 Mar to Christmas	The Lodge Loch Fitty, Kingseat by Dunfermline Fife Tel: Dunfermline (0383) 723162	Reduced evening boats. Mar. Apr. and Aug. Sept. Sessions: Day-10am-5pm Evenings-5.30pm-dark. Reductions for single anglers, and 'Father & Schoolboy Son' boats, restaurant, tackle shop, fish farm.
Free Loch	Ardlui	Pike		Ardlui Hotel, Ardlui by Arrochar Tel: Inveruglas 243	
Gladhouse Reservoir	Midlothian	Brown trout	1 Apr to 30 Sept	Lothian Regional Council Department of Water and Drainage, Comiston Springs Buckstone Terr. Edinburgh Tel: 031-445 4141	Local Nature Reserve Double-Sessions: May-Aug Day-8am-4.30pm Evening-5pm-sunset plus one hour. No Sunday fishing. Fly fishing only.
Glencourse Reservoir	Penicuik	Brown trout Brook trout Rainbow trout	1 Apr to 30 Sept	Lothian Regional Council Department of Water and Drainage, Comiston Springs Buckstone Terr, Edinburgh Tel: 031-445 4141	Fly fishing only 4 boats Sessions May to Aug
Harperrig Reservoir	West Calder	Brown trout	1 Apr to 30 Sept	Boat fishing: Lothian Regional Council Department of Water and Drainage, Comiston Springs, Buckstone Terr. Edinburgh Tel: 031-445 4141 Department of Water and Drainage, Lomond House, Livingston Tel: Livingston 414004 Bank fishing permits from Machine at Reservoir	Correct coins required for machine 50p, 10p, 5p denominations. Four boats. No Sunday fishing. Fly fishing only.
Harlaw Reservoir	Balerno	Brown trout Rainbow trout	1 Apr to 30 Sept	Boat fishing Lothian Regional Council Department of Water and Drainage, Comiston Springs. Buckstone Terr., Edinburgh Tel: 031-445 4141 Bank Flemings Grocer Balerno	Fly fishing only Bag limit-6 trout Limited number of bank permits
Holl Reservoir	Leslie	Brown trout	1 Apr to 30 Sept	Water Section, Fife Regional Council, Craig Mitchell House Flemington Road, Glenrothes. Tel: 0592-756541	Fly fishing only. No Sunday fishing.
Hopes Reservoir	Gifford	Brown trout Rainbow trout	1 Apr to 30 Sept	Lothian Regional Council Department of Water and Drainage, Alderston House, East Lothian. Tel: Haddington 4131	
Lindores Loch	Newburgh	Brown trout Rainbow trout	15 Mar- 30 Nov	F.G. Hamilton 18 Strathview Place, Comrie, Perthshire Tel: Comrie 70821.	Two sessions.
Linlithgow Loch	Linlithgow	Brown trout Rainbow trout	15 Mar to 31 Oct	Forth Area Federation of Anglers The Garden Shop, The Cross, Linlithgow Tel: Linlithgow 842943	Bank fishing on North bank. Fly fishing until 1 Oct

Water	Location	Species	Season	Permit available from	Other Information
Lochore	Ballingry	Brown trout	15 Mar to 5 Oct	Lochroe Meadows Country Park, Crosshill, Lochgelly, Fife. Tel: Ballingry (0592) 860086 Hobby and Model Shop Dunfermline Sports Shop, High St. Cowdenbeath Martins, 31 Main St. Kelty.	Reductions for clubs and groups. Sessions. Day 9am-5pm Evenings 5pm-dusk Fly fishing and Spinning. Bait fishing from bank from 1 July.
Loch Lomond	Balloch to Ardlui	Salmon Sea trout Brown trout Pike Poach Perch	11 Feb to 31 Oct 15 Mar to 6 Oct No close season	Loch Lomond Angling Improvement Association Messrs. R.A. Clement & Co C.A., 244 Ingram St. Glasgow. Permits from many hotels, shops and tackle dealers in the area. Ardlui Hotel, Ardlui Tel: (030 14) 243 Inversnaid Hotel Inversnaid Tel: Inversnaid 223.	Permit covers all Association waters. Boats for hire locally. No Sunday fishing.
Loch Lubnaig	Callander to Strathyre	Salmon Brown trout	1 Feb-31 Oct 15 Mar-6 Oct	Forth Area Federation of Anglers, J. Bayne, Main St. Callander Tel: (0877) 30218	
Lake of Menteith	Port of Menteith	Brown trout Rainbow trout	Apr to Oct	Lake Hotel Port of Menteith Tel: (08775) 258	
Morton Fisheries	Midcadder	Brown trout Rainbow trout	15 Mar to 31 Oct	Morton Fisheries, Waterkeepers Cottage Morton Reservoir Tel: Midcadder (0506) 88087	Advance bookings necessary Double sessions May-Aug 9am-5pm 5pm-dusk Bag limits 3-6 fish per rod.
North Third	Cambus-barron	Rainbow trout Brown trout		North Third Fishery "Greathill" Cambusbarron Stirling Tel: Stirling (0786) 71967	
Lochan Reoidhe	Aberfoyle	Brown trout	15 Mar-6 Oct	Forestry Commission David Marshall Lodge Aberfoyle	Fly fishing only Limited rods Boat available Advance Bookings accepted.
Rosebery Reservoir	Gore-bridge	Brown trout Rainbow trout	1 Apr to 30 Sept	Waterkeepers Cottage, Rosebery Reservoir Temple. Midlothian Tel: Temple (8300) 353	Three boats & bank fishing. Fly fishing only.
Swans Water Fishery	Bannockburn Stirling	Rainbow trout	All year	Swans Water Fishery Cultonhove Fish Farm Sauchieburn, Stirling Tel: (0786) 814805	
Threilpmuir Reservoir	Balerno	Brown trout Rainbow trout	1 Apr to 30 Sept	Flemings, Grocer, Main Street, Balerno.	Limited number of permits covers Harlaw Reservoir as well.
Loch Venachar	Callander	Brown trout	15 Mar to 6 Oct	J. Bayne, Main Street, Callander.Tel: (0877) 30218	
Loch Voil	Balquidder	Brown trout Salmon	15 Mar to 6 Oct	Ledcreigh Hotel, Balquidder Tel: Strathyre 230 Ferguson, Muirlaggan Farm, Balquidder Tel: (087 74) 219	Two caravans to let with free fishing

Water	Location	Species	Season	Permit available from	Other information
Whiteadder Reservoir	Gifford	Brown trout	1 Apr to 30 Sept	Waterkeepers House, Hungry Snout, Whiteadder Reservoir, Cranshaws, by Duns. Tel: (036 17) 257	Bank fishing from 1 June each year. Fly fishing only. 3 boats

FORTH AND LOMOND (CLYDE COAST)

Sea Angling
Helensburgh
Helensburgh is a small seaside town on the Firth of Clyde at the southern end of the Gareloch, easily reached by train or car.
Types of fish: Shore and boat – cod, flounder, coalfish, conger, rays, dogfish, whiting, dab, haddock, pollack and mackerel.
Boats: Modern Charters Ltd., Tel: Clynder (0436) 831312. A. Brown 041-882 4628; J. Ferguson 0389 51416; J. Allison 0436 84 2569; M. Kettle 0436 831312. Also Gourock skippers including Inverclyde Boat-Owners Association, 164 Burns Road, Greenock. Tel: 0475 34341..
Self Drive Boats: T. Lambert, Tel: Helensburgh 2083; R. Clark, Tel: Rhu 820344.
Tackle: 'Carousel', West Clyde Street, Helensburgh.
Bait: Ragworm, lugworm, may be dug locally. Mussels and crabs can be gathered from the shore.
Season for fishing: All year, especially winter for large cod.

Garelochhead
Garelochhead is the village at the head of the Gareloch, with the whole shoreline within easy reach. Upper and lower Loch Long and Loch Goil are only a few miles away.
Types of fish: Cod, coalfish, pollack, dab, flounder, plaice, whiting, haddock, pouting, rays, mackerel, spurdog, lesser spotted dogfish.
Bait: Garelochhead – cockles and mussels. Roseneath – lugworm, ragworm and cockles. Rhu – ragworm. Kilcreggan – ragworm. Coulport – cockles.
Season for fishing: December-March, migratory cod – June onwards.

Arrochar, Loch Long
The village lies at the northern end of the loch, and has waters sheltered by the high surrounding hills.
Types of fish: Shore – cod, conger, pollack, coalfish and rays. Boat – cod, haddock, whiting, conger, pollack, coalfish, mackerel, dogfish and rays.
Boats: Dinghies from Rossmay Boat Hire, (030 12) 250.
Tackle: Available from Mr. Findlater, Braeside Stores, Arrochar.
Bait: Fresh herring and mackerel, mussels and cockles usually available from the pier. Artificial baits, lures etc. available from shops in village.
Season for fishing: All year.

Clynder
Clynder is the fishing centre on the sheltered west side of the Gareloch and one mile north of the popular Rhu Narrows.
Types of fish: Shore: cod and mackerel. Boat: cod, conger, rays, plaice, flounders, dogfish, whiting, pouting and mackerel.
Boats: C. Moar (0436) 831333; Modern Charters (0436) 831312; Allisons Boat Hire (043684) 2237; Clynder Hotel (0436) 831248.
Tackle: The Modern Charters Ltd., Clynder.
Bait: Cockles, mussels, lug, ragworm, can be dug.
Season for fishing: All year, winter for large cod.
Further information from: Modern Charters Ltd., Victoria Place, Clynder. Tel: 0436 831312.

FORTH AND LOMOND (EAST COAST)

Anglers going afloat from Fife and Forth Harbours are advised to contact the coastguard at Fifeness for weather information. Tel: Crail (0333) 50666 (day or night).

Tayport
Tayport, on the Firth of Tay opposite Dundee, in the northern-most part of Fife, enjoys good shore fishing in sheltered waters. There are no hotels but there is a modern caravan and camping site with showers, laundry etc.
Types of fish: Cod, flounder and plaice from shore, with occasional sea trout (permit required).
Tackle: Available from W. Sturrock, Mainland Street, Tayport.
Bait: Lugworm, ragworm, mussels, cockles and crabs available locally at low water.
Season for fishing: April- January.
Further information from: James O'Brien, Secretary, Cupar, St. Andrews and District S.A.C., 40 King Street, Kirkcaldy.

St. Andrews
St. Andrews is a leading holiday resort with sea angling as one of its attractions. Fishing is mainly from boats, but good sport can be had from the rocks between the bathing pool and the harbour.
Tackle: J. Wilson & Sons, 169 South Street, St. Andrews.
Bait: Excellent supplies of Lugworm, ragworm and large mussels can be gathered in the River Eden.
Further information from: James O'Brien, Secretary, Cupar, St. Andrews and District S.A.C., 40 King Street, Kirkcaldy.

Boarhill and Kings Barns
Good beach fishing for cod and flatfish.

Anstruther
It is a fishing village with plenty of good boat and beach fishing. A very rocky coastline but can be very rewarding with good catches of cod, saithe, flounder, wrasse, and whiting. Be prepared to lose tackle.
Types of fish: Cod, saithe, wrasse, flounder, ling, conger and mackerel.
Boats: Plenty charter boats with local skippers who know all the hot spots.

Bait: Lug, rag, white rag, cockle, crab, mussel which can be dug locally.
Season: Boat – May-October. Beach – September-January.
Further inforamtion from: Mr. D. Williams, Secretary, Buckhaven & District SAC, 50 Lomond Gardens, Methil, Fife KY8 3JL.

Pittenweem

The nerve centre of the East Neuk with a large deep water harbour which boats can enter or leave at any stage of the tide. The European Cod Festival is now held here each year and produces large catches of cod. The harbour wall is very popular with young and old alike, with some good catches.
Types of fish: Cod, saithe, flounder, wrasse, ling, conger, whiting, mackerel from boats. Cod, saithe, flounder, wrasse and whiting from beach.
Boats: D. Stewart, 14 Marygate, Pittenweem. Tel: Anstruther (0333) 311276.
Bait: Lug, rag, can be dug locally.
Season: Boat – May-October. Beach – September-January.

Leven

A holiday resort with about 2 miles of lovely sandy beaches. Beach fishing is very popular with some very good catches.
Types of fish: Flounder, cod, bass, mullet, saithe.
Boats: No charter boats.
Tackle: Dave's Sport, Bridge Street, Leven.
Bait: Lug available locally.
Season: July-January.

Buckhaven

A small town on the north side of the Firth of Forth, which is renowned for its boat and beach fishing. The Scottish Open Beach Competition is fished from Buckhaven to Dysart each year with large entries from all over Scotland.
Types of fish: Cod, saithe, flounder, whiting, mackerel from beach. Cod, saithe, flounder, whiting, ling, mackerel and wrasse from boat.
Bait: Lug available at Leven.
Tackle: The Sports Shop, Wellesley Road, Buckhaven.
Boats: No charter hire.
Season: Boat – June-November. Beach – October-January.

Further information from: D. Williams, Hon. Sec., Buckhaven & District Sea Angling Club, 50 Lomond Gardens, Methil, Fife KY8 3JL.

Kirkcaldy

Beach fishing at east and west end of town.
Types of fish: Cod, flatfish, saithe, mackerel.
Bait: Beach off bus station.

Pettycur and Kinghorn

Rock and beach fishing off Pettycur Harbour and Kinghorn Beach.
Types of fish: Saithe, flatfish.
Boats: Small boats can be launched from beaches.
Bait: Plenty locally. Local caravan sites.

Burntisland

Permission required to fish the beach from harbour to swimming pool.
Types of fish: Saithe, flatfish, small cod.
Boats: None locally.
Bait: Lug available locally.
Further information from: J. O'Brien, Secretary, Cupar, St. Andrews and District SAC, 40 King Street, Kirkcaldy.

South Queensferry

A picturesque burgh overshadowed by the Forth Bridges.
Types of fish: Cod, whiting, coalfish, mackerel, flounder from boat and shore in season.
Tackle: J. Swan, High Street, South Queensferry.
Bait: Lugworm, ragworm, mussel, cockle, clams and crabs at low water in the area.
Season for fishing: May to October.
Further information from: B. Plasting, 53 Somerville Gardens, South Queensferry. Tel: 031-331 1605. There are 3 launching slips in the area, but currents can be dangerous and local advice should be obtained before setting out in dinghies.

Edinburgh

Scotland's capital city, on the south of the Forth estuary, has several miles of shoreline. Most of this is sandy, and can produce good catches of flatfish, although codling, Ray's bream, whiting,

eels and mackerel can be taken in season from the shore. Best marks are at Cramond, round the mouth of the River Almond, and the Seafield to Portobello area.
Tackle: Field and Stream, 61 Montrose Terrace, F. & D. Simpson, 28 West Preston Street, Shooting Lines Ltd., 23 Roseburn Terrace, John Dickson & Son, 21 Frederick Street, J. Robertson & Son, 17 North St. Andrew Street.
Bait: Lugworm, ragworm, mussels, cockles and clams from most beaches at low water.
Season for fishing: All year round.
Further information from: Mr G.A. Walker, 12/4 Murrayburn Park, Edinburgh. Tel: 031-442 3750.

Musselburgh

This town stands on the estuary of the River Esk, 6 miles to the east of Edinburgh, overlooking the Firth of Forth. It has a small but busy harbour at Fisherrow, catering mainly for pleasure craft.
Boats: Enquiries should be made at the harbour. Best shore marks range from Fisherrow harbour to the mouth of the Esk.
Tackle: T.H. Mealyou, 11 Newbiggin, Musselburgh.
Bait: Lugworm, ragworm, mussels, cockles and clams at low water.
Further information from: Brunton Hall, East Lothian. Tel: 031-665 6597.

Cockenzie

Mullet can be caught around the warm water outfall to the east of Cockenzie Power station and around the harbour. Other species include flatfish, codling and mackerel.

North Berwick

There is good boat fishing out of North Berwick and the coastline between the town and Dunbar is good for shore fishing.
Types of fish: Cod, haddock, plaice, mackerel and coalfish.
Boats: Launches occasionally run fishing trips from the harbour. Apply Fred Marr, Victoria Road, North Berwick.
Bait: Mussels, crabs and shellfish of various types available at low water.
Tackle: Tackle can be bought locally.

Dunbar

Dunbar claims to have the lowest
rainfall in Scotland and more
hours of sunshine than any other
Scottish resort. The coastline
from Dunbar to Eyemouth is very
popular for rock and beach
fishing.
Types of fish: Cod, haddock,
flounder, coalfish, mackerel,
wrasse and whiting.
Boats: Details can be obtained
from The Tourist Information
Centre, Dunbar, and Mr Hall,
The Fisherman's Cove, High
Street, Dunbar.
Tackle: Available from the
Fisherman's Cove, High Street,
Dunbar and Messrs Main,
Saddlers, West Port, Dunbar.
Bait: Mussels, lug and ragworm
available at low water, and also
from tackle dealers.
Season for fishing: Best April to
October.
Further information from:
Information Centre, Town
House, High Street. Tel: Dunbar
(0368) 63353 January-December.

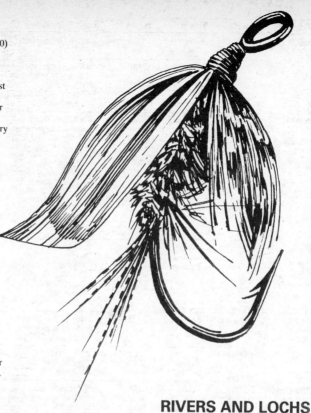

TAYSIDE

RIVERS AND LOCHS

Constituent Area Tourist Boards

City of Dundee Tourist Board
Director
City of Dundee Tourist Board
City Chambers
Dundee DD1 3BY
Tel: Dundee (0382) 23141

Perthshire Tourist Board
Director of Tourism
Perthshire Tourist Board
PO Box 33
George Inn Lane
Perth PH1 5LG
Tel: Perth: (0738) 27958

Angus Tourist Board
Tourist Manager
Angus Tourist Board
Market Place
Arbroath
Tel: Arbroath (0241) 72609/76680

RIVER PURIFICATION BOARD
TAY RIVER PURIFICATION BOARD
3 South Street
Perth PH2 8NJ
Tel: Perth 27989

RIVERS

Water	Location	Species	Season	Permit available from	Other information
Ardle	Kirkmichael	Salmon Trout	15 Jan-15 Oct 15 Mar-6 Oct	The Log Cabin, Hotel, Glen Derby Tel: Strathardle 288	No Sunday fishing.
	Blairgowrie	Salmon Trout	15 Jan-15 Oct 15 Mar-6 Oct	Corriefodly Hotel, Bridge of Cally. Tel: Bridge of Cally 236.	Sunday fishing for trout only.
Braan	Amulree	Brown trout	15 Mar to 6 Oct	Amulree Hotel, Amulree, by Dunkeld. Tel: Amulree 218.	

Water	Location	Species	Season	Permit available from	Other information
Dean	Glamis	Brown trout	15 Mar to 6 Oct	Canmore Angling Club Forfar.	
	Strathmore	Brown trout	15 Mar to 6 Oct	Strathmore Angling Improvement Association. Mrs. A. Henderson 364 Blackness Road, Dundee Tel: Dundee 68062	
Dochart	Killin	Brown trout	15 Mar to 6 Oct	D & S Allan, Tackle Dealer, Killin, Perthshire. Tel: Killin 362. All legal lures permitted.	
Earn	Crieff	Salmon Sea trout Brown trout	1 Feb to 15 Oct	Crieff Angling Club W. Cook & Son, Tackle Dealer, High Street, Crieff. Tel: Crieff 2081. Mr. A. Boyd, King Street, Crieff. Tel: (0764) 3871	No prawn, diving minnow or bubble floats.
	St Fillans	Salmon Sea trout Brown trout	14 Feb to 15 Oct 15 Mar to 6 Oct	St. Fillans & Loch Earn Angling Association J. MacPherson, Rannoch, 4 Earn View, St Fillans. Tel: St. Fillans 219. Lochearn Post Office, St. Fillans Post Office.	Salmon and Sea trout fishing for members only.
Ericht (and Ardle)	Bridge of Cally	Salmon Brown trout	1 Jan-15 Oct 15 Mar to 6 Oct	Bridge of Cally Hotel, Blairgowrie, Perthshire. Tel: Bridge of Cally 231	Fly fishing only after 15 Apr.
	Craighall	Salmon Brown trout	15 Jan-15 Oct 15 Mar to 6 Oct	Mr. P. Rattray, Craighall, Blairgowrie. Tel: Blairgowrie 2678	
Garry	Blair Atholl	Trout	15 Mar to 6 Oct	W. McEwan The Corner House Blair Atholl Tel: 246	
Gaur	Rannoch	Brown trout	15 Mar to 6 Oct	Moor of Rannoch Hotel, Rannoch Station, Perthshire. Tel: Bridge of Gaur 238	Free to guests
Lochay	Killin	Brown trout Pike Perch	15 Mar to 6 Oct	D & S Allan, Tackle Dealers, Main Street, Killin. Tel: Killin 362	
Lunan	Arbroath	Sea trout Brown trout	15 Mar to 6 Oct	Arbroath Angling Club T. Clark & Sons, 274 High St., Arbroath. Tel: Arbroath 73467	Fly, bait or Spinning.
Lyon	Aberfeldy	Salmon	15 Jan to 15 Oct	Fortingall Hotel, Fortingall, by Aberfeldy. Tel: Kenmore 367.	
South Esk	Kirriemuir	Salmon Sea trout Brown trout	16 Feb to 31 Oct	Kirriemuir Angling Club, 13 Clova Road, Kirriemuir Tel: Kirriemuir 3456 Permits issued only in advance.	No permits on Saturdays. No Sunday fishing.
Tay	Aberfeldy	Brown trout	15 Mar to 6 Oct	Jamiesons Sports Shop, Dunkeld St., Aberfeldy.	
	Aberfeldy	Salmon Brown trout	15 Jan-15 Oct 15 Mar to 6 Oct	Weem Hotel, Aberfeldy Tel: Aberfeldy 20381.	
	Grantully	Salmon Brown trout Grayling	15 Jan-15 Oct 15 Mar to 6 Oct	Grantully Hotel, Strathtay, Perthshire. Tel: Strathtay 207	

Water	Location	Species	Season	Permit available from	Other Information
	Ballinluig	Salmon Brown trout Grayling Pike Perch, Eels	15 Jan-15 Oct 15 Mar to 6 Oct	Logierait Hotel Ballinluig, Perthshire. Tel: Ballinluig 253	
	Dunkeld	Salmon Brown trout	15 Jan to 15 Oct 15 Mar to 6 Oct	Stakis plc Dunkeld House Hotel, Dunkeld, Perthshire. Tel: Dunkeld 243	Arrangements to be confirmed
	Dunkeld	Brown trout	15 Mar to 6 Oct	Top Shop, Atholl Street Dunkeld. Tel: Dunkeld 556	
	Stanley	Salmon Sea trout Brown trout	15 Jan to 15 Oct 15 Mar to 6 Oct	Ballathie Estate Office, Ballathie Farms, Near Stanley. Tel: Meikleour 250.	Spring fishing only available.
	Perth	Salmon Sea trout Flounders Roach	15 Jan to 15 Oct	Director of Finance, Perth & Kinross District Council, 2 High Street, Perth. Tel: Perth 39911 (Mon-Fri) Tourist Information Centre, Round House, Marshall Place, Perth.	Advisable to book in advance. Only 20 permits per day. Only 2 permits may be booked in advance by any one person. No weekly permits issued after end Aug. (Sat)
Tummel	Kinloch Rannoch	Brown trout	15 Jan to 15 Oct	Manager, West Tempar Estate, Kinloch Rannoch. Tel: Kinloch Rannoch 338	
	Pitlochry	Salmon Sea trout	15 Jan to 15 Oct	Pitlochry Angling Club, c/o Tourist Office, Pitlochry. Tel: Mr. Gardiner Pitlochry 2157 (evenings)	Permits available Mon-Sat.
	Moulinearn to Ballinluig	Salmon Sea trout	15 Jan to 15 Oct	Pitlochry Angling Club, c/o Tourist Office, Pitlochry. Tel: Mr Gardiner, Pitlochry 2157 (evenings)	Only available Jul, Aug, Sept.
	Pitlochry to Ballinluig	Brown trout Grayling	16 Mar to 6 Oct	Pitlochry Angling Club, Pitlochry Tourist Office, Milton of Fonab Caravan Site Ballinluig Post Office Malloch's Highland Gathering, Athol Road, Pitlochry.	Five miles of river both banks. Map and rules on permit.

LOCHS AND RESERVOIRS

Water	Location	Species	Season	Permit available from	Other Information
Loch Bhac	Blair Atholl	Brown trout	15 Mar to 6 Oct	Pitlochry Angling Club c/o Airdanair Hotel, Atholl Road, Pitlochry Tel: Pitlochry 2266	Fly fishing only. 10 a.m. to dusk.
Butterstone Loch	Dunkeld	Rainbow trout Brown trout	1 Apr to 31 Oct	The Bailiff, Lochend Cottage, Butterstone Loch, by Dunkeld. Tel: Butterstone 238	Fly fishing only. Twelve boats. Day session: 9a.m.-5p.m.. Evening session: 5.30 p.m.-dusk.
Castlehill Reservoir	Glendevon	Brown trout	1 Apr to 30 Sept	Tormaukin Hotel, Glendevon. Tel: Glendevon 252.	Fly fishing only.
	Glendevon	Brown trout	1 Apr to 30 Sept	Water Section, Fife Regional Council, Craig Mitchell House, Flemington Road, Glenrothes. Tel: 0592-756541. Permits also available from Castlehill Boathouse. Tel: 025981-239	Fly fishing only.

Please mention this Pastime Publications guide.

Water	Location	Species	Season	Permit available from	Other information
Crombie Reservoir	Crombie Country Park	Brown trout	Apr to Sept	Monikie Angling Club, Bailiff Tel: Newbigging 300	
Den of Ogil Reservoir		Brown trout	1 Apr to 6 Oct	Canmore Angling Club, Forfar.	
Dunalastair Loch	Kinloch Rannoch	Brown trout	15 Mar to 6 Oct	Dunalastair Hotel, Kinloch Rannoch. Tel: Kinloch Rannoch 323 Lassintullich Fisheries, Kinloch Rannoch. Tel: Kinloch Rannoch 238	Five boats available. Five boats available. Half price for single rod.
Loch Earn	St. Fillans Lochearn head	Brown trout Rainbow trout	1 Apr to 6 Oct	St. Fillans and Lochearn Angling Association, St. Fillans, Perthshire. Tel: St. Fillans 219 Post Office, St. Fillans Post Office, Lochearnhead.	
Loch Eigheach	Moor of Rannoch	Brown trout	15 Mar to 6 Oct	Rannoch and District Angling Club, John Brown, The Square, Kinloch Rannoch. Tel: Kinloch Rannoch 331	Bank fishing only.
Loch Faskally	Pitlochry	Salmon Brown trout Pike Perch	Mar, May to Oct Apr to Sept	P. Williamson, Boathouse, Loch Faskally, Pitlochry. Tel: Pitlochry 2919/2612	Any legal lure for salmon.
Glendevon (Upper) Reservoir	Glendevon	Brown trout	1 Apr to 30 Sept	Water Section Fife Regional Council, Flemington Rd., Glenrothes. Tel: Glenrothes 756541	Fly fishing only. No Sunday fishing.
Glendevon (Lower) Reservoir	Glendevon	Brown trout	1 Apr to 30 Sept	Water Section Fife Regional Council, Flemington Rd., Glenrothes. Tel: Glenrothes 756541	Fly fishing only. No Sunday fishing.
Glenfarg Reservoir	Glenfarg	Brown trout	1 Apr to 30 Sept	Water Section Fife Regional Council, Flemington Rd., Glenrothes. Tel: Glenrothes 756541.	Fly fishing only.
Loch Kinardochy	Strath-tummel	Brown trout	15 Mar to 6 Oct	Pitlochry Angling Club, c/o Airdaniar Hotel Atholl Road, Pitlochry. Tel: Pitlochry 2266.	No bank fishing. 10a.m. to dusk. Fly fishing only.
Loch Laidon	Rannoch Moor	Brown trout	15 Mar to 6 Oct	Moor of Rannoch Hotel, Rannoch Station, Perthshire. Tel: Bridge of Gaur 238.	Boat available to guests and visitors.
Loch Leven	Kinross	Brown trout (Loch Leven strain)	Apr to Oct	The Pier, Kinross. Tel: Kinross 63407	Fly fishing only. Boat fishing only.
Lintrathen Reservoir	Kirriemur	Brown trout	Apr to Oct	Lintrathen Angling Club Day permits: Tayside Regional Council, Water Services Dept., 10 Ward Street, Dundee. Tel: Dundee 21164. Club bookings: Dr. Parratt, 91 Strathearn Road, West Ferry, Dundee. Tel: Dundee 77305.	Twelve boats Sunday fishing. 10 a.m. to 1 hour after sunset. Double sessions from mid-May to mid-Aug. Fly fishing only.
Lassintullich Fisheries Dunalastair Loch	Kinloch Rannoch	Brown trout	15 Mar to 6 Oct	Lassintullich Fisheries, Tel: (08822) 238	Five boats. No bank fishing. Fly fishing only.

Water	Location	Species	Season	Permit available from	Other information
Monikie Reservoir	Monikie	Trout	Apr to Sept	Monikie Country Park Monikie Angling Club Bailiff. Tel: Newbigging 300	Fly fishing. Boat fishing. Telephone Bookings 9.30-10.30 am 1.00-1.30 pm 4.30-6.30 pm
Monzievaird	Crieff	Brown trout Rainbow trout	Apr to Oct	Loch Monzievaird Limited Dalchonzie, Comrie. Tel: Comrie (Perthshire) 273	
Loch Rannoch	Kinloch Rannoch	Brown trout	15 Mar to 30 Sept	Loch Rannoch Conservation Association, Cuilmore Cottage, Kinloch, Rannoch. Loch Rannoch Hotel, Bun Rannoch Hotel.	
Rescobie Loch	Forfar	Brown trout Rainbow trout	15 Mar to 31 Oct	Bailiff, Rescobie Loch Tel: (030781) 384 Fly only.	Fly Fishing Only
Sandy-knowes Fishery	Bridge of Earn	Rainbow trout	15 Mar to 31 Oct	M.A. Brien, The Fishery Office, Sandyknowes Fishery Bridge of Earn. Tel: (0738) 813033	Bank fly fishing only. Session times 10 a.m.-2 p.m. 2 p.m.-6 p.m., 6 p.m.-10 p.m. Bag limit-4 trout per session. Open 7 days per week. No Sunday evenings.
Loch Tay	Killin	Salmon Trout	15 Jan-15 Oct 15 Mar-6 Oct	Killin Hotel, Killin. Tel: Killin 296. Claichaig Hotel, Killin. Tel: Killin 270/ 565.	Ghillies available.
	Killin	Trout	15 Mar to 6 Oct	D & S Allan, Tackle Dealers, Killin Tel: Killin 362.	All legal lures permitted.
	Milton Morenish	Salmon	15 Jan to 15 Oct	Loch Tay Highland Lodges, Milton Morenish, by Killin,	
		Trout	15 Mar to 6 Oct	Tel: Killin (05672) 323	
	Ardeonaig	Salmon Trout	15 Jan-15 Oct 15 Mar to 6 Oct	Ardeonaig Hotel, South Lochtayside by Killin, Tel: Killin 400	Six boats available. Special offers mid-week fishing, ask for prices.
	Kenmore	Salmon Trout	15 Jan-15 Oct 15 Mar to 6 Oct	Kenmore Hotel, Kenmore, by Aberfeldy. Tel: Kenmore 205.	
	Lawers	Salmon Brown trout	15 Jan-15 Oct 15 Mar to 6 Oct	Ben Lawers Hotel, Lawers, Aberfeldy, Perthshire. Tel: Killin (056 72) 436	
Loch Turret	Crieff	Brown trout	1 Apr to 30 Sept	Director of Finance, Central Scotland Water Development Board, 30 George Square, Glasgow. Tel: 041-248 5855 W. Cook & Son, 19 High Street, Crieff. Tel: Crieff 2081.	Four boats available with outboards.

TO ASSIST WITH YOUR BOOKINGS
OR ENQUIRIES
YOU WILL FIND IT HELPFUL TO MENTION THIS
Pastime Publications Guide.

TAYSIDE
Sea Angling

Arbroath
Situated on the east coast of Angus, 17 miles north-east of Dundee, Arbroath is easily accessible by road and rail. It is the centre for commercial fishing, and famous for its smokies. Pleasure boats ply for short cruises to local sea cliffs and caves, from the harbour. There are about 10 boats between 15ft and 35ft used for lobster and crab fishing, taking out parties for sea angling.
Types of fish: Cod, coalfish, mackerel, flounder, conger, plaice, haddock and pollack.
Boats: Available through local fishermen and part time lobster and crab fishermen at reasonable prices.
Tackle: Available from Tom Clark & Sons, 274 High Street, Arbroath. Tel: Arbroath 73467.

Dundee
Dundee is situated on the estuary of the River Tay and has sea fishing in the city centre, while Broughty Ferry, a suburb of Dundee, Easthaven and Carnoustie, all within easy reach by road and rail, have sea fishing from rocks, piers or from boats.

There are good marks around the Bell Rock about 12 miles offshore.
Types of fish: Cod, flatfish from shore plus cod, haddock, coalfish, ling, pouting and plaice from boats.
Tackle: All types of tackle available from Messrs John R. Gow and Sons, 12 Union Street, Dundee. Shortcast Ltd., 8 Whitehall Crescent, Dundee. Fagan, Union Street, Dundee. McGill Bros Ltd., 18 Victoria Road, Dundee.
Bait: Available locally.
Season for fishing: All year.
Further information from: Messrs John R. Gow and Sons, 12 Union Street, Dundee.

NORTHEAST and SPEY VALLEY
RIVERS AND LOCHS

Constituent Area Tourist Organisations

Aviemore and Spey Valley Tourist Organisation
Area Tourist Officer
Aviemore and Spey Valley Tourist Organisation
Grampian Road, Aviemore
Inverness-shire PH22 1PP
Tel: Aviemore (0479) 810545

Banff and Buchan Tourist Board
Tourism Manager
Banff and Buchan Tourist Board
Collie Lodge
Banff AB4 1AU
Tel: Banff (026 12) 2789

Kincardine and Deeside Tourist Board
Tourist Officer
Kincardine and Deeside Tourist Board
45 Station Road, Banchory
Kincardineshire AB3 3XX.
Tel: Banchory (033 02) 2066

City of Aberdeen Tourist Board
Director
City of Aberdeen Tourist Board
St Nicholas House, Broad Street
Aberdeen AB9 1DE
Tel: Aberdeen (0224) 632727

Gordon District Tourist Board
Director
Gordon District Tourist Board
St Nicholas House, Broad Street
Aberdeen AB9 1DE
Tel: Aberdeen (0224) 632727

Moray District Council
Chief Tourist Officer
Moray District Council
17 High Street, Elgin
Morayshire IV30 1EG
Tel: Elgin (0343) 2666

RIVER PURIFICATION BOARD
NORTH EAST RIVER PURIFICATION BOARD
Woodside House,
Persley,
Aberdeen AB2 2UQ
Tel: Aberdeen 6966147

RIVERS

Water	Location	Species	Season	Permit available from	Other information
Avon	Ballindalloch	Salmon Sea trout	11 Feb to 30 Sept	Delnashaugh Hotel, Ballindalloch, Banffshire. Tel: Ballindalloch 210	
	Tomintoul	Salmon Sea trout	Feb to end Sept	Gordon Arms Hotel, Tomintoul, Banffshire. Tel: Tomintoul 206.	No prawn. Fly fishing during Sept. Max breaking strain 10lb. No lead attached to fly.

Water	Location	Species	Season	Permit available from	Other information
	Tomintoul	Salmon Sea trout	May to 30 Sept	Richmond Arms Hotel, Tomintoul.	Fly fishing only in September. Permits given to hotel guests only. Tel: 209
Bervie	Laurence- kirk Fordoun	Salmon Sea trout Brown trout		W. Davidson 26 Provost Robson Dr. Laurencekirk. Tel: Laurencekirk 8140	
Carron	Stonehaven	Brown trout	15 Mar to 6 Oct	Davids Sports Shop, 31 Market Square, Stonehaven. Tel: Stonehaven 62239.	Stonehaven Angling Assoc. Visitors permits. Sea Pool to Railway Viaduct.
Cowle	Stonehaven	Salmon Sea trout Brown trout	15 Mar to 6 Oct	Davids Sports Shop 31 Market Square, Stonehaven Tel: Stonehaven 62239.	Stonehaven Angling Assoc. Visitors permits. Sea Pool to Railway Viaduct.
Bogie	Huntly	Salmon Sea trout Brown trout	11 Feb to 31 Oct 1 Apr to 6 Oct	G. Manson, Sports Shop, Gordon Street, Huntly. Tel: Huntly 2482 Clerk of Fishings, 27 Duke Street, Huntly. Tel: Huntly 2291	Permit covers Bogie, Deveron and Isla
Dee	Braemar	Salmon	1 Feb to 30 Sept	Mar Lodge Hotel, Braemar. Tel: Braemar 216	
	Braemar	Salmon	1 Feb to 30 Sept	Invercauld Arms Hotel, Braemar. Tel: Braemar 605	Fishing on adjacent beats can be arranged on request.
	Banchory	Salmon Sea trout	1 Feb to 30 Sept	Banchory Lodge Hotel, Banchory. Tel: Banchory 2625	Rods available by booking in advance.
	Blairs	Salmon Sea trout	1 Feb to 30 Sept	Ardoe House Hotel, Blairs, by Aberdeen. Tel: Aberdeen 867355	
Deveron	Banff	Salmon Sea trout Brown trout	11 Feb to 31 Oct	Jay-Tee Sports Shop, Low Street, Banff. Tel: Banff 5821 County Hotel, High Street, Banff. Tel: (02612) 5353	
	Huntly	Salmon Sea trout Brown trout	11 Feb to 31 Oct 1 Apr to 6 Oct	G. Manson, Sports Shop, Gordon Street, Huntly. Tel: Huntly 2482 J. Christie, 27 Duke Street, Huntly. Tel: Huntly 2291.	Permit covers Deveron, Bogie and Isla.
	Huntly	Salmon Sea trout Brown trout	Feb to Oct	Castle Hotel, Huntly. Tel: Huntly 2696	
	Rothiemay	Salmon Sea trout Brown trout	11 Feb to 31 Oct	Forbes Arms Hotel, Rothiemay, Huntly. Tel: Rothiemay 248.	Fly fishing and spinning. Worm in spate only.
	Turriff	Salmon Sea trout Brown trout	11 Feb to 31 Oct	Turriff Angling Assoc. I. Masson, 14 Main Street, Turriff. Tel: Turriff 62428	No day tickets. Six weekly tickets available to visitors. Restrictions on spinning.
Don	Grandhome	Salmon Sea Trout	11 Feb to 31 Oct	D. Hunter Mains of Grandhome Woodside Aberdeen Tel: (0224) 723408	
	Monymusk	Salmon Brown trout	11 Feb to 31 Oct Apr-Sept	Grant Arms Hotel, Monymusk, Aberdeenshire. Tel: Monymusk 226	Fly or spinning only.

Water	Location	Species	Season	Permit available from	Other information
Don cont'd	Kemnay	Salmon Brown trout	11 Feb to 11 Oct	F.J.& S.L. Milton, Kemnay House, Kemnay, Aberdeenshire. Tel: Kemnay 2220.	Advance booking essential.
	Kildrummy Fishings	Salmon Brown trout	11 Feb-31 Oct 15 Mar to 6 Oct	T. Hillary, Achnavenie, Kildrummy, Alford Tel: Kildrummy 208	Best April, May, June Approx. 4 mile north bank.
	Strathdon	Salmon Brown trout	11 Feb to 31 Oct	Colquhonnie Hotel, Strathdon, Aberdeenshire. Tel: Strathdon 210	
	Strathdon	Salmon Brown trout	11 Feb to 31 Oct	Glenkindie Arms Hotel, Glenkindie, Strathdon. Tel: Glenkindie 288	
	Kintore	Salmon Brown trout	11 Feb to 31 Oct	Kintore Arms Hotel, Kintore. Tel: Kintore 32216 J. Copeland, Newsagent, 2 Northern Road, Kintore. Tel: Kintore 32210. S.P. Amin Post Office The Square, Kintore. Tel: Kintore 32201	
	Alford	Salmon Brown trout	11 Feb to 31 Oct	Forbes Arms Hotel, Bridge of Alford, Tel: Alford 2108	
	Inverurie	Salmon Sea trout Brown trout	11 Feb to 31 Oct 1 Apr to 30 Sept	J. Duncan, 4 West High St., Inverurie. Tel: Inverurie 20310 P. McPherson, Ironmonger, 49 Market Place, Inverurie. Tel: Inverurie 21363	No worm fishing till 1 May. No natural minnow. Reductions for juveniles and OAPs.
Dulnain	Grantown-on-Spey	Salmon Sea trout Brown trout	11 Feb to 30 Sept 15 Mar to 30 Sept	Strathspey Angling Association, Mortimer's, 61 High Street, Grantown-on-Spey. Tel: Grantown-on-Spey 2684	Visitors resident in Grantown, Cromdale, Duthil, Carrbridge, Dulnain Bridge and Nethybridge areas. 12 miles of river.
Feugh	Feughside	Salmon Brown trout		James Somers & Sons, 40 Thistle Street, Aberdeen. Tel: Aberdeen 633910	
Fiddich	Dufftown	Salmon Sea trout Brown trout	May to Sept	E. & D. Smith, The Square, Dufftown.	Fly or worm.
Findhorn	Findhorn (Estuary)	Sea trout	11 Feb to 6 Oct	Post Office, Findhorn. Kimberley Inn, Findhorn. Crown and Anchor Hotel, Findhorn	Bait, fly, lures. Fly only 1 May-15 Jun.
	Forres	Salmon Sea trout	11 Feb to 30 Sept	J. Mitchell, Tackle Shop, 97b High Street, Forres. Tel: Forres 72936	All visiting anglers must reside in parishes of Forres and Rafford. Fishing times 8 am to 6 pm.
Isla	Huntly	Salmon Sea trout Brown trout	11 Feb to 31 Oct 1 Apr to 6 Oct	G. Manson, 45 Gordon St., Huntly. Tel: Huntly 2482 J. Christie, 27 Duke Street, Huntly. Tel: Huntly 2291	Permit covers Isla, Deveron and Bogie
Livet	Tomintoul	Salmon Sea trout		Richmond Arms Hotel, Tomintoul. Tel: Tomintoul 209	
Lossie	Elgin	Salmon Sea Trout Brown Trout	11 Feb to 15th Oct 15 Mar to 6 Oct	Elgin and District Angling Association, The Tackle Shop, High Street, Elgin.	
Muckle Burn	Forres	Salmon Sea trout	1 Apr to 30 Sept	Tackle Shop, 97b High St., Forres. Tel: Forres 72923	Reductions for juveniles.

Water	Location	Species	Season	Permit available from	Other information
Spey	Aberlour	Salmon Sea trout Brown trout	11 Feb to 30 Sept	J.A.J. Munro, 95 High Street, Aberlour. Tel: Aberlour 220 Lour Hotel, Aberlour, Tel: Aberlour 224. Aberlour Hotel, Aberlour. Tel: Aberlour 287 Dowans Hotel, Aberlour Tel: Aberlour 488	Visitor tickets available from J.A.J. Munro. 3 tickets available in each of village hotels. First fish kept by angler, others sold for village fund. No day tickets on Sat or local holidays.
	Fochabers	Salmon	11 Feb to 30 Sept	Gordon Arms Hotel, Fochabers. Tel: (0343) 820508/9	
	Grantown-on-Spey	Salmon Sea trout Brown trout	11 Feb to 30 Sept 15 Mar to 30 Sept	Strathspey Angling Association, Mortimer's, 61 High Street, Grantown-on-Spey. Tel: Grantown-on-Spey 2684 Palace Hotel, Grantown-on-Spey, Tel: Grantown-on-Spey 2706	7 miles both banks. No prawn. No Sunday fishing. Visitors must resided in Grantown, Cromdale, Dunhill, Carrbridge, Dulnain Bridge and Nethy Bridge.
	Boat of Garten	Salmon Sea trout Brown trout	11 Feb to 30 Sept 15 Mar to 30 Sept	Craigard Hotel, Boat of Garten. Tel: Boat of Garten 206 The Boat Hotel, Boat of Garten. Tel: Boat of Garten 258 Ben-o-Gar, Disher Street, Boat of Garten. Tel: Boat of Garten 372.	River Spey and several trout lochs.
	Nethy Bridge Boat of Garten	Salmon Sea trout Brown trout	11 Feb to 30 Sept	Abernethy Angling Associaton Boat of Garten. Tel: Boat of Ben-o-Gar Stores, Boat of Garten. Tel: 372.	
	Aviemore	Salmon Sea trout Brown trout	11 Feb to 30 Sept	Fisheries Manager, Inverdruie Fisheries, Aviemore. Lynwilg Hotel, Loch Alvie, Aviemore. Tel: Aviemore 810602 Kinrara Estate Office, Grantown-on-Spey.	Four beats available.
	Aviemore	Salmon Sea trout Rainbow trout Brown trout	11 Feb-30 Sept 15 Mar-6 Oct	Osprey Fishing School, The Fishing Centre, Aviemore Tel: Aviemore 810767/810911	Fly fishing or spinning. River Spey, River Feshie and lochs arranged.
		Salmon Sea trout Brown trout	11 Feb to 30 Sept	Alvie Estate Office, Kincraig, by Kingussie. Tel: Kincraig 255 Dalraddy Caravan Park, Aviemore. Tel: Aviemore 810330	Fly fishing or spinning. Permit also covers River Feshie and lochs Alvie and Insh.
	Kingussie	Salmon Sea trout Brown trout	15 Mar to 30 Sept	Badenoch Angling Association, Secretary, Mrs. J. Waller 38 Burnside Avenue, Aviemore. Local tackle shops in Kingussie and Newtonmore.	Spinning allowed when fly fishing applicable.
	Newtonmore	Salmon Sea trout Brown trout	15 Mar to 30 Sept	Badenoch Hotel Newtonmore. Tel: Newtonmore 246	
Truim		Salmon	Apr to Sept	Badenoch Angling Association. J. Dallas, Jeweller, 9 High Street, Kingussie.	
Ugie	Peterhead	Salmon Sea trout Brown trout	11 Feb to 31 Oct	G. Milne, Newsagent, 3 Ugie Road, Peterhead. Dicks Sports, 54 Broad Stret, Fraserburgh. Robertson Sports, 1-3 Kirk St., Peterhead. Tel: Peterhead 72584.	Bag limit – 8 fish per day. Worming only in spates. No spinning (Apr-Aug inc.)
Urie	Inverurie	Salmon Sea trout Trout	11 Feb-31 Oct 1 Apr to 30 Sept	James Duncan (Grocer), 4 West High St., Inverurie. Tel: Inverurie 20310 P. McPherson, Ironmonger 45 Market Place, Inverurie. Tel: Inverurie 21363	No worm fishing until 1 May. No natural minnow at any time.

Please mention this Pastime Publications guide.

Water	Location	Species	Season	Permit available from	Other information
Ythan	Ellon	Salmon Sea trout Brown trout	11 Feb to 31 Oct	Buchan Hotel, Ellon, Aberdeenshire. Tel: Ellon 20208	Machar Pool for hotel guests only, £7 day.
	(Estuary) Newburgh	Salmon Sea trout	11 Feb to 31 Oct	Mrs. Forbes, 3 Lea Cottages, Newburgh. Tel: Newburgh 297	8 boats available. No lead core lines. No more than 2 lures or flies at a time. No live bait.
	Fyvie	Salmon Sea trout	11 Feb to 31 Oct	Fyvie Angling Association. G.A. Joss, Clydesdale Bank Plc, Fyvie, Turriff. Tel: (06516) 233	
	Methlick	Salmon Sea trout	11 Feb to 31 Oct	Haddo House Angling Association, Secretary, Kirton, Methlick, Ellon, Aberdeenshire.	

LOCHS AND RESERVOIRS

Water	Location	Species	Season	Permit available from	Other information
Aboyne Loch	Aboyne	Pike Perch		The Warden, Aboyne Loch Holiday Park. Tel: Aboyne 2244	Fishing parties restricted on Sat, Sun and Wed afternoon.
Loch Alvie	Aviemore	Brown trout	15 Mar to 6 Oct	Lynwilg Hotel, Aviemore. Tel: Aviemore 810602	Three boats.
		Brown trout Pike		Alvie Estate Office, Kincraig, by Kingussie. Tel: Kincraig 255 Dalraddy Caravan Park, Aviemore. Tel: Aviemore 810330	Boat fishing only. Fly fishing or spinning. Permit also covers Rivers Feshie and Spey and Loch Insh.
Avielochan	Aviemore	Rainbow trout Brown trout	Apr to Sept	Mrs. M. McCook, Avielochan, Aviemore. Tel: Aviemore 810450 Mortimer's, 61 High Street, Grantown-on-Spey.	Bank fishing only. Spinning area designated.
Loch of Blairs	Forres	Brown trout Rainbow trout	Easter- mid-Oct	Moray District Council, Department of Recreation, 30-32 High Street, Elgin Tel: Elgin 45121. J. Mitchell, 97b High St Forres. Tel: Forres 72936	Two sessions. Boat fishing. Fly only. Sunday fishing. Four boats available.
Loch Dallas	Boat of Garten	Brown trout Rainbow trout	Apr to Sept	Mortimer's, 61 High Street, Grantown-on-Spey.	Fly fishing only.
Loch Ericht	Dalwhinnie	Brown trout	15 Mar to 6 Oct	Badenoch Angling Association. Loch Ericht Hotel, Dalwhinnie.	
Glen Latterach Reservoir	Elgin	Brown trout	1 Apr to 30 Sept	Dept. of Water Services, Grampian Road, Elgin. Tel: Elgin 41144	
Loch Insh	Kincraig	Brown trout Char	15 Mar to 6 Oct	Loch Insh Watersports Centre, Kincraig, Kingussie. Tel: Kincraig 272	
		Salmon Sea trout Brown trout	11 Feb to 30 Sept	Alvie Estate Office, Kincraig, by Kingussie. Tel: Kincraig 255 Dalraddy Caravan Park, Aviemore. Tel: Aviemore 810330	Boat fishing only. Fly fishing or spinning. Permit also covers Rivers Feshie and Spey and Loch Alvie.
Loch Laggan	Dalwhinnie	Brown trout	15 Mar to 6 Oct	Badenoch Angling Association Local tackle shops in Kingussie and Newtonmore.	
Millbules Loch	Elgin	Brown trout Rainbow trout	Easter- mid-Oct	Moray District Council Department of Recreation, 30-32 High Street, Elgin. Tel: Elgin 45121 Warden at Millbules.	Boat fishing. Fly fishing only. Four boats available.
Loch Mor	Dulnain Bridge	Brown trout Rainbow trout	Apr to Sept	Mortimer's, 61 High Street, Grantown-on-Spey Tel: Grantown-on-Spey 2648	

Water	Location	Species	Season	Permit available from	Other information
Loch Morlich	Aviemore	Brown trout Pike	15 Mar to 30 Sept	The Warden, Campsite, Glenmore Forest Park, Aviemore. Tel: Cairngorm 271	Reductions for children. Spinners and fly only.
Loch Na Bo	Lhanbryde	Brown trout	1 Apr to 30 Sept	Keepers Cottage, Loch Na Bo Tel: Lhanbryde 2215	Fly fishing only.
Loch Saugh	Fettercairn	Brown trout Rainbow trout	15 Mar to 6 Oct	Brechin Angling Club. D.E. Smith, 3 Friendly Park, Brechin. White Heather Inn, Auchenblae. Tel: Auchenblae 305 Ramsay Arms Hotel, Fettercairn. Tel: Fettercairn 334 J & J Coghill, Newsagents, High St, Brechin. W. Phillips, Tackle, High St, Montrose.	
Rothiemurchus Estate and Inverdruie Fisheries (Lochs Pityoulish, An Eilean & Morlich)	Aviemore	Sea trout Rainbow trout Brown trout Pike	Check with Manager Aviemore	Inverdruie Fisheries Coylum Bridge. Aviemore.	
Spey Dam	Laggan	Brown trout	1 Apr to 30 Sept	Badenoch Angling Association, A. McDonald, 6 Gergask Avenue, Laggan.	Boat available.
Loch Vas	Aviemore	Brown trout Rainbow trout	Apr to Sept	Mortimer's, 61 High Street, Grantown-on-Spey. Tel: Grantown-on-Spey 2648	Boat fishing only.

NORTH EAST AND SPEY VALLEY

Sea Angling

Further information from: The Harbour Master, Nairn.

Season for fishing: Migratory fish season, October. Best months – late July, early August.

Moray Firth
The Moray Firth has always been famous for its fishing grounds and most of the towns along the south coastline depend largely on commercial fishing for their prosperity; cod, haddock, flatfish of many kings, pollack, coalfish and mackerel being landed.

Nairn Nairn is set on the pleasant coastal plain bordering the southern shore of the Moray Firth. There is a beautiful stretch of sands to the east. Most fishing is done from two small piers at the entrance to the tidal harbour.
Types of fish: Mackerel, small coalfish, pollack, dab and cod.
Boats: One or two, privately owned, will often take a passenger out. Enquiries should be made at the harbour.
Tackle: P. Fraser, 41 High Street, Nairn. Harbour Street General Store, Harbour Street.
Bait: Lugworm available on the beach at low water. Mackerel etc. mostly taken on flies.

Lossiemouth and Garmouth
Lossiemouth, a small, prosperous town, is a unique combination of white fish centre, seaside, shops and hotels. The angler will find unlimited sport of a kind probably new to him, for off the east and west beaches sea trout and finnock abound, and spinning for these into the sea, especially into the breakers, is a magnificent sport.
Types of fish: Sea trout, conger from the pier, coalfish, flatfish, 6½ miles of shore fishing. Haddock, cod, plaice and coalfish from boats. Shore fishing – sea trout between harbour and Boar's Head Rock and at the old cement works Garmouth.
Tackle: Angling Centre, Moss Street, Elgin; The Tackle Shop, High Street, Elgin.
Bait: Lugworm on the west beacn and the harbour at low water. Also plenty of mussels to be collected. Spinners, Pirks.
Permits: Angling Centre, Moss Street, Elgin.

Buckie
Buckie is a major commercial fishing port on the eastern side of Spey Bay. It has become increasingly popular over the last few years as a tourist area and is well supplied with hotels, golf courses and caravan sites. It offers a varied coastline in the form of sandy beaches and quite spectacular rugged cliff formations.
Types of fish: Cod, coalfish, conger, pollack, mackerel, haddock, whiting, flatfish.
Tackle: Slater Sports, 5 High Street, Buckie.
Bait: Lugworm, ragworm, mussels, cockles and crabs freely available along the shoreline eastwards.
Season for fishing: April-October. Winter months best for cod.

Portknockie
Portknockie is a quaint little fishing village to the west of Cullen Bay. The small harbour is used by two small mackerel boats.

Types of fish: Excellent rock fishing here for cod, coalfish, and some mackerel from the piers. Good boat fishing for haddock, ling and gurnard.

Boats: There are no boats for hire as such, although it is possible to get out in two small (18ft) mackerel boats.

Tackle: Wood, General Dealer, has a small supply.

Bait: Lugworm and mussels in the harbour at low water.

Further information from: Moray District Council, Tourist Information Centre, 17 High Street, Elgin, IV30 1EG will provide information for sea anglers.

Portsoy

One of the numerous small towns that line the Banffshire coast. It is a former seaport but the harbour is silting up.

Types of fish: Coalfish and mackerel from the small pier and some good rock fishing east and west for cod. From boats, mackerel, cod, haddock, plaice, coalfish and dab.

Tackle: Peter Lyon, 36 Low Street, Banff.

Bait: Some lugworm at low water mark.

Stonehaven

Stonehaven is a holiday resort 15 miles south of Aberdeen on main road and rail routes. Magnificent catches of cod and haddock are taken regularly by boat. Anglers obtain great co-operation from angling boat skippers and local professional fishermen. On either side of Stonehaven there are good rock fishing marks which should be approached with care

especially during strong easterly winds.

Types of fish: Cod, haddock, pollack, coalfish, flounder, catfish and mackerel from the shore. Cod, haddock, coalfish, pollack, ling, catfish, plaice and other flatfish, ballan wrasse, cuckoo wrasse, whiting and Norway haddock from boats.

Boats: Boats may be available from harbour.

Tackle: Available from David's, Market Square, Stonehaven.

Bait: Mussels, lugworm and other bait available in the area or contact Mrs E. Cargill, 16 King Street, Stonehaven.

Season for fishing: All year.

Further information from: Information Centre, The Square. Tel: Stonehaven (0569) 62806 Easter-September.

Gardenstown and Crovie

These are traditional fishing villages. Mackerel are plentiful, June-September. Anglers would be well advised to follow local boats which are fishing commercially.

Types of fish: From shore – coalfish, pollack, flatfish, conger. From boats – mackerel, cod, haddock, flounder, plaice, conger, dab, catfish, gurnard and ling.

Bait: Available on beach, but local people prefer to use flies.

Fraserburgh

Situated on the north-east shoulder of Scotland, Fraserburgh has the Moray Firth to the west and north and the North Sea to the east. The Burgh was primarily given over to the herring and white fish industry, but has

developed as a holiday resort with the decline of commercial fishing in the North Sea. Tickets and permits for game fishing from the beaches can be had at Weelies, Grocer, College Bounds.

Types of fish: Shore – cod, coalfish and mackerel. Boat – as shore.

Tackle: Available from Caledonian Fish Co., Shore Street. P. & J. Johnstone, Balclava Sports Shop, Charlotte Street, Fraserburgh.

Bait: Mussels and lugworm can be dug from the beach.

Season for fishing: May- October.

Peterhead

Peterhead is an important fishing port situated north of Buchan Ness, the most easterly point of Scotland. Excellent breakwaters, 1900ft and 2800ft long, are the main shore marks for holiday anglers. However passengers are at times taken out by private boats.

Types of fish: From the pier – mackerel, coalfish, dab and cod. From boats – cod, haddock, dabs, ling, coalfish and mackerel.

Boats: There are a number of privately owned boats which will sometimes take out passengers. Enquiries should be made at the harbour.

Tackle: Available from the Sports Shop, 71 Marischal Street, Peterhead; Robertsons Sports, 1 Kirk Street, Peterhead.

Bait: Lugworm can be dug from shore at low water while mussels can be gathered from the rocks.

Further information from: Harbour Office, West Pier, Peterhead. Tel: Peterhead 4281.

GREAT GLEN and SKYE

RIVERS AND LOCHS

Constituent Area Tourist Boards

Fort William and Lochaber Tourist Board
Area Tourist Officer
Fort William and Lochaber Tourist Board, Travel Centre, Fort William
Inverness-shire PH33 6AN
Tel: Fort William (0397) 3781

Isle of Skye and South West Ross Tourist Board
Area Tourist Officer
Isle of Skye and South West Ross Tourist Board
Tourist Information Centre, Portree
Isle of Skye IV51 9BZ
Tel: Portree (0478) 2137

Inverness, Loch Ness and Nairn Tourist Board
Area Tourist Officer
Inverness, Loch Ness and Nairn Tourist Board
23 Church Street
Inverness IV1 1EZ
Tel: Inverness (0463) 234353

RIVER PURIFICATION BOARD
HIGHLAND RIVER PURIFICATION BOARD
Strathpeffer Road
Dingwall IV15 9QY
Tel: Dingwall 62021

RIVERS

Water	Location	Species	Season	Permit available from	Other information
Ailort	Arisaig	Salmon Sea trout	11 Feb to 31 Oct	Lochailort Inn, Lochailort, Inverness-shire.	
Broadford	Skye	Salmon Sea trout	11 Feb to 31 Oct	Broadford Hotel, Broadford, Isle of Skye.	
Coe	Glencoe	Salmon Sea trout	11 Feb to 31 Oct	Forestry Commission, Ballachulish. Warden, Glencoe Campsite, National Trust for Scotland, Achnambeithach Farm, Glencoe.	
Croe		Salmon Sea trout	11 Feb to 31 Oct	National Trust for Scotland. Morvich Farm, Inverinate.	
Enrick	Drumna drochit	Salmon Brown trout	15 Jan-15 Oct 15 Mar-6 Oct	Kilmartin Hall, Glenurquhart, Inverness-shire. Tel: Glenurquhart 269	
Farrar	Struy	Salmon	11 Feb-15 Oct	Glen Affric Hotel, Tel: Cannich 214	
Garry	Invergarry	Salmon Brown trout	15 Jan to 15 Oct 15 Mar-6 Oct	Rod & Gun Shop, Station Square, Fort William. Garry Gualach Adventure Centre, Invergarry. Tel: Tomdoun 230	
Glass	Cannich	Salmon	11 Feb to 15 Oct	Glen Affric Hotel, Cannich Tel: Cannich 214	
Moriston	Glen- Moriston Estuary Beat Dundreggan Combined Beats	Salmon Brown trout-	15 Jan-30 Sept Spring Jun onwards Mar to Sept Sept	Glenmoriston Estate Office, Glenmoriston, nr Inverness. Tel: Glenmoriston (0320) 51202	Estate Office only. Discounts for hotel and holiday home guests.
Nairn	Nairn	Salmon Sea trout Brown trout	11 Feb to 30 Sept 15 Mar to 6 Oct	Nairn Angling Association. P. Fraser, High St., Nairn. Clava Lodge Hotel, Culloden Moor Meallmore Lodge Hotel, Daviot.	
Ness	Inverness	Salmon	15 Jan to 15 Oct	Inverness Angling Club, John Graham, 71 Castle Street, Inverness. Tel: Inverness 33178	No day permits on Saturdays.
Ose	Skye	Salmon Sea trout	11 Feb to 31 Oct	Ullinish Lodge Hotel Struan, Isle of Skye. Tel: Struan 214	
Scaddle	Ardgour	Salmon Sea trout	2 Jun to 30 Sept	Ardgour Hotel, Ardgour by Fort William Tel: (08555) 225	
Sligachan	Skye	Salmon Sea trout	end Jun early Oct	Sligachan Hotel, Sligachan, Isle of Skye. Tel: Sligachan 204	
Snizort	Skye	Salmon Sea trout Brown trout	15 Mar to 31 Oct	Skeabost House Hotel, Skeabost, Isle of Skye. Tel: Skeabost Bridge 202	
Spean	Spean Bridge	Salmon Sea trout Brown trout	11 Feb to 31 Oct	Spean Bridge Hotel, Spean Bridge, Inverness-shire Tel: Spean Bridge 250	

LOCHS

Water	Location	Species	Season	Permit available from	Other information
Loch Arkaig	Fort William	Sea trout Brown trout Salmon (occasional) Pike	Mar-Oct	Locheil Estate Fishings, West Highland Estates Office, 33 High St., Fort William. Tel: Fort William 2433 Tel: Gairlochy 217	

Please mention this Pastime Publications guide.

Water	Location	Species	Season	Permit available from	Other information
Ardtornish Estate Waters	Morvern	Salmon Sea trout Brown trout	Apr-Oct	Ardtornish Estate Office, Morvern, by Oban, Argyll. Tel: (096 784) 288	Four boats for hire.
Balmacara Estate Lochs	Kyle of Lochalsh	Brown trout	Apr-Oct	Balmacara Hotel, by Kyle of Lochalsh, Wester Ross. Tel: (059 986) 283	No Sunday fishing.
Loch Beannachran	Glen Strathfarrar	Brown trout	15 Mar-6 Oct	Glen Affric Hotel Cannich Tel: Cannich 214	
Loch Benevean (Bheinn a' Mheadhoin)	Cannich	Brown trout	15 Mar-6 Oct	J. Graham & Co., 71 Castle Street, Inverness. Tel: Inverness 331 78 Glen Affric Hotel, Cannich Tel: Cannich 214	Fly fishing only.
Loch Cluanie	Glen-moriston	Brown trout Pike	15 Mar to 6 Oct	Dochfour Estate Office, Dochgarroch, by Inverness. Tel: Dochgarroch 218	One boat Two rods per boat.
Lochs Connan (Duagraich & Ravag)	Skye	Brown trout	15 Mar to 6 Oct	Ullinish Lodge Hotel, Struan, Isle of Skye Tel: Struan 214	Two boats. Residents only
Loch Dochfour	Inverness	Brown trout	15 Mar to 6 Oct	Dochfour Estate Office, Dochgarroch, by Inverness Tel: Dochgarroch 218	No Sunday fishing. Bank fishing only.
Loch Eilt (and hill lochs)	Glenfinnan	Salmon Sea trout Brown trout		Lochailort Inn, Lochailort, Inverness-shire Tel: Lochailort 208	
Loch Garry (and Loch Inchlaggan)	Invergarry	Brown trout Rainbow trout	May-Sept	Garry Gualach Adventure Centre, Invergarry, Inverness-shire. Tel: Tomdoun 230 Tomdoun Hotel, Invergarry. Tel: Tomdoun 218	
Glenmoriston hill lochs	Glen-moriston	Brown trout	1 May to 11 Aug	Glenmoriston Estate Office, Glenmoriston, Inverness-shire. Tel: Glenmoriston 51202	Fly fishing only. Sunday fishing permitted.
Loch Lochy	Fort William	Brown trout	15 Mar to 6 Oct	None required.	
Loch Loyne	Glen-moriston	Brown trout Pike	15 Mar to 6 Oct	Cluanie Hotel, Glenmoriston, Inverness-shire. Tel: (0320) 40238	
Loch Monar	Inverness-shire	Brown trout	15 Mar to 6 Oct	Glen Affric Hotel, Cannich Tel: Cannich 214	
Loch Morar (and hill lochs	Mallaig	Salmon Sea trout Brown trout	11 Feb to 1 Nov 15 Mar to 6 Oct	Morar Fishings, Allt an Loin, Morar. Tel: Mallaig 2388 Morar Motors, Morar.	Eight boats available. Designated areas for fly fishing only. Spinning & trouting outwith fly area.
				Tackle Shop, Mallaig Morar Hotel, Morar	Three boats available.
Loch Mullardoch	Cannich	Brown trout	15 Mar to 6 Oct	Glen Affric Hotel, Cannich Tel: (04565) 214	
Loch Ness	Glen-moriston	Salmon Brown trout	15 Jan to Oct	Glen Moriston Estate Office, Glenmoriston, by Inverness Tel: (0320) 51202	25% discount for holiday and hotel guests.
	Foyers	Salmon Brown trout	15 Jan to Oct	Foyers Hotel, Foyers, Inverness-shire Tel: Gorthleck 216	

Water	Location	Species	Season	Permit available from	Other information
Loch Oich	Inver-garry	Salmon	15 Jan to Oct	Rod and Gunshop Fort William	
		Trout	15 Mar-6 Oct		
Loch Quoich	Tomdoun	Brown trout	15 Mar to 6 Oct	Tomdoun Hotel, Invergarry. Tel: (08092) 218 Lovat Arms Hotel, Fort Augustus.	
Loch Ruthven	Foyers	Brown trout	15 Mar to 6 Oct	Grouse and Trout Hotel Flichty, Inverness-shire. Tel: (08083) 314	Fly fishing only.
		Brown trout	Apr-Sep	J. Graham & Co. 71 Castle Street, Inverness Tel: Inverness 33178	Fly fishing only.
Loch Shiel	Acharacle	Salmon Sea trout Brown trout	May-Sept	D. Macaulay, Dalilea Farm, Acharacle, Tel: (096 785) 253	Four boats available.
	Glenfinnan		Apr-Oct	Stage House Inn, Glenfinnan, Inverness-shire. Tel: (039 783) 246	Seven boats available
	Glenfinnan			Glenfinnan House Hotel, Glenfinnan. Tel: (039 783) 235	Three boats available.
Storr Lochs (and other hill lochs)	North Skye	Brown trout	15 Mar to 6 Oct	Portree Angling Association. Masonic Buildings, Portree. Isle of Skye.	
South Skye Fishings	South Skye	Sea trout Brown trout	Apr-Oct	Fearann Eilean Iarmain, Isle of Skye. Tel: Isle of Ornsay (04713) 266 Telex 75252 Iarmain G	Boats by arrangement. No Sunday fishing.
Tomich hill lochs	Tomich	Brown trout	15 Mar to 6 Oct	Glen Affric Hotel Cannich Tel: Cannich 214	
Whitebridge Lochs (Knockie & Killin)	White-bridge	Brown trout	Mar-Oct	Whitebridge Hotel, Stratherrick, Gorthleck, Inverness-shire. Tel: Gorthleck 226	

GREAT GLEN AND ISLE OF SKYE

Sea Angling

Isle of Eigg
The Isle of Eigg lies 5m SW of Skye.
Types of fish: Pollack, conger, spurdog, skate, cod, mackerel.
Boats: Available from Eigg Estate, Estate Office, Isle of Eigg, Inverness-shire.
Tackle: As boats.
Bait: Lugworm, ragworm, shellfish, mackerel, available from Estate Office.
Season for fishing: Summer-Autumn.

Isle of Skye
The many lochs and bays around the beautiful Isle of Skye provide ideal facilities for sea angling. There is a great variety of fish, most of which can be caught from the shore because of the deep water found close inshore off rocky shores and headlands. Local residents are very knowledgeable about fishing in their own area. Loch Snizort has now been found to hold a number of large common skate and anglers could well contact these during a session there.

Isle of Skye (Portree)
Portree, the capital of Skye, is situated half way up the east coast of the island. There is a very good harbour where a considerable number of small craft are available for private hire. There are good fishing marks in and round the harbour. Ample free anchorage and berthing available for visiting craft. Slipping, re-fuelling and watering facilities are easily accessible.

Types of fish: Cod, haddock, whiting, coalfish, pollack and mackerel.
Boats: For information on boats contact: Tourist Information Centre, Meall House, Portree. Tel: (0478) 2137. Greshornish House Hotel, Edinbane, by Portree. Tel: (047082) 266, has one boat available.
Bait: Unlimited mussels and cockles available in tidal area of Portree Bay.
Tackle: Portree Electrical Stores, Wentworth Street, Portree. A. McKenzie, The Harbour Shop, Portree. Skeabost House Hotel, Skeabost, by Portree. Tel: Skeabost Bridge (047032) 202.
Season for fishing: May-September.
Further information from: Isle of Skye & South West Ross Tourist Board, Tourist Information Centre, Portree (0478) 2137.

Isle of Skye (Camastianavaig by Portree)

To reach this sheltered bay which lies 4 miles south east of Portree, turn off the A850 to Braes. Although local tactics are the use of feathers, bottom fishing with trace or paternoster has yielded heavy bags with skate of 62½lbs, cod 6lbs, whiting 3lbs, haddock 3lbs, spurdog 12lbs, gurnard 2lbs, pollacks 12lbs, coalfish 14lbs, all from boats.

Types of fish: Shore – coalfish, pollack, wrasse and mackerel. Boat – cod, haddock and spurdog.

Tackle: Obtainable at Portree.

Bait: Lugworm at Broadford Bay and Balmeanac Bay. Cockles and mussels at Portree Loch.

Season for fishing: June- October.

Isle of Skye (Uig)

Uig, a picturesque village amidst some of the finest scenery in the north west, has excellent fishing on its doorstep. Loch Snizort and small islands at its entrance, together with the Ascrib Islands opposite, are well worth fishing. Fishing can be arranged as far round the coast as Score Bay, known to some ring net fishermen as the 'Golden Mile'.

Types of fish: Shore – coalfish, mackerel, pollack, conger and dogfish. Boat – coalfish, mackerel, pollack, conger, whiting, haddock, dogfish, flatfish, skate, cod and gurnard.

Boats: Available locally at Uig, Waternish and Kilmuir.

Season for fishing: May-September.

Isle of Skye (Skeabost Bridge)

Skeabost Bridge is situated 5 miles from Portree at the south east end of Loch Snizort.

Types of fish: There is no shore fishing but many types of sea fish can be caught from boats.

Boats: Available from Skeabost House Hotel. Tel: Skeabost Bridge (047 032) 202.

Tackle: Tackle available for hire or sale from the Skeabost House Hotel.

Bait: Available locally.

Season for fishing: July- October.

Isle of Skye (Glendale by Dunvegan)

Glendale Estate is owned by the crofters of Glendale and stretches from Dunvegan Loch, southside, to the Maidens beyond Loch Bracadale and Neist Point. The seas around the area abound in a great variety of sea fish. There is now a sea angling club in this area which covers Loch Bay, Loch Dunvegan, Loch Poolteil and Loch Bracadale. The Club Secretary can advise names and numbers of local boatmen. Strong gear is recommended and fishing is usually for one tide of 5-6 hours.

Types of fish: Shore fishing at Poolteil Pier, Glendale and Neist Point Lighthouse. All types of fish from boats.

Further information from: L. Shurmer, 13 Skinidin, by Dunvegan, Skye. Tel: Dunvegan 380.

Kyle of Lochalsh

The village of Kyle, on the mainland opposite Kyleakin on the Isle of Skye, is a railhead and a car ferry link with Skye and the Hebrides.

Types of fish: Conger, coalfish, pollack and whiting from the harbour. Boat – pollack, cod, coalfish, mackerel and whiting.

Tackle: Available from John MacLennan & Co., Marine Stores, Kyle of Lochalsh.

Bait: Mussels from Fishery Pier and clams and cockles at spring tides.

Season for fishing: June-September.

Further information from: Isle of Skye & South West Ross Tourist Board, Tourist Information Centre, Kyle of Lochalsh. Tel: (0599) 4276.

NORTH SCOTLAND — RIVERS AND LOCHS

Constituent Area Tourist Boards

Caithness Tourist Organisation
Area Tourist Officer
Caithness Tourist Organisation
Whitechapel Road, Wick
Caithness KW1 4EA
Tel: Wick (0955) 2596/2145

Ross and Cromarty Tourist Board
Area Tourist Officer
Ross and Cromarty Tourist Board
Information Centre, North Kessock
Inverness IV1 1XB
Tel: Kessock (0463 73) 505

Sutherland Tourist Board
Area Tourist Officer
Sutherland Tourist Board
The Square, Dornoch
Sutherland IV25 3SD
Tel: Dornoch (0862) 810400

RIVER PURIFICATION BOARD

HIGHLAND RIVER PURIFICATION BOARD
Strathpeffer Road
Dingwall IV15 9QY
Tel: Dingwall 62021

RIVERS

Water	Location	Species	Season	Permit available from	Other information
Alness	Alness	Salmon Sea trout	11 Feb to 31 Oct	Coul House Hotel, Contin by Strathpeffer, Ross-shire Tel: Strathpeffer 21487	Six boats available on rotation. Four rods per boat. Fly fishing only.
Badachro	Gairloch	Salmon		Shieldaig Lodge Hotel, Gairloch. Tel: Badachro 250	

Water	Location	Species	Season	Permit available from	Other information
Balgy	Torridon	Salmon Sea trout	Easter– 15 Oct	Loch Torridon Hotel, Torridon by Achnasheen, Ross-shire Tel: Torridon 242	
Blackwater **(Ross-shire)**	Strath- peffer	Salmon Sea trout		Craigdarroch Lodge Hotel, Contin, by Strathpeffer, Ross-shire Tel: Strathpeffer 21265	
Brora	Brora	Sea trout Finnock Brown trout	1 Jun ·to 15 oct	Three-quarter mile of tidal water No permit required.	Fly or worm fishing only. No Spinning tackle.
Conon	Strath- peffer	Salmon Sea trout	26 Jan to 30 Sept	Craigdarroch Lodge Hotel, Contin, by Strathpeffer, Ross-shire. Tel: Strathpeffer 21265 Loch Achonochie Angling Club. (Under review)	
	Contin·	Salmon Sea trout	26 Jan to 30 Sept	Coul House Hotel, Contin by Strathpeffer Ross-shire Tel: Strathpeffer 21487	Lower Middle and Upper Brahan and Coul Water Beats available at various times.
	Dingwall	Sea trout		Dingwall and District Angling Club	Fly only. Breast waders prohibited.
Dionard	Durness	Salmon Sea trout		Cape Wrath Hotel, Durness.	
Halladale	Forsinard	Salmon	1 May to 30 Sept	Forsinard Hotel, Forsinard, Sutherland Tel: Halladale 221	
Helmsdale	Helmsdale	Salmon	11 Jan to 31 Oct	A Jappy, Dunrobin Street Helmsdale Tel: (04312) 654.	Association Beat
Kerry	Gairloch	Salmon Sea trout Brown trout		Creag Mor Hotel, Charleston Gairloch, Ross-shire Tel: (0445) 2068	
Kirkaig	Lochinver	Salmon	1 May to 15 Oct	Culag Hotel, Lochinver, Sutherland Tel: Lochinver 209/255	
Kyle of **Sutherland**	Bonar Bridge	Brown trout Sea trout Salmon		Bonar Bridge Angling Club, Secretary, W. Shannon Tel: Edderton (086282) 288 River Boats as available.	
Meig	Strathconon	Brown trout	1 May to 30 Sept	East Lodge Hotel & Inn Strathconon. Tel: Strathconon 222 River Beats as available	
Mudale	Altnaharra	Salmon Sea trout	12 Jan to 30 Sept	Charles McLaren Angling Centre, Altnaharra, Sutherland Tel: (054 981) 225	Angling instruction available
Naver	Bettyhill	Salmon	12 Jan– 30 Sept	Bettyhill Hotel Bettyhill, Sutherland Tel: Bettyhill 202.	
Oykel	Sutherland	Salmon Sea trout	11 Jan to 30 Sept	Culag Hotel, Lochinver tel: Lochinver 209/255 Renton Finlayson Estates Office, Bonar Bridge, Inveroykel Lodge Hotel Strathoykel by Argay Sutherland. Tel: Rosehall 200	
Polly	Ullapool	Salmon Sea trout Brown trout	May-Sept	Mrs. A. MacLeod, Inverpolly Ullapool, Ross-shire Tel: Lochinver 482	Fly fishing only No Sunday fishing
Thurso	Thurso	Salmon	11 Jan to 5 Oct	Thurso Fisheries Ltd, Thurso East, Thurso Tel: (0847) 63134.	Fly fishing only.

Water	Location	Species	Season	Permit available from	Other information
Torridon	Torridon	Salmon Sea trout	1 Apr to 30 Sept	Tigh An Eilean Hotel, Shieldaig, Strathcarron. Tel: 05205 251	Fly only.
Ullapool	Ullapool	Salmon Sea trout Brown trout	May to 30 Sept	Loch Broom Hardwear Shop, Ullapool. Tel: (0854) 2356	
Wick	Wick	Salmon Sea trout	11 Feb to 31 Oct	Wick Angling Association 80 Wick Sports Shop High Street Wick	

LOCHS

Water	Location	Species	Season	Permit available from	Other information
Loch Achall	Ullapool	Salmon Sea trout Brown trout	1 Apr to 20 Sept	Loch Broom Hardwear Shop, Ullapool. Tel: (0854) 2356	Boat and bank fishing.
Loch Achonochie	Strathpeffer	Salmon Brown trout	1 Apr to 30 Sept	Loch Achonochie Angling Club	
Loch Achility	Strathpeffer	Brown trout	15 Mar to 6 Oct	Craigdarroch Lodge Hotel, Contin	
Assynt Angling Club (numerous hill lochs)	Lochinver	Brown trout	15 Mar to 6 Oct	Assynt Angling Club, Tourist Information Office, Lochinver. Tel: (05714) 330 and local hotels and shops.	No Sunday fishing. No dogs. Boats on some lochs. Spinning restricted to certain lochs.
Loch Assynt (and Lochs Awe, Gillaroo, Grugach Borralam Cam Letteressie Loch)	Inchnadamph	Salmon Brown trout	1 Apr-15 Oct 1 Apr to 6 Oct	Inchnadamph Hotel, Inchnadamph, Sutherland Tel: (05712) 202	No Sunday fishing Boats available
Loch A'chroisg	Achnasheen	Pike Perch		Ledgowan Lodge Hotel Achnasheen, Ross-shire Tel: Achnasheen 252.	Free to Residents.
Loch Badachro (and numerous other lochs)	Gairloch	Salmon Brown trout	Apr-Oct	Shieldaig Lodge Hotel Gairloch, Ross & Cromarty. Tel: Badachro 250	No Sunday fishing. Fly only. Nine boats.
Loch Badanloch (and other hill lochs)	Kinbrace	Brown trout	15 Mar to 6 Oct	Richard McNicol, Badanloch, Kinbrace, Sutherland. Tel: Kinbrace 232 Navidale House Hotel, Helmsdale, Sutherland Tel: Helmsdale 256.	Five boats.
Balmacara hill lochs	Kyle of Lochalsh	Brown trout	Apr-Oct	Balmacara Hotel, Kyle of Lochalsh Tel: Kyle of Lochalsh 283.	
Loch Beannachairan	Strath-conon	Brown trout	1 May to 30 Sept	East Lodge Hotel & Inn Strathconon, Ross-shire Tel: (099 77) 22	Restrictions on spinning. No Sunday fishing.
Loch Beannachan	Lairg	Brown trout	1 May to 30 Sept	Sutherland Arms Hotel, Lairg Sutherland. Tel: Lairg 2291	
Bettyhill hill lochs (Loch Meadie and others)	Bettyhill	Brown trout	Mar-Jul	Bettyhill Hotel, Bettyhill, Sutherland Tel: Bettyhill 202	
Loch Brora	Brora	Salmon Sea trout Brown trout	1 May to 15 Oct	Estate Office, Gordonbush Brora, Sutherland Tel: Brora 323 Rob Wilson, Fountain Square,	

Water	Location	Species	Season	Permit available from	Other information
				Brora, Sutherland Tel: Brora 373 See under 'Golspie Angling Club Waters'.	
Loch Borralie	Durness	Brown trout		Cape Wrath Hotel, Keoldale, by Lairg, Sutherland. Tel: (097181) 274.	
Loch Caladail	Durness	Brown trout		Cape Wrath Hotel, Keoldale, by Lairg, Sutherland. Tel: (097181) 274.	
Cape Wrath hill lochs (30 plus)	Durness	Brown trout		Cape Wrath Hotel. Keoldale by Lairg, Sutherland Tel: (037181) 274	
Loch Calder	Thurso	Brown trout	15 Mar-6 Oct	None required	All legal methods
Loch Craggie	Tongue	Brown trout		Ben Loyal Hotel, Tongue Tel: Tongue 216. Tongue Hotel, Tongue. Tel: Tongue 206.	
Loch Craggie (and Loch Ailsh)	Rosehall	Sea trout Brown trout Rainbow trout		Oykel Bridge Hotel, Rosehall, Sutherland. Tel: Rosehall 218.	
Loch Culag (Fionn Loch and numerous others)	Lochinver	Brown trout Rainbow trout	15 Mar to 6 Oct	Culag Hotel, Lochinver Tel: Lochinver 209/255	
Loch Damph	Loch Torridon	Brown trout	1 Apr to Oct	Tigh An Eilean Hotel, Shieldaig, Strathcarron. Tel: 05205 251	One boat.
Dornoch & District Angling Assoc. (6 lochs)	Dornoch	Brown trout	15 Mar to 6 Oct	Dornoch & District Angling Association William A. MacDonald, Castle Street, Dornoch. Tel: Dornoch 801301	No Sunday fishing. Fly fishing only.
Drumbeg hill lochs (20 lochs)	Assynt	Brown trout	Apr-Sept	Drumbeg Hotel, Assynt, by Lairg, Sutherland Tel: Assynt 236	Seven boats available No Sunday fishing. Fly fishing only.
Loch Fannich	Achnasheen	Brown trout	15 Mar to 6 Oct	Strathgarve Lodge Hotel, Garve, Ross-shire Tel: Garve 204	
Fionn Loch	Gairloch	Salmon Brown trout		Creag Mor Hotel Gairloch, Ross-shire Tel: Gairloch 2068	Fly only for salmon and sea trout.
Forsinard Lochs (Loch Sletill and many others)	Forsinard	Brown trout	1 May to 30 Sept	Forsinard Hotel, Forsinard, Sutherland Tel: Halladale 221	Fly fishing only.
Loch Garve	Garve	Brown trout		Strathgarve Lodge Hotel, Garve, Ross-shire. Tel: Garve 204.	
Loch Glasgarnock	Garve	Brown trout		Altguish Inn, Aultguish, Ross-shire. Tel: (09975) 254	
Golspie Angling Club waters (Loch Brora Loch Lundie Loch Horn)	Fly fishing only. Bank and boat fishing.	Salmon Sea trout Brown trout	15 Mar to 15 Oct	Golspie Angling Club, Lindsay & Co. Main St. Golspie. Tel: (04083) 212.	Fly fishing only. Bank and boat fishing.
Loch Kernsary (Tournaig Goose Ghiuragarstidh)	Gairloch	Brown trout	15 Mar to 6 Oct	National Trust for Scotland Inverewe Visitor Centre, Poolewe, Ross-shire Tel: (044586) 229.	
Leckmelm Hill Lochs	Ullapool	Brown trout	May to Sept	Leckmelm Holiday Cottagaes, Leckmelm, Ullapool Tel: (0854) 2471.	Bank fishing only. No Sunday fishing.

Water	Location	Species	Season	Permit available from	Other information
Loch Loyal	Tongue	Brown trout		Ben Loyal Hotel, Tongue, Tel: (08005) 216.	
	Altnaharra by Lairg	Brown trout		Charles McLaren Angling Centre Altnaharra by Lairg. Tel: (054981) 225	Angling Instruction available boats on some lochs. Caravan accommodation.
Loch Maree	Ross-shire	Salmon Sea trout Brown trout	May-Oct	Loch Maree Hotel, Achnasheen, Tel: Loch Maree 200 Shieldaig Lodge Hotel, Gairloch Tel: Badachro 250. Kinlochewe Hotel, Kinlochewe Tel: Kinlochewe 253.	Several boats. One boat. Four boats.
Loch Meadie	Altnaharra by Lairg	Brown trout		Charles McLaren Angling Centre, Altnaharra, by Lairg Tel: (054 981) 225.	Angling instruction available Boats on some lochs. Caravan accommodation.
Loch Meig	Strath-peffer	Brown trout	1 Jun to 30 Sept	Loch Achonochie Angling Club East Lodge Hotel, Strathconon. Tel: Strathconon 222	
Melvich hill lochs (Loch Akran and others)	Melvich	Brown trout	Jun-Sept	Melvich Hotel, Melvich by Thurso, Caithness. Tel: Melvich 206.	Eight Boats available. Fly fishing only.
Loch Merkland	Lairg	Brown trout		Overscaig Hotel, Overscaig, by Lairg, Sutherland Tel: Merkland 203.	Boats and ghillies available.
Loch More	by Lairg	Salmon Sea trout Brown trout		Wetsminster Estate Office, Achfary, by Lairg, Sutherland. Tel: Lochmore 221.	Self catering accommodation available.
Loch Morie	Head of River Alness	Brown trout Arctic Char	15 Mar- 6 Oct	Coul House Hotel Contin, by Strathpeffer, Ross-shire Tel: Strathpeffer 21487. Boat available.	
Scourie Lochs (over 200 available)	Scourie	Salmon Sea trout Brown trout	1 Jul-15 Oct 1 May-30 Sept	Scourie Hotel, Scourie by Lairg, Sutherland Tel: Scourie 2396.	Twelve boats available No Sunday fishing. Fly fishing only.
Loch Shin	Lairg	Brown trout	30 Apr to 30 Sept	Lairg Angling Club, J.M. Ross, Secretary, Post Office, House, Lairg, Sutherland Tel: Lairg 2010 Local Tackle Shop club warden at boathouse	Note: Permits not issued at Post Office, Nine boats available with outboards. No booking for half days. Advance bookings. Tel: Lairg 2010 or Lairg 2025. Up to three rods per boat.
Loch Sionascaig (and other lochs)	Ullapool	Brown trout		Inverpolly Estate Office, Inverpolly Ullapool Tel: Lochinver 252.	
Loch Stack	by Lairg	Salmon Sea trout Brown trout		Westminster Estate Office Archfary, Lairg, Sutherland. Tel: (097 184) 221.	Self catering accommodation available.
Tongue Lochs (Several hill lochs)	Tongue	Brown trout	15 Mar to 6 Oct	Ben Loyal Hotel, Tongue Tel: Tongue 216 Tongue Hotel, Tongue Tel: Tongue 206.	
Loch St Johns	Dunnet	Brown trout	15 Mar to 6 Oct	Northern Sands Hotel, Dunnet, Caithness.	Two boats. Two session 8.30am to 6pm 6pm to dusk Fly fishing only.
Ulbster Estates Lochs (Ten hill lochs)	Halkirk	Brown trout	15 Mar to 6 Oct	Ulbster Arms Hotel, Halkirk, Cathness. Tel: Halkirk 206.	No Sunday fishing. Fly fishing only. One boat on each of eight lochs.

NORTH SCOTLAND

Sea Angling

Gairloch

Gairloch Bay is very popular with sea anglers. There is good fishing in this lovely sea loch, especially around Longa Island which lies near the entrance to the Loch.
Tackle: Available from Wild Cat, Achtercairn. Gordon of Alford, Strath. K. Gunn, Strath and Sand Holiday Centre. Angie Allan's also supplies tackle.
Boats: Sea Anglers Aid. Tel: Gairloch (0445) 2116. Mr Griffen, Burnside Terrace. Tel: Gairloch (0445) 2464. Mr Mackenzie, Seacrest, Port Henderson. Tel: Badachro (044 583) 263. Mr J.A. Grant, 2 Woodlands Road, Dingwall.

Poolewe and Aultbea

Situated amidst magnificent scenery, the sheltered waters of Loch Ewe offer the sea angler opportunities of fine catches. Suitable accommodation is available in surrounding villages and local advice is always available.
Types of fish: Shore – pollack, coalfish, dab, codling. Boat – haddock, cod, codling, gurnard, skate, whiting, mackerel, flatfish.
Boats: Several boats available locally.
Bait: Mussels, lugworm, cockles, etc. from shore. Artificial and preserved baits from W.A. Neate, Bridgend Stores, Aultbea.
Season for fishing: April- October incl.

Little Loch Broom

Ten miles north east Aultbea. Contact: Janoz Ertz (085 483) 262.

Ullapool & The Summer Isles

Loch Broom and the waters encircled by the Summer Isles offer excellent sea angling. The banks can be approached from Ullapool, which is an attractive holiday village sited on a peninsula projecting into Loch Broom. The numerous banks and islands offer superb fishing and beautiful scenery in sheltered waters. Many attractions on shore via local shops; hotels and sporting facilities available throughout the season. Morefield Motel, Ullapool. Tel: Ullapool (0854) 2161 offers day charters. Achiltibuie, a small village, also gives access to fishing grounds.
Types of fish: Shore – codling, coalfish, conger, pollack, mackerel, dabs, thornbacks, dogfish, flounders and plaice. Boat – as above plus haddock, whiting, wrasse, ling, megrim, gurnard, spurdog and turbot.
Tackle: Lochbroom Hardwear, Ullasport.
Boats: H. MacRae. Tel: Ullapool (0854) 2361. D. Maclean. Tel: Ullapool (0854) 2440. I. MacLeod, Achiltibuie. Tel: Achiltibuie (085 482) 200.
Season for fishing: June- October inclusive. Big skate best in autumn.

Lochinver

Lochinver is one of the major fishing ports in the north of Scotland. With a population of some 300 inhabitants it has a safe all-tides harbour with excellent shore services, including good moderately-priced accommodation and two fishing tackle shops. Excellent sea fishing within a short distance from the port, specialising in jumbo haddock, cod, skate and conger. Boats available. A large fleet of fishing vessels operates from the harbour and bait is readily available.
Types of fish: Cod, haddock, whiting, saithe, gurnard, ling, pollack, mackerel, wrasse, conger, skate. Coalfish, pollack, cod and mackerel from the shore.
Boats: Norman Macaskill – *M.V. Stardust*, fast purpose built Aquastar 33. 10 rods. Weekdays and weekends. Jim Crooks - M.V. Opsrey. 4 rods, 4 hour trips. Rods for hire.
Tackle: Tackle is available from Newsagent, Lochinver and the Lochinver Fish Selling Co.
Season for fishing: April- October.
Further information from: N.A. MacAskill, 8 Cruamer, Lochinver, Sutherland. Tel: Lochinver (057 14) 291.

Drumbeg

Seven miles north of Lochinver. Contact: Lachie MacRae. Drumbeg (057 13) 243.

Caithness

With the prolific fishing grounds of the Pentland Firth, the north of Caithness has built up a reputation as being one of the premier sea angling areas in Scotland. It is now recognised that the chance of taking a halibut on rod and line is better in Pentland waters than anywhere else; more halibut have been taken here than in any other part of the British Isles. The presence of Porbeagle shark in these waters has been proved by the capture of two specimens, with many more hooked and lost. Among the notable fish caught were European halibut records of 194 lbs. in 1974, 215 lbs. in 1975, 224 lbs. in 1978 and 234 lbs. in 1979. This fish represented a world record catch for the species. The Scottish shore record ling of 12lbs 4oz was caught in these waters. With countless numbers of rocky coves and sandy beaches there is much for the shore angler to discover along the whole of the north coast of Scotland. Accommodation is available to suit everyone, from first class hotels, private B. & B. to caravan and camping sites with full facilities. It is also possible to have a full sea angling package holiday with full board at a hotel and all boat charges included. The number of angling boats available increases each year, but it is still advisable to book boat places in advance.

Thurso and Scrabster

Thurso is the main town on the north side of Caithness and gives access through Scrabster to the waters of the Pentland Firth, where there are first class fishing grounds. Thurso Bay and the Dunnet Head area are sheltered from prevailing winds and it is reasonably easy for anglers to get afloat to the marks. Scrabster 1¼ miles from Thurso, is the main harbour in northern Caithness. Most of the angling boats are based here. There is also some excellent rock fishing, while conger may be caught from the harbour walls.

Types of fish: Cod, ling, haddock, conger, pollack, coalfish, dogfish, spurdog, plaice, wrasse, mackerel, dab, whiting, rays, halibut, porbeagle shark.
Boats: W. Kirk, 26 Traill Street, Castletown, Tel: Castletown (084 782) 662. G. Maynard, 23 Holborn Place, Scrabster, Tel: Thurso (0847) 64872. P.A. Mathieson, The Boatyard, Scarfskerry, by Thurso, Tel: Barrock (0847) 85332. J.W. Oag, Corbiegoe, Thrumster, Tel: Thrumster (0955) 85207. Mr. F. Johnson, 110 High Ormlie, Thurso. Tel: (0847) 63313/65406.
Tackle: A. Harper, The Drill Hall, Sinclair Street, Thurso. Pentland Sports Emporium, 14 Olrig Street, Thurso. A. & D. Mackay, Shore Street, Thurso. Wilson & Nolf, 1 Francis Street, Wick. The Gun Shop, Dunnet.
Bait: Mussels, lugworm can be gathered at low water, mackerel and squid from fish shops and local fishermen. Most species take lures, feather and rubber eels, etc. and most fishing done with this type of artificial bait.
Season for fishing: April-November.
Further information from: Mr. Ian Myles, Secretary, Ormlie Lodge A.C., Thurso. (0847) 62000 and Caithness Tourist Organisation, Whitechapel Road, off High Street. Tel: Wick (0955) 2596 Jan-Dec.

Dunnet
Dunnet is situated 8 miles east of Thurso at the end of the famous Dunnet Sands, which are over 2½ miles long. Few anglers fish this beach, as there is excellent boat fishing nearby. There is plenty of lugworm and the beach is well worth trying. Information about boats can be obtained from the

Northern Sands Hotel, Dunnet and the Seaforth Motel, Castletown, Caithness.
Types of fish: As for Thurso.
Boats and Tackle: As for Thurso.
Bait: Mussels from the rocks at low tide and lugworm all along Dunnet Sands.
Season for fishing: Shore – July and August. Boat – April-November.

Keiss
Good shore fishing is to be had around Keiss, a small fishing village between John o'Groats and Wick. It might be difficult to get out in a boat, but enquiries can be made at the Sinclair Bay Hotel (Tel: Keiss (0955 83) 233). The shore fishing is from the rocks around Keiss, and from the beach at Sinclair's Bay to the south of the village. Here some very good plaice have been taken and also anglers have caught sea trout while spinning for mackerel.
Tackle: Tackle shops at Wick.
Bait: Mussels and lugworm can be obtained at low tide.

Sutherland and Easter Ross Brora
Brora is a village situated on the A9, 12 miles south of Helmsdale. There is a small harbour and a few boats are available to sea anglers. There are rail links to Brora from the south and ample hotel accommodation and caravan facilities.
Types of fish: Cod, coalfish, cod, ling, haddock, rays and conger from boats.
Boats: B. Yates, 21 Johnson Place, Brora and some owners are willing to take visitors at nominal costs.
Tackle: Rob Wilson, Fountain Square, Brora.
Bait: Can be dug locally.
Season for fishing: July-September.

Grannies Heilan' Hame, Embo
This is a caravan holiday centre with extensive amenities 14 miles north of Dornoch. Manager is Willie MacKintosh, Tel: Dornoch 383.
Types of fish: Spinning for sea trout from the beach up to the mouth of Loch Fleet. Coalfish,

mackerel and flatfish from the pier. The rocks provide good cod fishing. From boats, coalfish, mackerel, plaice, cod, haddock and whiting at times.
Boats: Contact the manager.
Bait: Lugworm can be dug at the ferry landing area and there are plenty of mussels and cockles near Loch Fleet.
Season for fishing: April-Septmeber.

Dornoch
Dornoch gives access to the fishing banks off the north coast of the Dornoch Firth. There is good shore fishing from the rocks at Embo, but to get afloat it is necessary to make arrangements in advance. Youngsters can enjoy good fishing from Embo Pier.
Types of fish: Sea trout from shore. Flat fish, haddock and cod from boats.
Boats: Boats are difficult to hire but there are one or two in Embo which is three miles from Dornoch.
Tackle: W.A. Macdonald, Castle Street, Dornoch.
Season for fishing: April-September.

Tain
Tain lies on the south side of the Dornoch Firth and gives access to excellent sea trout fishing, both shore and boat, in sheltered waters of the Firth.
Types of fish: Shore – wrasse, flatfish, pollack, mackerel. Boat – haddock, cod, skate, mackerel.
Boats: Available in Balintore, 6 miles from Tain.
Bait: Available from the shore.
Tackle: R. McLeod & Sons, 14 Lamington Street, Tain.
Further information from: G. McLeod, 14 Lamington Street, Tain.

Portmahomack
This fishing village is well situated in a small bay on the southern shore of the Dornoch Firth, 9 miles east of Tain and 17 miles from Invergordon to the south. There is a well-protected harbour and a good, safe sandy beach.
Types of fish: Cod from the shore. Haddock and cod from boats.
Tackle: Available at Tain.

Season for fishing: Spring to Autumn.

Ballintore
Small village five miles south of Portmahomack.

Boats: Steve Coates, Ballintore (086 283) 2863.

North Kessock, Avoch and Fortrose
These villages lie along the north-west side of the Moray Firth

north of Inverness. This sheltered sea loch provides good fishing. Information regarding boats can be obtained from East Ross & Black Isle Tourist Office, Muir of Ord.

WESTERN ISLES

RIVERS AND LOCHS

Area Tourist Board
Outer Hebrides Tourist Board
(formerly Western Isles Tourist Board)
Area Tourist Officer
Outer Hebrides Tourist Board
4 South Beach Street
Stornoway
Isle of Lewis PA87 2XY
Tel: Stornoway (0851) 3088

RIVER PURIFICATION AUTHORITY
WESTERN ISLES ISLANDS AREA
(No formal Board constituted)

RIVERS

Water	Location	Species	Season	Permit available from	Other information
LEWIS					
Creed	Stornoway	Sea trout	11 Feb to 16 Oct	Factor, Stornoway Trust Estate Office, Stornoway, Isle of Lewis. Tel: Stornoway 2002.	Four beats available Day lets available
LOCHS					
An Ois	Stornoway	Sea trout	11 Feb to 16 Oct	Factor, Stornoway Trust Estate Office, Stornoway, Isle of Lewis. Tel: Stornoway 2002	Four beats from the shore Day lets available.
Clachan	Stornoway	Sea trout	11 Feb to 16 Oct	Factor, Stornoway Trust Estate Office, Stornoway, Isle of Lewis. Tel: Stornoway 2002.	Two beats from shore. Day lets available
Breugach	Stornoway	Brown trout	15 Mar to 6 Oct	The Sports Shop, 6 North Beach Street, Stornoway	
Keose (and Ham Bhraer Na Muline)	10 mls South of Stornoway	Brown trout	15 Mar to 15 Sept	Loch Keose Angling Assoc. Tourist Information Centre, Stonoway, Isle of Lewis Smith, Keose Glebe, Lochs Isle of Lewis.	No Sunday fishing.
HARRIS Drinisinader (and other lochs in Horsacleit Lodge Fishings)	Tarbert	Salmon Sea trout Brown trout	25 Feb-31 Oct 15 Mar to 6 Oct	The Manager, 7 Diraclete, Tarbert, Isle of Harris Tel: Harris 2464	
NORTH UIST Eashader (and other lochs)	Loch-maddy	Brown trout	15 Mar to 6 Oct	Secretary, North Uist Angling Club, 19 Dunossil Place, Lochmaddy, North Uist	
Fada (and many other lochs)	Loch-maddy	Brown trout	15 Mar to 30 Sept	Lands Officer, Depts. of Agriculture and Fisheries for Scotland, Balivanich Isle of Benbecula Tel: Benbecula 2346	
Scadaway and numerous lochs in southern part of island)	Loch-mabby	Brown trout	15 Mar to 6 Oct	Lochmalddy Hotel, Lochmaddy North Uist. Tel: Lochmaddy 331	

Water	Location	Species	Season	Permit available from	Other information
BENBECULA Langivat (Harivay and numerous other lochs)	Benbecula	Sea trout Brown trout	15 Mar to 6 Oct	Creagarry Hotel, Isle of Benbecula Tel: Benbecula 2024	No Sunday fishing. No spinning
Olavat (and other lochs)	Benbecula	Brown trout	15 Mar to 30 Sept	Lands Officer, Dept of Agriculture and Fisheries for Scotland, Balivanich, Isle of Benbecula. Tel: Benbecula 2346.	
SOUTH UIST All hill and Machair Lochs	South Uist	Salmon Sea trout Brown trout	Jul-Oct Apr-Sept	Resident Manager Lochboisdale Hotel, Lochboisdale South Uist. Tel: Lochboisdale (08784) 367	Fourteen boats available on lochs. Fly fishing only.

WESTERN ISLES

Sea Angling

The Outer Hebrides

The Outer Hebrides form a north-south chain of islands off the west coast of Scotland. Separated from the mainland by the Minches, much of their rod and line fishing remains to be discovered, not only due to a lack of boats in the area, but also due to a lack of communications between and within the islands. Several of the islands, Barra, Lewis, Harris and Benbecula have regular air services and car ferries run from Oban and Ullapool on the mainland and Uig on Skye.

Isle of Harris (Tarbert)

The largest community on the southern part of the largest of the Hebridean islands, Tarbert stands on a very narrow neck of land where the Atlantic and the Minch are separated by only a few hundred yards of land. It is the terminal for the car ferry from Uig on Skye and Lochmaddy on North Uist.

Types of fish: Boat – mackerel, ling, coalfish, cod, rays, pollack and conger. Shore – plaice, haddock and flounder.
Boats: Check with Tourist Information Centre, Tarbert (0859) 2011.

Tackle: Available from J.S. Morrison, Tarbert.
Bait: Mussels available on the shore, lugworm, cockles.
Season for fishing: May-October.
Further information from: D.B. Deas, Hon. Sec. Harris Sea Angling Club, Invercarse, Kendebis, Isle of Harris.

Isle of Lewis (Stornoway)

Stornoway, the only town in the Outer Hebrides, is easily accessible by air from Glasgow Airport (1½ hours) and Inverness (25 mins.); there is also a drive-on car ferry service from Ullapool (3 hours crossing). Another car ferry service connects Uig (Skye) to Tarbert (Harris), which is only an hour's drive from Stornoway. Stornoway is now recognisded as a mecca for sea angling in Scotland. There is an enthusiastic sea angling club with club boats and lincensed premises which overlook the harbour. Each August the club runs the Western Isles (Open) Sea Angling Championships. Many skate over the 'ton' have been caught, the heaviest so far being 192 lbs. The Scottish blueshark record of 85½ lbs. was off Stornoway in August 1972. Visiting anglers may become temporary members of the Stornoway Club (one minute from the town hall) and can make arrangements for fishing trips with club members in the club boats. Accommodation can be arranged through the Outer Hebrides Tourist Board, Administration and Information Centre, 4 South Beach Street, Tel: Stornoway (0851) 3088.

Types of fish: Conger, cod, skate, rays, ling, pollack, whiting, dabs, bluemouth, flounder, dogfish, wrasse, haddock..
Tackle: Available from Electro Sports, North Beach Street and C. Morrison & Sons, Point Street, Stornoway. C. Engebret & Co., Sandwick Road.
Bait: Mussels in harbour area; mackerel from local boats.
Further information from: The Secretary, Stornoway S.A.C., South Beach Quay, Stornoway, PA87 2BT. Tel: Stornoway (0851) 2021.

Isle of Eriskay

Sea angling boat hire and accommodation. Contact: Mr. C. Macleod, 1 Rudha Fhraoich, Eriskay, Isle of South Uist, Eriskay (08786) 223.

Isle of Barra

Sea angling boat hire and accommodation. Contact: George Macleod, Castlebay Hotel, Isle of Barra. Tel: Castlebay (08714) 223.

TRADES DESCRIPTION ACT

The accommodation mentioned in this holiday guide has not been inspected, and the publishers rely on information provided. The publishers have every confidence in their advertisers but cannot be held responsible for the accuracy of the descriptions published.

NORTHERN ISLES

LOCHS

Area Tourist Boards

Orkney Tourist Board
Information Centre
Broad Street, Kirkwall
Orkney KW15 1Dh
Tel: Kirkwall (0856) 2856.

Shetland Tourist Organisation
Area Tourist Officer
Shetland Tourist Organisation
Information Centre
Market Cross, Lerwick
Shetland ZE1 0LU
Tel: Lerwick (0595) 3434

PURIFICATION AUTHORITY
ORKNEY ISLANDS AREA
SHETLAND ISLANDS AREA
(No formal Boards constituted)

Water	Location	Species	Season	Permit available from	Other information
ORKNEY					
Boardhouse	Mainland	Brown trout	15 Mar-6 Oct	None required	Boats available locally
Harray	Mainland	Brown trout	15 Mar-6 Oct	None required	All legal methods permitted Anglers are recommended
Hundland	Mainland	Brown trout	15 Mar-6 Oct	None required	to join Orkney Trout Fishing Accos. Kirkwall
Kirbister	Mainland	Brown trout	15 Mar-6 Oct	None required	who make facilities available to visitors.
Stenness	Mainland	Sea trout	25 Feb-31 Oct	None required	
		Brown trout	15 Mar-6 Oct	None required	
Swannay	Mainland	Brown trout	15 Mar-6 Oct	None required	
SHETLAND 1000 lochs & Voes	Shetland Islands	Sea trout	25 Feb-31 Oct	Shetland Anglers Association,	
		Brown trout	15 Mar-6 Oct	3 Gladstone Terrace, Lerwick, Shetland	

NORTHERN ISLES

Orkney
The waters around Orkney attract many sea anglers each year as big skate, halibut and ling are there for the taking. Ling of 36 lbs. skate of 214 lbs. taken by Jan Olsson of Sweden and the former British record halibut (161½ lbs.) taken by ex-Provost Knight of Stromness provide the bait which attracts anglers to these waters. The Old Man of Hoy, Scapa Flow and Marwick Head are well-known names to sea anglers. The Brough of Birsay, Costa Head and the Eday and Stronsay Firths are equally well known as marks for big halibut and skate. Fishing from Kirkwall or Stromness, there is easy access to Scapa Flow where wrecks of the German Fleet of the First World War provide homes for large ling and conger. In the fish rich sea surrounding Orkney the angler will find some excellent shore fishing, nearly all of which remains to be discovered. Furthermore, skate of over 100 lbs. are still common while specimens of 200 lbs. have been recorded. More halibut have been caught in the waters to the south separating Orkney from the mainland than elsewhere in the U.K. Shark have also been sighted and hooked but none so far have been landed. Around the islands, in bays and firths, there is excellent sport for the specimen fish hunter and the Orcadians are eager to help sea anglers share the sport they enjoy. There is a regular car ferry service from Scrabster (Thurso) to Orkney and daily air services from Edinburgh, Glasgow and other points of the U.K.

Types of fish: Sea trout, plaice, pollack and coalfish, mackerel, wrasse from the shore. Skate, halibut, ling, cod, pollack, haddock, coalfish, plaice and dogfish from the boats.
Boats: Booking for boats should be done via St. Ola Hotel, Kirkwall, Orkney. Barony Hotel, Tel: Birsay 327.
Tackle: Available from Stromness and Kirkwall.
Bait: Available from most beaches and piers.
Season for fishing: June- October.
Further information from:
Orkney Tourist Board Information Centre, Broad Street, Kirkwall. Tel: Kirkwall (0856) 2856.

Shetland
The Shetlands offer the best skate fishing to be had in Europe; during the years 1970-74 more than 250 skate over 100 lbs. were caught. These included a European record of 226½ lbs., and 12 other skate over 190 lbs. During the same period, Shetland held nine British records, ten Scottish records and six European

Please mention this Pastime Publications guide.

records, giving some indication that the general fishing is of no mean standard. Halibut and porbeagle of over 300 lbs. have been taken commercially in the Sumburgh area with porbeagle shark now being landed by anglers from this area. Two Scottish record porbeagle of 404 lbs. have been taken by Peter White and bigger fish are landed every year by commercial boats. Shore- fishing remains for the most part to be discovered.

Types of fish: Shore – coalfish, pollack, dogfish, mackerel, dabs, conger and cod. Boat – skate, halibut, ling, cod, torsk, haddock, whiting, coalfish, pollack, dogfish, porbeagle shark, Norway haddock, gurnard, mackerel, cuckoo and ballan wrasse.

Boats: Many boats available for hire throughout the islands. Boats can also be arranged through the Shetland Tourist Organisation.

Tackle: Available from J.A. Manson, 88 Commercial Street, Stove and Smith, 97 Commercial Street, Hay & Co., Commercial Road, and Cee & Jays, Commercial Road, all Lerwick.

Tackle hire can also be arranged through the Shetland Tourist Organisation.

Bait: Fresh, frozen or salted fish bait available from fishmongers. Worm bait, crabs, etc. from beaches.

Season for fishing: Limited to May to October by weather conditions.

Further information from: Mr. Jim Watt, Shetland Association of Sea Anglers, Information Centre, Lerwick, Scotland, Tel: Lerwick 3434.

RIVERS INDEX

Please mention this Pastime Publications guide.

LOCHS INDEX

LOCHS INDEX contd.

SEA ANGLING INDEX

Please mention this Pastime Publications guide.

ANGLING IN SAFETY

Each angling season brings its gloomy headlines of one or other angling accident, all of them hazardous, many of them fatal. What we rarely hear about are the dozens of 'near-misses', where fishing trips have been spoiled by incidents which may result in nothing more than a red face or a ducking, but which linger on in the memory as a 'might have been' something more serious.

In recognition of the hazardous aspects of angling, The Royal Society for the Prevention of Accidents in association with the Shakespeare Company have produced a valuable leaflet called *The Safe Angler*. With the kind permission of ROSPA we are pleased to publish extracts from this pamphlet here in other places throughout the guide. The message is simple — heed it.

ANGLING ACCIDENTS
In any activity close to water there is always some danger of drowning. One can lose a life in a few inches of water if one stumbles, is stunned and has both nose and mouth under water.

Fishing from a boat
The greatest danger is when boating, where every year a number of anglers lose their lives. This is due to various causes some of which are avoidable by observing the following rules:

- Do not take a boat out until you are fully experienced in seamanship.

- Understand navigation and make sure that your boat has the necessary navigation aids and distress signals.

- Check on the weather forecast. Beware so-called 'freak' conditions, they happen more often than you may think. It may be disappointing to postpone a trip because the weather is unsuitable, but to ignore a bad forecast and to take on conditions which are hazardous is plain stupidity.

- Wear a life jacket or some form of buoyancy aid. This will keep you afloat in an emergency and also help to conserve energy.

- Make sure someone knows where you aim to fish and roughly how long you will be away. Leave your name and address visible inside your car.

- Check the state of the craft. Some fishing boats are totally unseaworthy.

- Watch the weather. If it should blow up rough seek a sheltered area and stay there until the storm blows over.

- At least 50% of the trout fishermen one sees fishing from boats will be standing up because this makes casting: particularly long casting, easier. A standing angler is more likely to topple into the water than one sitting. It also frightens and disturbs fish which either see the angler or his shadow, or are disturbed because a standing caster rocks the boat, sending out waves which 'put the fish down'. Fish sitting down and you will catch more fish and fish more safely.

- Whenever possible fish two to a boat. Fishing alone where help is not available is ill-advised.

- If the boat capsizes, stay with it, hold on to it unless you are so close to the shore that you can reach it by swimming.

- Do not wear waders in boats.

River Fishing
Wading accidents have occurred usually because the river has risen swiftly and the angler has not noticed it. Fast rivers will rise very quickly. A ghillis on the Wye in Wales describes that river as 'coming up a matchstick a minute'. Observe the following rules:

- Keep your weather eye open and watch the colour of the water. It will start to colour up as soon as flood water starts to come down.

- Try to keep calm if you tumble or plunge into deep water. Do not fight the current, because you may become exhausted. Go with it until you find shallow water or a bank where you can scramble ashore.

- A wading staff is a very useful aid.

- Make sure the soles of your waders grip properly.

Falls

Anglers often fish from coastal rocks and cliffs and perhaps some very rocky areas when trout or salmon fishing. It is easy to fall or stumble and this can result at the best in bruises and abrasions and at the worst, broken bones, being stunned and even death.

River banks in winter can be dangerous because snow, ice or mud could cause you to slip into very cold water. The same applies only to a slightly lesser degree with the sides of lakes. Falls may be prevented if you observe the following rules:

● Move slowly and carefully.

● Only go where you are certain you can go safely.

● Make sure you are wearing the right type of footwear. Worn rubber soles are a menace on wet rock or mud. Nailed soles can be dangerous on some surfaces.

● Fish in company and carry a whistle which will allow you to signal that you need aid (or that you have hooked a salmon). Carry a torch at night.

● If you do take a ducking, get rid of the water in your waders and jog off to your car or where you can get warm. Jogging makes the blood circulate and will help to keep you warm.

Injuries

Articles of fishing tackle can be dangerous, particularly hooks and sea leads. When bank fishing on reservoirs or casting sea leads from beaches and piers it is easy to hook someone behind you or to hit them with the lead. There is always the danger of hooking yourself when fishing, particularly in the hand. It is sensible to observe the following rules:

● When you are back casting watch out for people behind you, especially where the public have access.

● Wear polarising glasses when fly fishing, particularly with big lures and salmon flies. You will probably fish better because you can see into the water, but more importantly, you are protecting your eyes.

● If you hook yourself it is best to see a doctor as soon as possible. However, always carry sufficient first aid equipment to temporarily deal with a hook injury i.e. a pair of pliers which can cut wire, antiseptic and dressings. If the hook is not deep it is possible to push it so that the point and barb are forced out of the skin. They can then be cut off with a pair of pliers and the hook withdrawn.

● Every angler should be able to swim, know basic rescue, personal survival, resuscitation and have a knowledge of first aid.

● Take care with dangerous fish. A small shark thrown up against you by a rocking boat can inflict a nasty wound. If you are a beach fisherman, learn what a weaver looks like and never fish barefoot where they are likely to be about. The weaver sting is very painful. FINALLY, SAFETY WHEN FISHING IS A MATTER OF COMMON-SENSE AND NOT TAKING CHANCES.

Useful Publications

Anglers who fish at sea should obtain a copy of the *Seaway Code* which gives excellent advice on safety for small boat users. This may be purchased from the Department of Trade.

The *Code of Practice for Handling Fish*, obtainable from the National Anglers Council, is also recommended for all anglers. The National Anglers Council run Proficiency Awards for Game, Coarse and Sea Fishing.